MELBOURNE
THE MAKING OF A DRINKING AND EATING CAPITAL

MELBOURNE
THE MAKING OF A DRINKING AND EATING CAPITAL

Michael Harden

additional photography by Dan Magree

hardie grant books
MELBOURNE · LONDON

'07 LUIS PATO, PORTUGUESE B...
'07 GRANBAZAN, ALBARINO

ROSÉ

'08 CHIVITE, GARNACHA, S...
'07 ROUET, ROSÉ de PROVENCE

RED

'07 MASSOLINO, DOLCETTO
'06 AUROCH, TEMPRANILLO, T...
'06 VALLADO, DOURO TINTO, P...
'07 SABON, CÔTES du RHÔNE

SWEETIES ~ '06 DR. LOOSEN, RIE...
'01 ...di GRESY, MOSCATO PASSI...

☆: ½ BOTTLE = ½ PRICE

Italy
Frangelico
AMARO
MONTENEGRO
LIQUORE ITALIANO
ITALIA
Berta
GRAPPA
DI

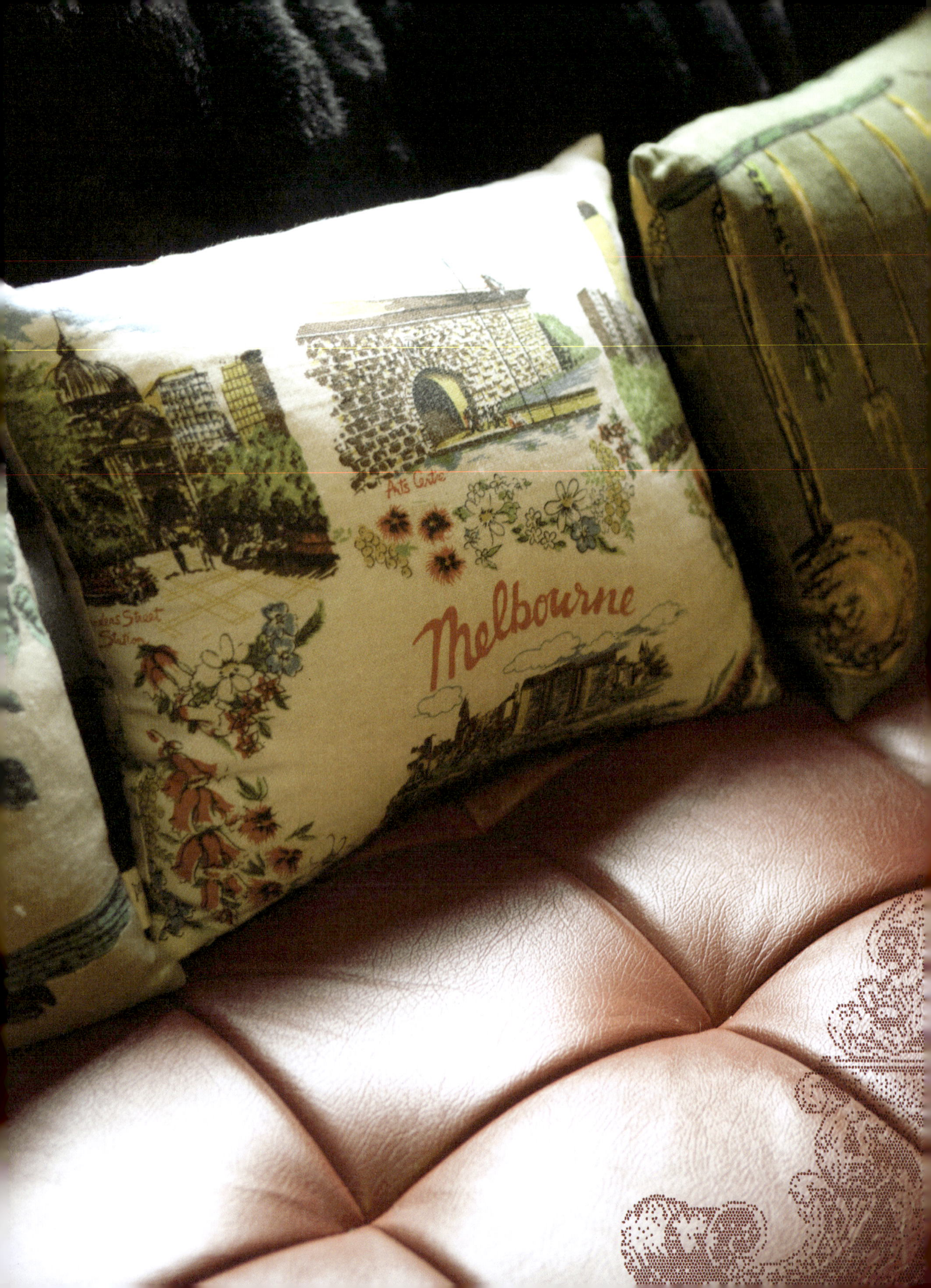
Arts Centre
Melbourne

Foreword

The Labor Party came to government in April 1982 bristling with ideas for change in every aspect of public administration and social policy. We had as a party worked hard in Opposition to present a comprehensive programme to the electorate. Now we could act.

As a reader of Victorian history and a lawyer I was aware of the legend around the grog shops of the gold fields of the 1850s and '60s. The liquor industry had an iron grip on the liquor laws from early colonial days and there was a long-standing alliance between the industry and the temperance movement. Both were generous donors to political parties.

All the marginal changes around hotel trading, service and hours never shook the power of the peak industry bodies, who maintained dominance. For most of the twentieth century there were entrenched beliefs around the links between alcohol and starting price book makers, domestic violence, family disharmony, crime and the road toll. In today's language, 'the perfect storm' was awaiting any political party that chose to go there.

The path to public policy reform can be a complex one. The securing of a coalition for change around an issue of consequence may need different strategies in the party room of the government, the electorate and the Parliament.

Frequently, timing and the emergence of other issues can be critical. For a new government sometimes labelled as 'wowserish', making nude bathing and prostitution legal in our first term was probably enough some said. However, we had wide commitments to social change – equal opportunity, gender equality, third party insurance, workers' compensation, preventative health care, freedom of information, to name some of the more controversial.

The initiative to commission the Nieuwenhuysen report and consequent Act should be seen in that context. A new defiant approach to 140 years of custom and law where the dominant consideration had been protecting vested commercial interests in the name of managing a social ill. It was hypocrisy of a high order and entrenched vested interests we took on.

Michael Harden's analysis tells it all in comparatively few pages. He then takes the reader through the places that have evolved in the past twenty years following the Act. Places where people meet at all hours and talk about social issues – the arts, politics, sport and all the things that make our city what it is. Places tourists read and hear about, and wish to experience.

No one who was around when the Act was planned and passed could have foreseen the direction of this evolution. It needed an enlightened thinker like John Nieuwenhuysen to show the way.

Honourable John Cain
Premier of Victoria 1982–1990

Published in 2009 by
Hardie Grant Books
85 High Street
Prahran, Victoria 3181, Australia
www.hardiegrant.com.au
www.hardiegrant.co.uk

All rights reserved. No part of this publication may be reproduced, stored in a retrieval system or transmitted in any form by any means, electronic, mechanical, photocopying, recording or otherwise, without the prior written permission of the publishers and copyright holders.

The moral rights of the authors have been asserted.

Copyright main text © Michael Harden 2009
Copyright breakout text © Claude Forell or Jeni Port as credited 2009
Copyright photography © individual photographers as credited 2009
(see pages 216–17 for a full list of photography credits)

Cataloguing-in-Publication data is available from the National Library of Australia.
ISBN 978 174066 745 6

Design by Trisha Garner
Jacket photography by Dan Magree
Colour reproduction by Splitting Image Colour Studio
Printed and bound in China by C & C Offset Printing

10 9 8 7 6 5 4 3 2 1

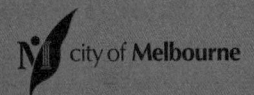

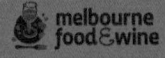

Contents

Foreword by John Cain	*vii*
Introduction	*xi*
Before and Beyond the Swill	1
The Laws of Dining	32
Revolution Not Evolution	58
Hopes, Fears and the Word Made Law	78
The Taste of Freedom	102
Raising the Bar	138
Freedom of Choice	176
Afterword by John Nieuwenhuysen	208
Notes	214
Photography Credits	216
Acknowledgements	218
Index	219

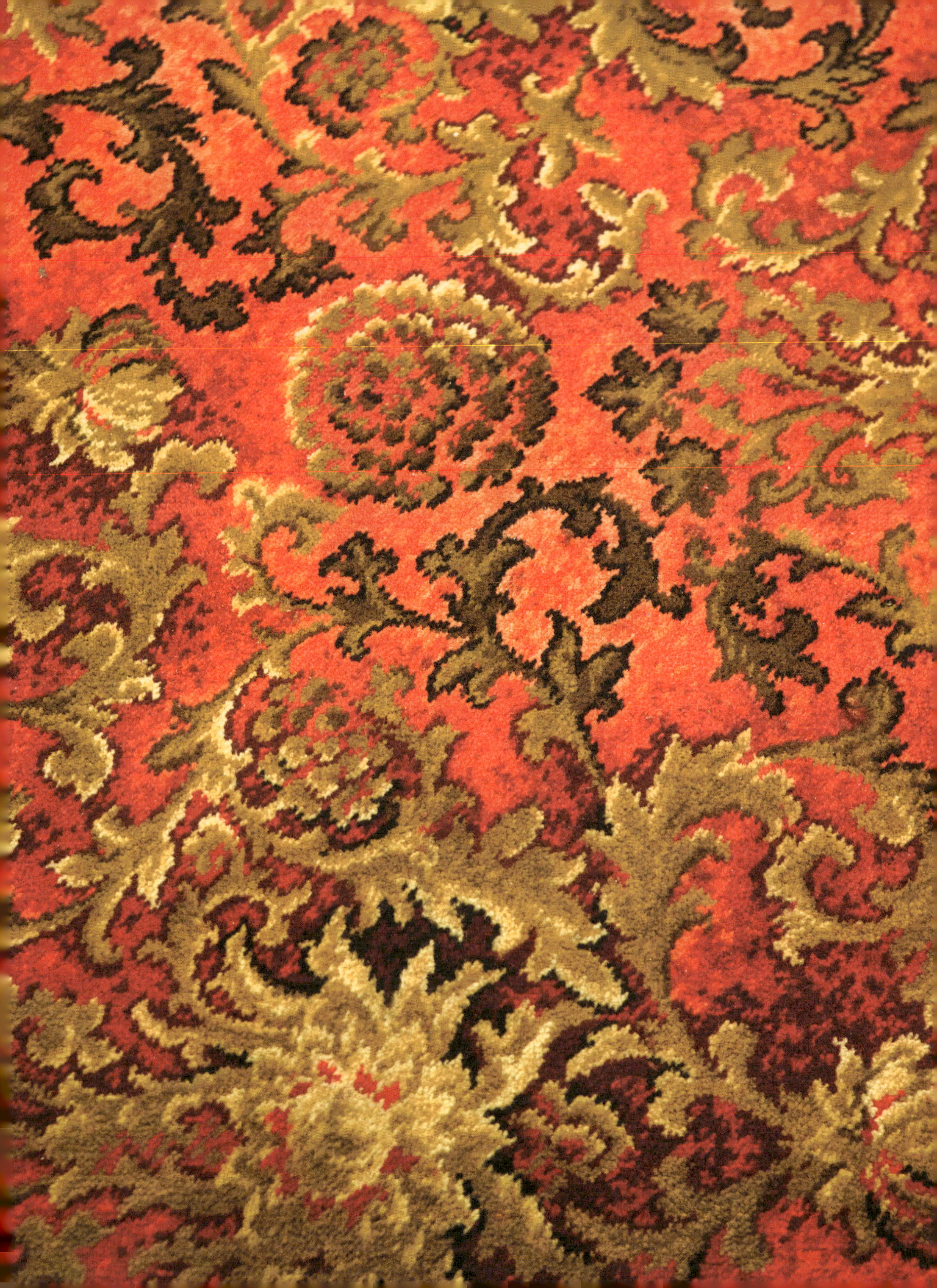

Introduction

How easy it is to forget the recent past. In overlooking events that occurred one or even two decades ago there is great potential for missing how far we have travelled, how different we are from how we were, how much change has occurred in a relatively short space of time.

The restaurant and bar scene of Melbourne and its surrounding region is arguably one of the finest and most diverse on the planet. Blessed with access to fine produce, creative minds, entrepreneurial spirit and a gregarious public that considers eating and drinking in public an inalienable right, Melbourne has become synonymous with sophisticated dining and a relaxed, liberal approach to imbibing. Although this food and wine culture may appear firmly entrenched, so completely has it insinuated itself into the lay of the land, it has certainly not always been the case. When Dr John Nieuwenhuysen, an economist working at the University of Melbourne, was asked by the Victorian government in the mid-1980s to review the state's existing licensing laws, the hospitality industry was struggling under the yoke of a bewildering thicket of laws that were the most conservative and confusing in Australia.

Small bars were illegal and therefore non-existent, though a sly-grog trade thrived in many of the city's billiard halls and espresso bars. Restaurant Licences allowing customers to drink alcohol during certain, strictly enforced hours (and only under the protective embrace of a substantial meal) were expensive and hard to come by. Liquor licensing commissioners had the power to refuse or revoke a licence if they didn't approve of the menu, the wine list or even the decor. The BYO (bring your own) licence reigned supreme at this time; diners hauled Eskies full of grog bought at nearby bottle shops into restaurants and drank them dry, while the restaurant owners tried to make a profit and a living from food alone. Nightclubs were legally obliged to force-feed their late-night patrons. Vineyards that did not have the capacity to make their own wine were forbidden cellar doors. Pubs clung fiercely to their monopoly of being the only places to get a drink without a meal, gained through the decades-long obligation of providing dining rooms and accommodation to punters largely uninterested in eating or sleeping. It was an antiquated, clunky and protectionist system that not only stifled the industry's creativity but did almost nothing to discourage entrenched and longstanding binge-drinking behaviour.

There had been numerous reviews and amendments to Victoria's licensing laws since the first statutes were put in place in the middle of the nineteenth century, but these changes were more about tinkering with and patching the existing system than reforming it. The changes that John Nieuwenhuysen proposed after studying the existing laws for more than a year were a complete overhaul, a revolution rather than an evolution. The fierceness of much of the opposition to his proposals, which would change Victoria's licensing laws from Australia's most conservative to its most liberal, illustrates just how radical his review was considered. The fact that it took nearly two years for an ostensibly supportive government to act on the review and turn much of it into law also shows how politically sensitive the whole alcohol issue had become. Those opposed to the changes promoted doomsday scenarios of Victoria drowning in an unrestricted, free-flowing ocean of booze.

It is nearly a quarter of a century since the *Liquor Control Act 1987* came into force in Victoria, and the changes to the hospitality industry have been nothing short of remarkable. The Act, and its subsequent amendments, has cultivated the 'Melbourne-style bar' – an eccentric, creative, unique type of watering hole that has colonised many of Melbourne's disused, unloved and out of the way places and helped revive an ailing CBD. It has allowed the freedom and flexibility that has seen the notions of restaurant, cafe, bar and bottle shop blend and mix to create hybrid businesses that would have been unrecognisable – not to mention illegal – just a couple of decades ago. It has fostered the growth of the Victorian wine industry by creating a demand for local wines in the city and by attracting people to visit an ever-increasing number of vineyards and wineries with attached cellar doors, restaurants, cafes and art galleries. In short, the public has been given the style and shape of eating and drinking venues it wants because the Act has delivered businesses the flexibility to respond to demand.

There are always questions about the availability of alcohol and whether there should be restrictions placed on the number of outlets, the hours they are allowed to operate and where they should be allowed to set up shop. These questions will continue to be asked as long as there is alcohol and the problems that inevitably follow it. They will be asked particularly of places where the licensing laws are most liberal, such as in Victoria, and the questions should be asked. But cast your eye over the state's vibrant hospitality scene, which is full of creative people looking for ways to push boundaries, challenge assumptions and find new ways to do things in a system that allows them that freedom. Look at how integral eating and drinking in public have become to the city's identity. These are powerful responses to questions that should be asked of any new freedoms with inherent risks.

The fact that people responded so positively, quickly and in such numbers to the changes put forward by John Nieuwenhuysen seems to show that the laws that sprung from his proposals were good ones. The fact that the changes have become so much a part of day-to-day life that most people have forgotten the restrictive past, or have never experienced any other way, also leads to the conclusion that these were changes not just practical and workable but also worthwhile and positive. They improved what came before them. What more can you ask of change?

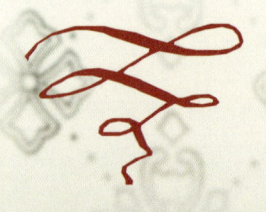

5
FIVE
5
FIVE

LA GITANA
LA GITANA

SALOM
ogressive
ourses
n Curley
Veltliner
McLaren

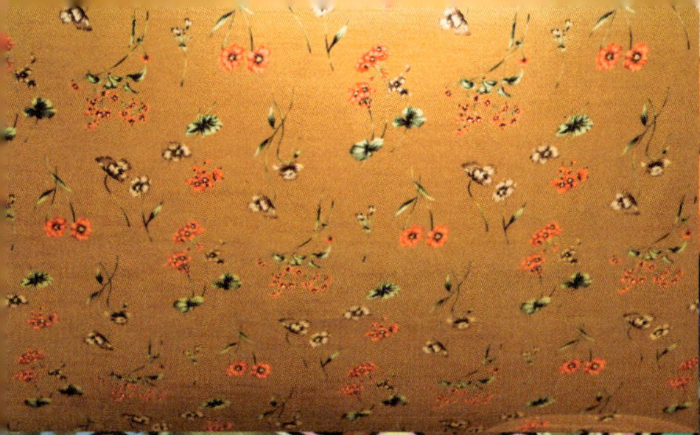

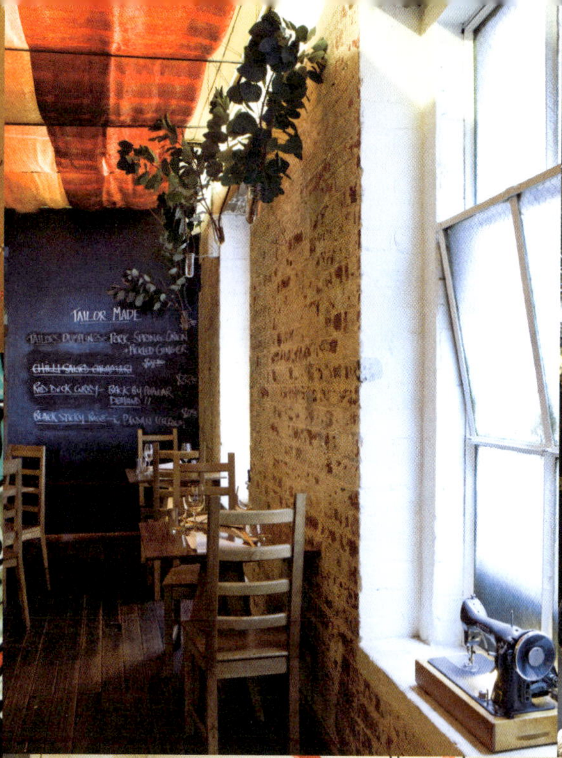
TAILOR MADE

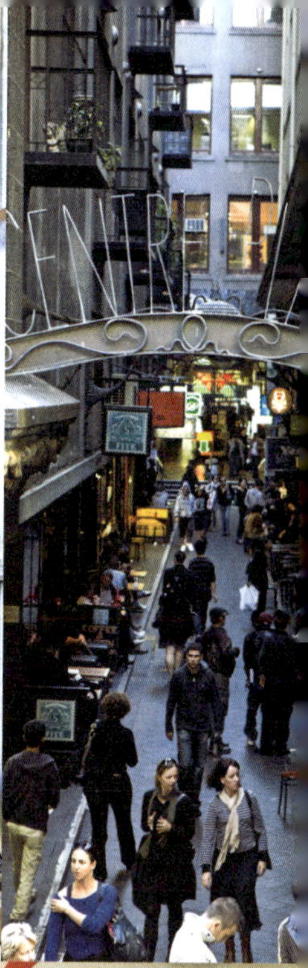

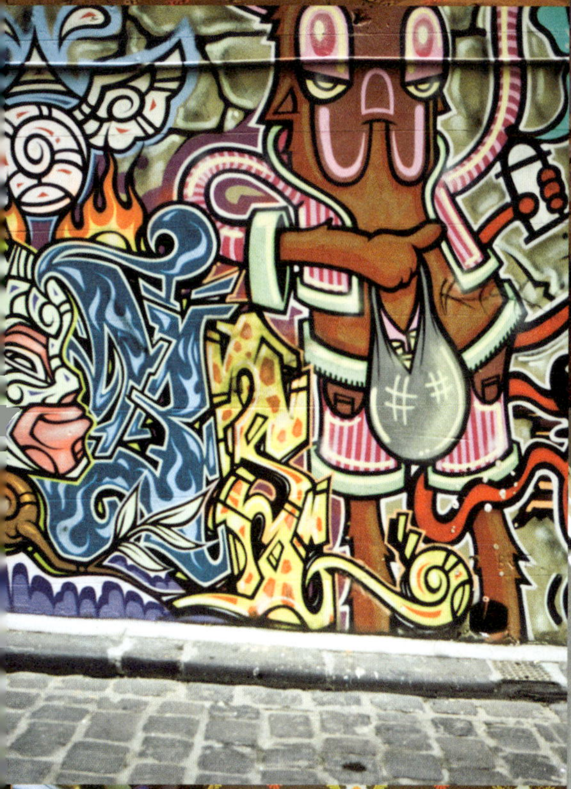

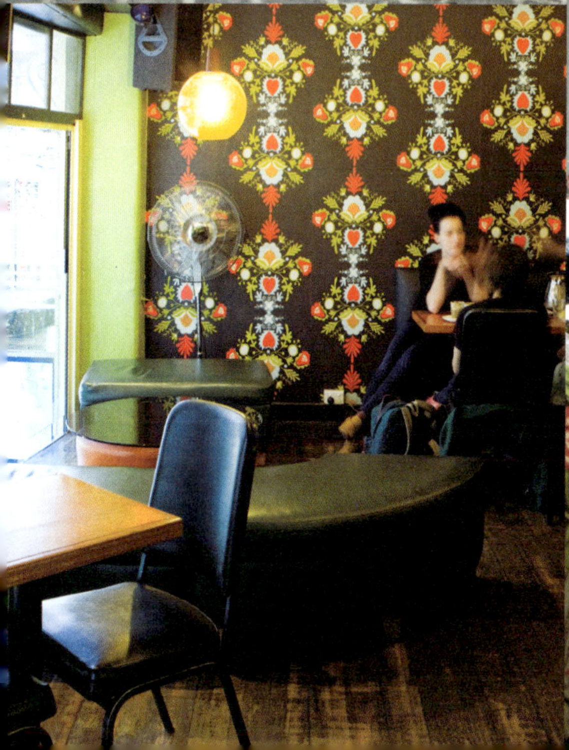

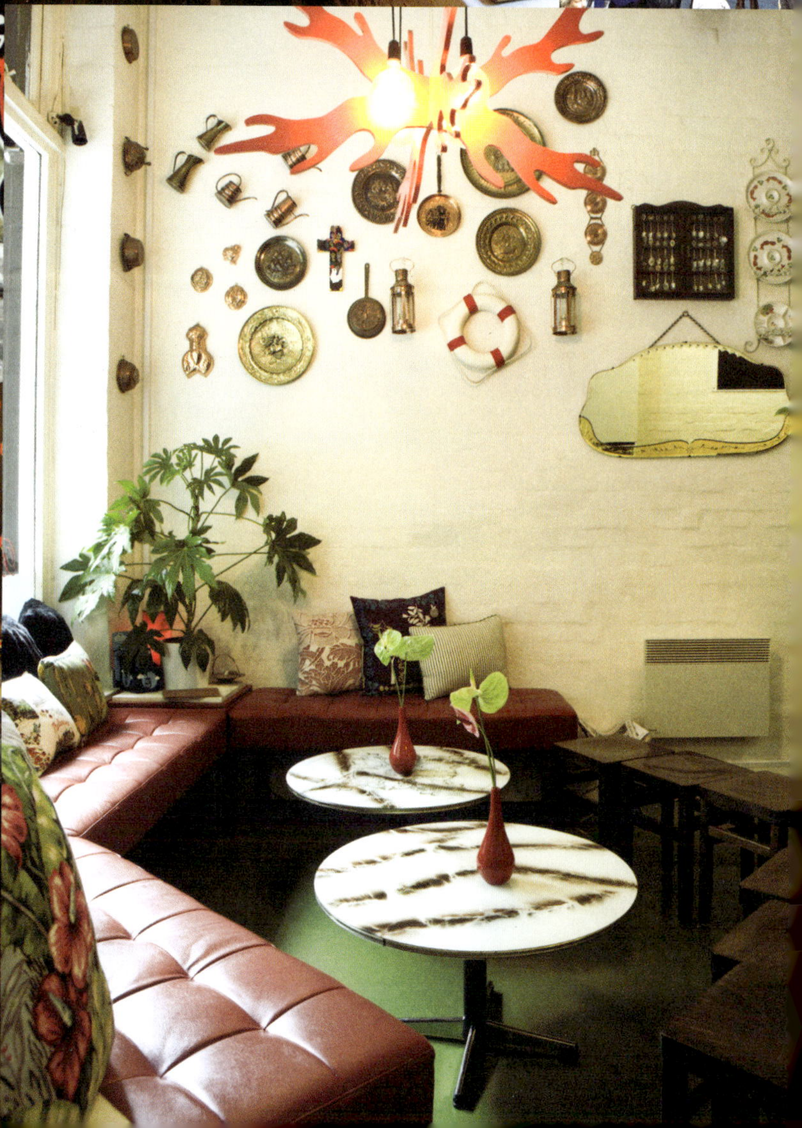

But the Act is in many ways unsatisfactory. It should be repealed and replaced with a much simpler system reflecting the ethos of today, not that of a society just emerged from 50 years of six o'clock closing.

JOHN NIEUWENHUYSEN, 1986

Before and Beyond the Swill

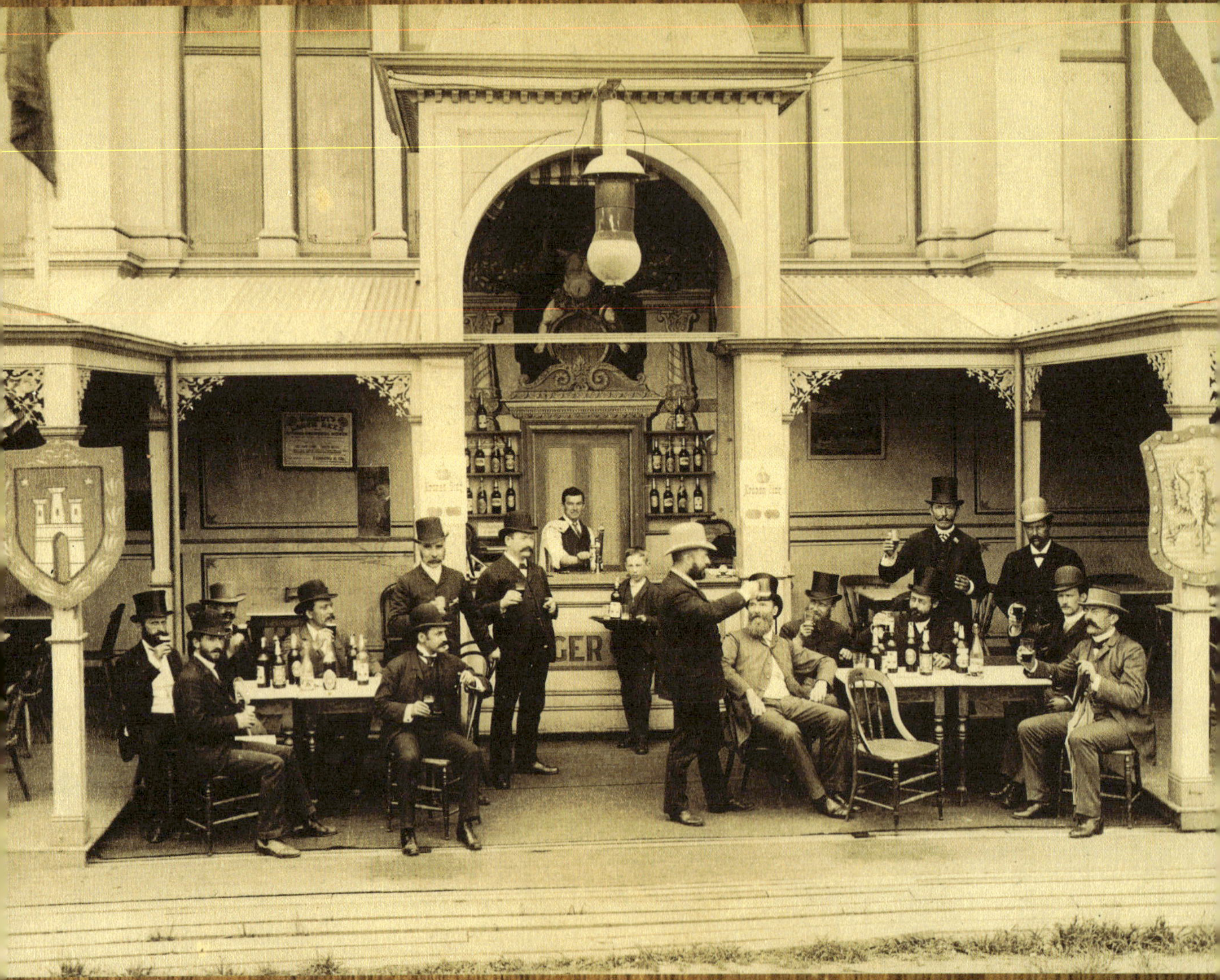
GER

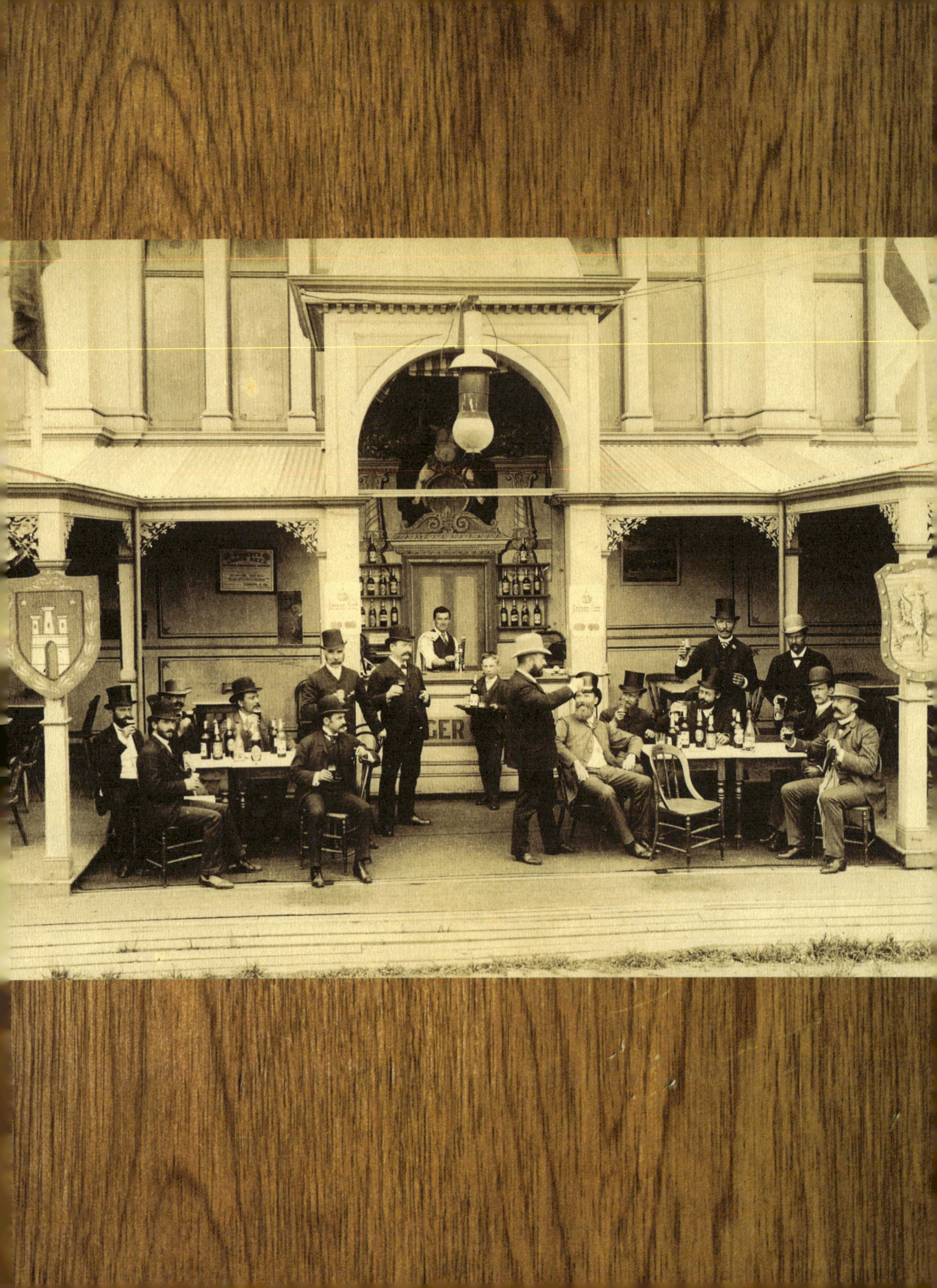

Alcohol has always been a slippery beast for legislators. When the Nieuwenhuysen report into liquor law in Victoria was commissioned in October 1984, more than 100 alcohol-related pieces of legislation had been passed since the first Victorian statute dealing with liquor was enacted in 1852. There had been some major reforms in alcohol licensing along the way, but the gist of most of these changes and reversals, amendments and appendices was to control the sale – and therefore the consumption – of alcohol. The supposed end, of course, was to limit the effects of alcohol's various associated ills.

The foundation on which all these laws rested was the belief that the problems associated with alcohol could be best addressed by restricting how and when people drank. This was an easier route to take than the more esoteric one of figuring out why people drank as much as they did in the first place. But legislation has never been a safe haven for shades of grey, and so the restrictive, doing-it-for-their-own-good path was the one taken. Not surprisingly, this single-minded approach on behalf of successive administrations was the major factor in creating an entrenched, uncompetitive liquor monopoly, along with some spectacularly hideous drinking habits. It also saw Victoria's licensing laws degenerate into the Byzantine and ultimately ridiculous tangle that John Nieuwenhuysen confronted in 1984.

So, how did Victoria's liquor laws get into such a mess? Just as drinking – and drinking to excess – has a long and proud Anglo-Saxon history, so too have the laws trying to keep a lid on it. Victoria's legislation has its own particular story, but initially its laws were inherited from Britain, whose restrictive liquor licensing goes back to the late fifteenth century. These laws were emulated in Australia shortly after settlement, with the first liquor licences granted in Sydney in 1792; naturally, they were applied to the new settlement in Victoria as well. Once in place, and with the weight and gravitas of history behind them, it was always going to be hard for local legislators to think outside of the imposed box, as the next century or so proved.

One notable difference from British legislation, and one that would have a far-reaching effect on how Victorians accessed their booze, was the abandonment

{*Opposite*} Beer drinkers sampling lager from Germany during the Melbourne Centennial Exhibition, 1888

> Restrictions on selling alcohol on the goldfields were openly flaunted, with sly-grog shops set up in tents along the roads to the goldfields

of the distinction between inns and public houses. Under British laws, inns provided food and accommodation to travellers, while public houses basically served alcohol. Early laws in Australia granted publicans licences to sell alcohol, so long as they also provided food and accommodation. By combining the functions of public house and inn, the Australian law not only created an identifiable pub architecture – bars downstairs, accommodation upstairs – but also a situation ripe for complication. How could a traveller arriving late at night get food and drink when the hotel was prohibited from operating after a certain hour? And if hotels were entitled to serve travellers after hours, what constituted a bona-fide traveller? How far were they to have travelled and for what purpose? And so on. The tangle had started from the very earliest days and would only get knottier as the years went on.

As with nearly every aspect of the fledgling Victorian colony, the existing and quite basic liquor laws were overwhelmed during the stampede that followed the discovery of gold in 1851. Melbourne's population soared from 23,000 in 1851 to 130,000 in 1858, swelled mostly by thousands of binge-drinking single men who flocked to the Victorian countryside to find their fortunes. Restrictions on selling alcohol on the goldfields were openly flaunted, with sly-grog shops set up in tents along the roads to the goldfields. Women roamed the tent cities, selling rum by the cup out of milk cans.

The response of government was to deregulate the industry under the *Wines, Beer and Spirits Sale Act 1864*. Ostensibly, this radical move was to bring licensing laws into line with existing behaviour. But more importantly for what was to come, it saw the government grasp the concept of raising greater revenue through granting more licences.

The years following the Act witnessed a huge increase in the number of businesses licensed to sell alcohol. In 1878, Victoria boasted 4320 hotels, 334 licensed grocers, 113 wine saloons, 500 spirit merchants and 104 brewers. Many places were able to obtain licences that enabled them to trade around the clock. Accommodation rules were relaxed and consumption of alcohol in Victoria rocketed – though Western Australia and Queensland still led the way as far as volume per capita was concerned.

Given that deregulation came into being just as the temperance movement hit its straps and the publicans' protests about unfair competition became louder, it is not surprising that the relative free-for-all was snuffed out by yet another Act – the 1870 amending act. This brought liquor laws back to more comfortable and familiar restrictive territory.

The powerful alliance between the increasingly vocal temperance movement and the collective might of the publicans would become one of the main forces to shape

{*Opposite*} Binge drinkers, as typified in the early press

EVENING SERVICE.

[SCENE—*The Pig and Whistle,* —— *Street, Melbourne.* TIME—*Sunday evening.*]

DISTINGUISHED PHILANTHROPIST : Constable, I fear liquor is being sold in this establishment to-night.

POLICEMAN : Liquor, Sir ; bless your 'art, Sir, no. Werry serious landlord here, Sir. Always has a prayer meetin' o' Sundays, and they're now a singin' o' hymns.

(*Moral.*—Never alter a law which works so well as that which now keeps the public houses closed on Sunday).

And at the end of a week depart swearing they'll never drink again.

Supplement to "The Australasian Sketcher," December 29, 1887.

"DIVIDED ATTENTION."

(Taken from Mr. Calqhoun's Prize Painting at the Students' Exhibition, Melbourne National Gallery, 1887.)

THE BANNER OF TRUTH.
A Weekly Record of Passing Events, and

POLICE NEWS

Nº 10.   MELBOURNE, JANUARY 27, 1877.   ONE PENNY.

MIRACULOUS ESCAPE FROM A SHARK.

A METROPOLITAN INTERIOR.

Victorian licensing laws for close on a century. The temperance movement was the political voice of hardening attitudes towards alcohol in the community. Blaming alcohol for many of society's ills was not unique to Victoria, or even Australia at the time. Across the Western world there was a growing perception that alcohol was at the root of most crime and was responsible for the overflowing gaols. It was seen to undermine culture, promote lunacy and infidelity and, because of the vast sums of money spent on it, contribute to economic malaise.

Melbourne was the scene of Australia's first temperance rallies, and in 1885 a petition in support of 'local option' was delivered to the government, signed by 45,000 Victorian women – almost a quarter of the female adult population – on a roll of paper measuring half a kilometre in length. Local option gave residents the right to veto, even reduce, the number of licences in their own towns and suburbs. The first success came with the 1885 licensing act, which allowed all Victorians on the electoral roll to reduce the number of hotels in their locality to one for every 500 inhabitants. It was an odd alliance, but both pub owners and temperance leaders agreed on the good sense of limiting the number of businesses able to serve alcohol. This well-supported petition, and many others like it, was integral in tightening licensing laws, and it heralded the arrival of one of Victoria's first successful lobby groups.

On paper, it would seem that the goals of the temperance movement and those of publicans, or 'licensed victuallers' as they were known, should have been at opposite ends of the spectrum. But circumstances in the last decades of the nineteenth century led to strange bedfellows. For the publicans, their profits took a mighty hit through the combination of proliferating licensed premises following the 1870 Act, the levelling in population growth as the gold rush petered out and the economic crash that hit Victoria in the 1890s. For the temperance movement, of course, it was always looking for ways to reduce the effects of alcohol on society and it had fixed on local option as the best way to go about it.

It was a formidable double act. Both groups had already proved successful in lobbying the government for changes to the licensing laws to suit their own goals, but together they almost had the ability to draft legislation. It may have seemed an ideal situation for them, but the outcomes in the following decades did not always turn out as planned.

In 1906, the Victorian government established the Licences Reduction Board, whose task it was to reduce the number of businesses selling alcohol; compensation was offered to those whose licences were withdrawn or were voluntarily surrendered. Between 1907 and 1916, some 1054 hotels were closed down. At the same time, the Licensing Court was established, supposedly to create a more systematic approach to the laws. But it ended up being more concerned with policing (and raising) the standards of pubs than with systematising the laws. This saw a further reduction in the number of hotels, as establishments that did not come up to scratch were closed down. It also created the sense of mutual obligation that was to turn the liquor industry into something of a closed shop until the 1980s. Because the law demanded that hotels meet standards in food and accommodation – the parts of a hotel business that often ran at a loss and were subsidised by the sale of alcohol – hotel owners could demand a certain amount of government protection in return, as they were spending money to uphold the laws' emphasis on the ever-higher standards.

Hotels at this time were also coping with increased pressure from suppliers. Carlton and United Breweries (CUB) was founded in 1907; it was a combination of six of the state's thirty-seven breweries and accounted for more than half of the total beer supply in Victoria. Through takeovers from 1909 until the early 1980s, CUB was able to gain a substantial dominance of the market and, through control of the restricted number of licenses through ownership, leasing and finance agreements, could effectively block any potential competitors' entry into the market. To maintain dominance, it was very much in the interests of CUB to keep the number of outlets restricted, and it formed yet another group to lobby fiercely against any changes that would ease the licensing restrictions in place.

> On paper, it would seem that the goals of the temperance movement and those of publicans should have been at opposite ends of the spectrum

{*Opposite*} Women from the temperance movement bring their protests – and their suitcases – to the street, 1938

10 BEFORE AND BEYOND THE SWILL

{*Left*} Vertical drinking, 1950s style

> Hoards of shouting, shoving men charged every bar every evening, ordering multiple beers before the imposed witching hour

The temperance movement was pleased with any drop in the number of alcohol-related businesses in Victoria, but its work was by no means over. Undaunted by the relatively limited success of local option, it began to lobby furiously for a reduction in hotel trading hours. In a way, it was the Germans and the outbreak of World War I that helped seal the success of this, as well as the fate of Victorian drinkers for the next fifty years. The idea of alcohol weakening the foundations of society grew in strength and popularity with the outbreak of war. How were Australians ever going to help defeat 'the Kaiser' if their combat-aged men were boozing on in pubs until all hours of the night? The 1915 Temporary Restriction Bill initially reduced the 6 am to 11.30 pm trading hours to 9 am to 9 pm; a year later it forced pubs and licensed grocers to cease trading at 6 pm. As John Nieuwenhuysen wrote in his *Review of the Liquor Control Act 1968*:

> In retrospect it was a temperance victory of most dubious merit since it created the notorious '6 o'clock swill'. The high turnover drinking in compressed opening hours hardly assisted the creation of satisfactory drinking habits or premises. Indeed the regulations of the time must have been a major cause of the poor standards of the premises which subsequent legislation ... was intended to remedy.[1]

Dubious indeed was the ridiculous and barbaric spectacle of the swill, as hoards of shouting, shoving men charged every bar every evening, ordering multiple beers before the imposed witching hour. Couple this with the spectacle of these same men – now drunk – all being pushed out onto the streets of Melbourne at the same time and you would have to concede the Temporary Restriction Bill was one of the most short-sighted and naive pieces of legislation ever passed in Victoria. Several other states, including New South Wales, Tasmania and South Australia, also introduced swill-friendly closing hours.

The Bill did nothing to raise the tone of hotels, and economic conditions over the following decades did nothing to improve the reputation of Australian pubs. With the Great Depression, followed closely by World War II and the post-war shortages and rationing of beer and building materials, the Licences Reduction Board found it difficult to force pub owners to comply with its stated aim of constant upgrading and improvement. Pubs found their own level, hemmed in on every side by restrictive laws. As Keith Dunstan puts it in his book *Wowsers*:

> After World War I, except for a few rare establishments, seats were never provided, there was no entertainment except a radio droning out the races or the football and the only decoration was the tiles on the wall, which enabled the bar to be washed down with greater ease after 6 pm.[2]

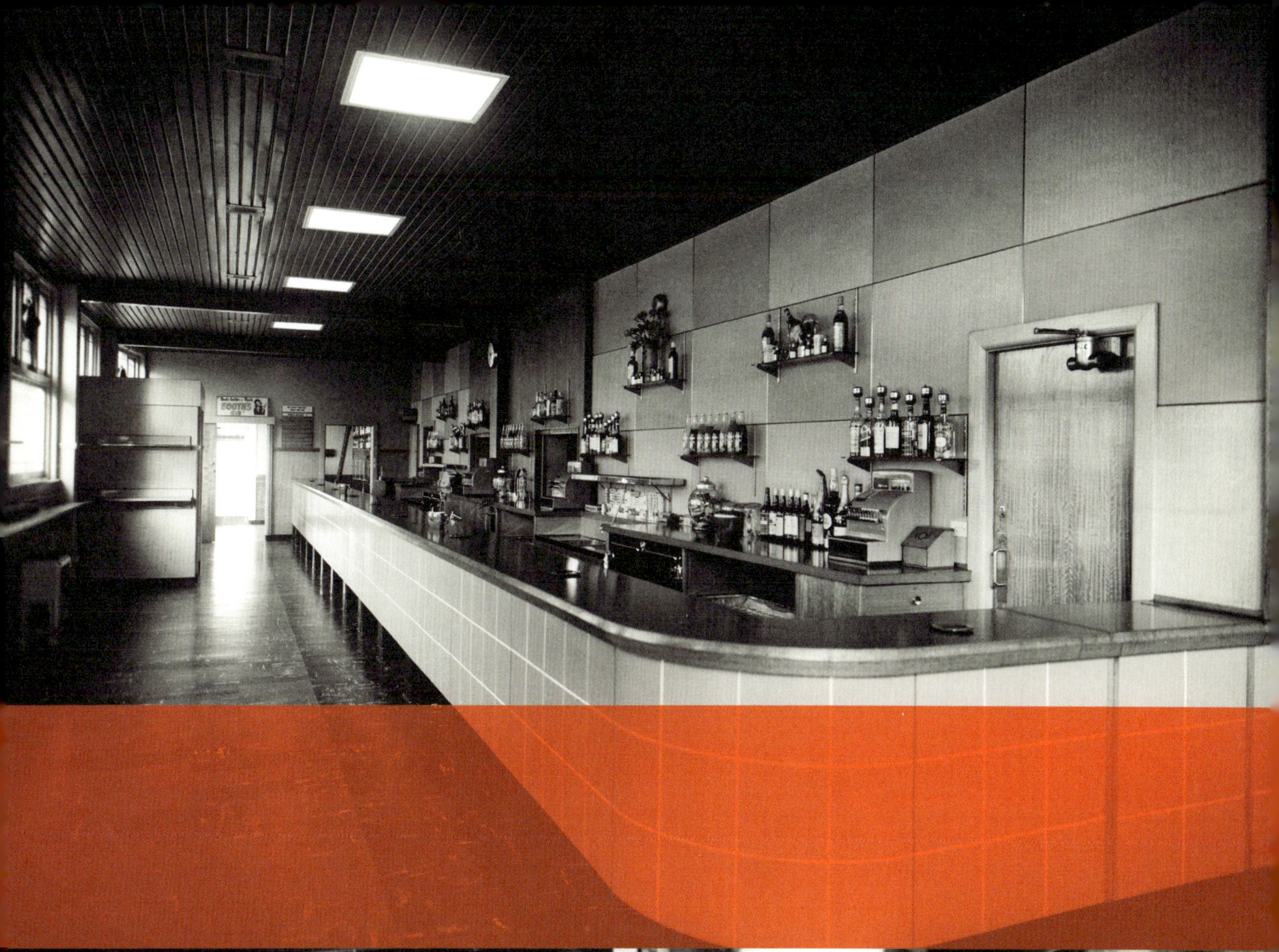

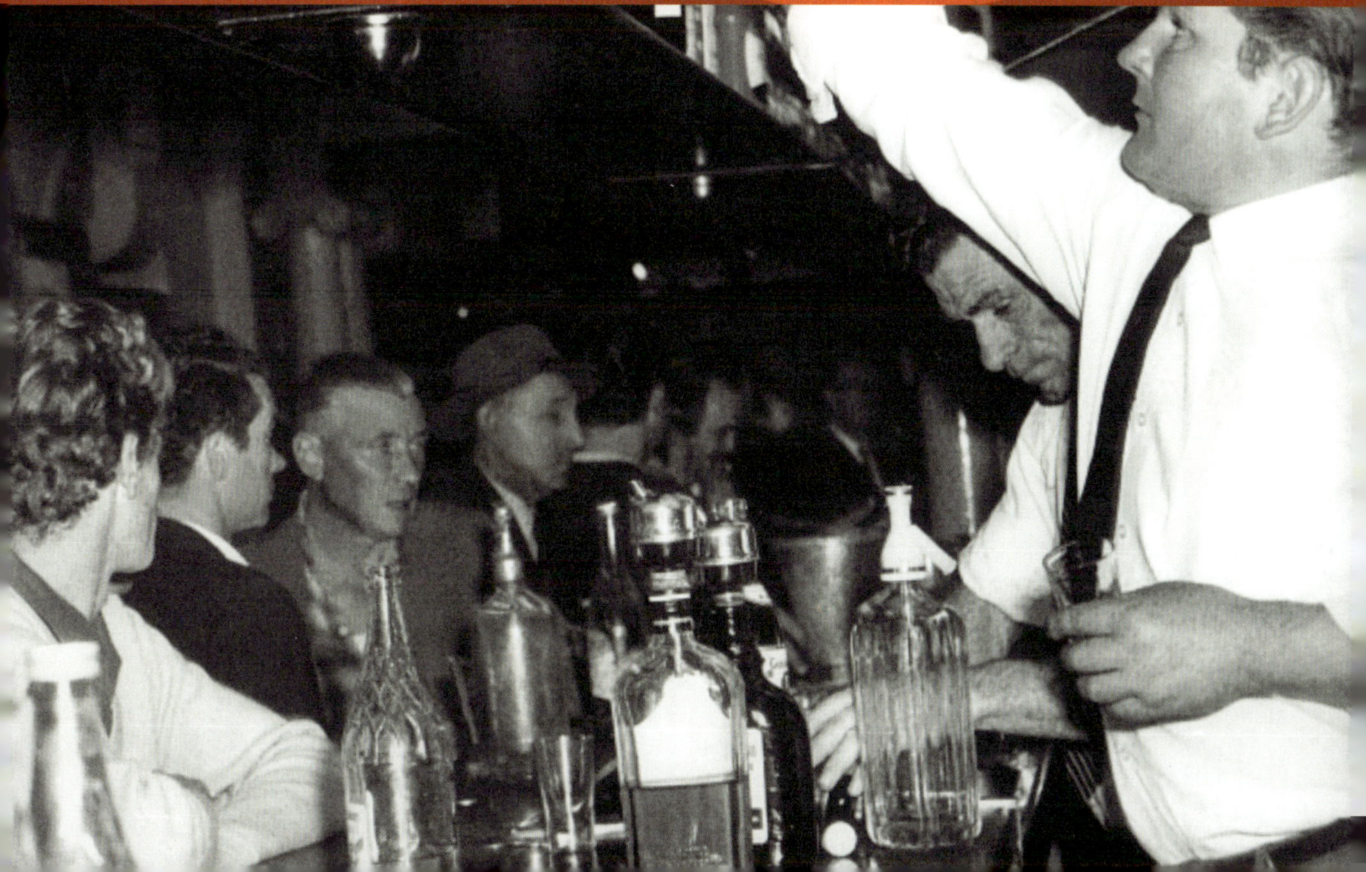

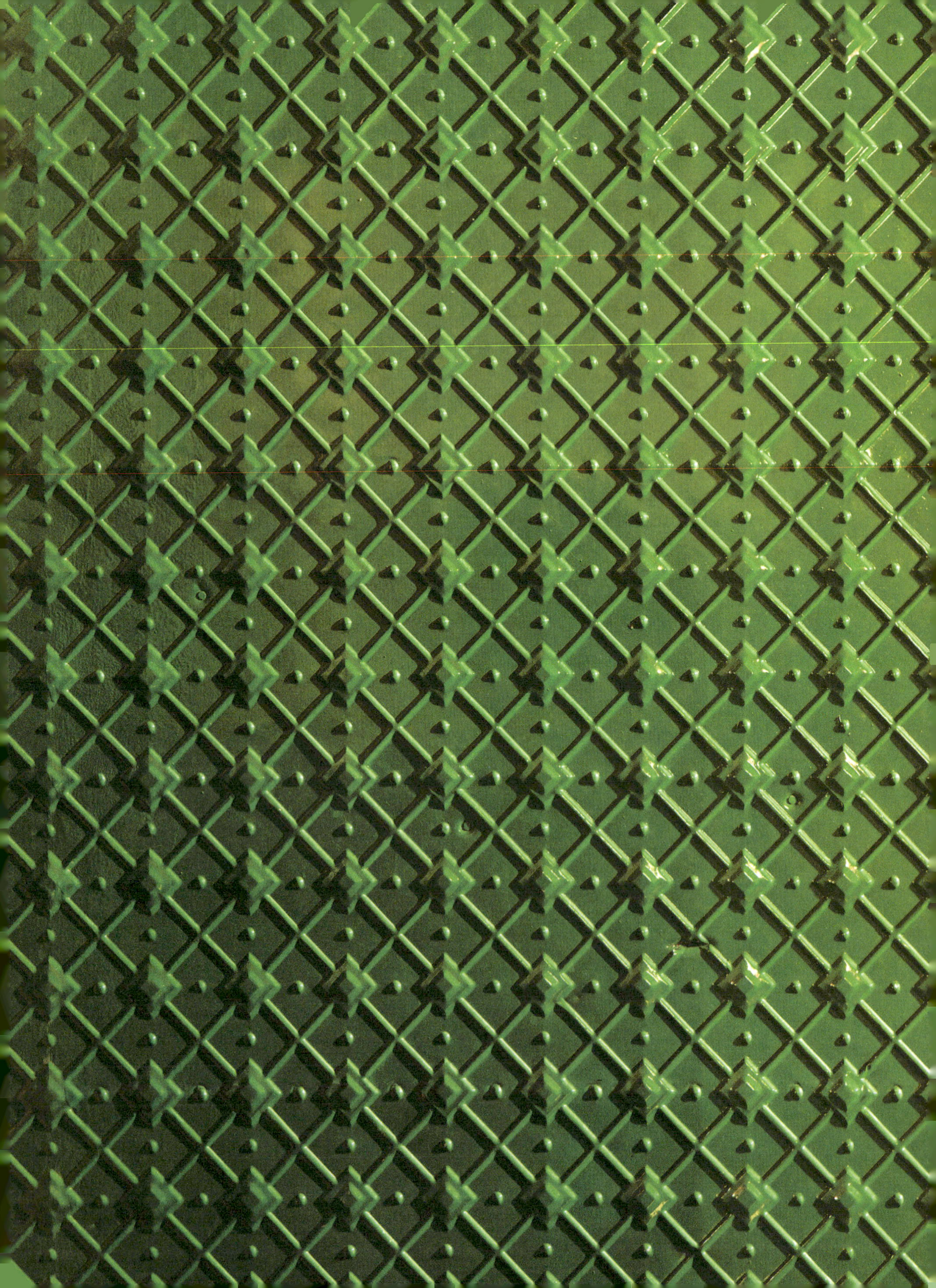

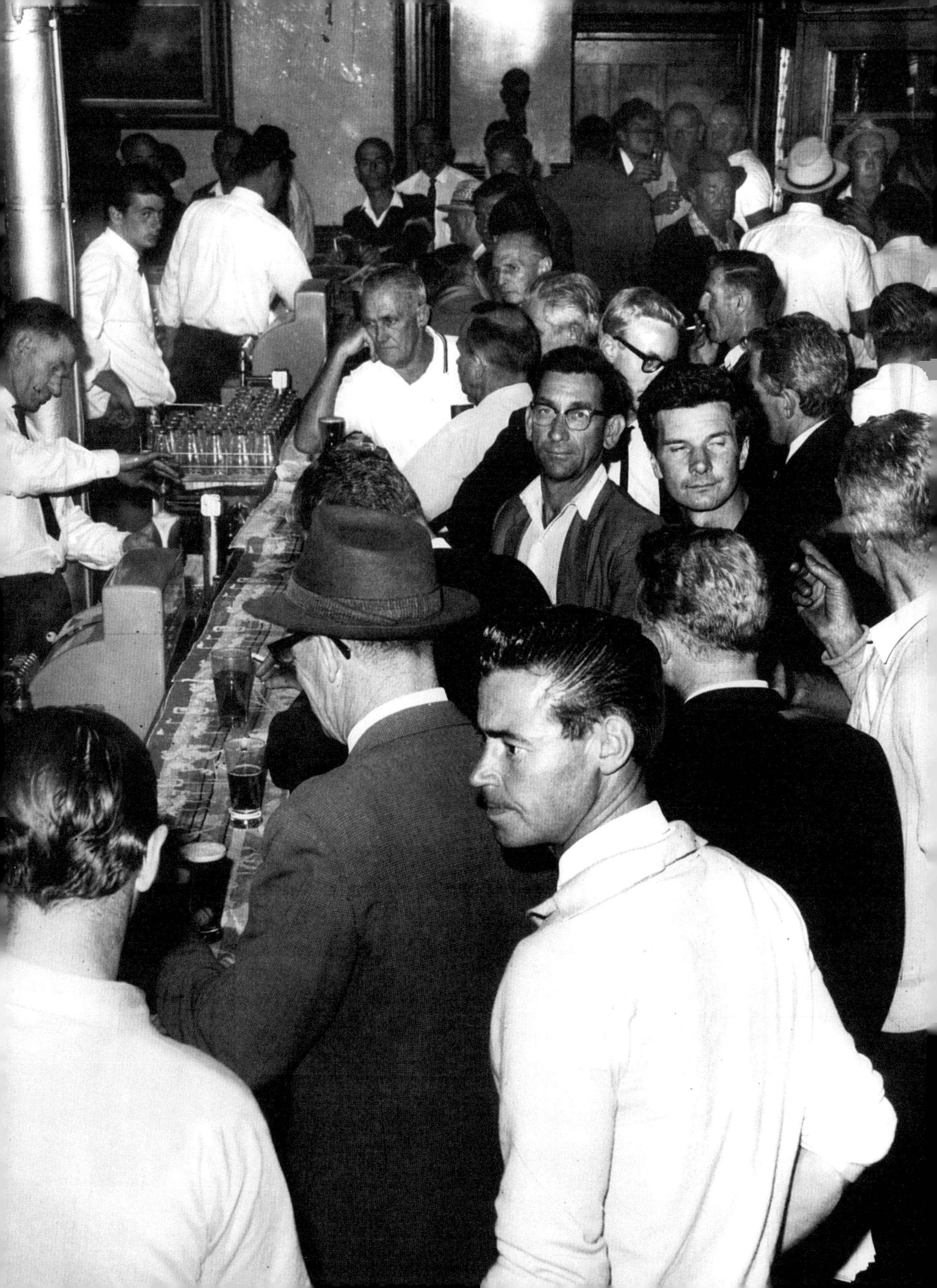

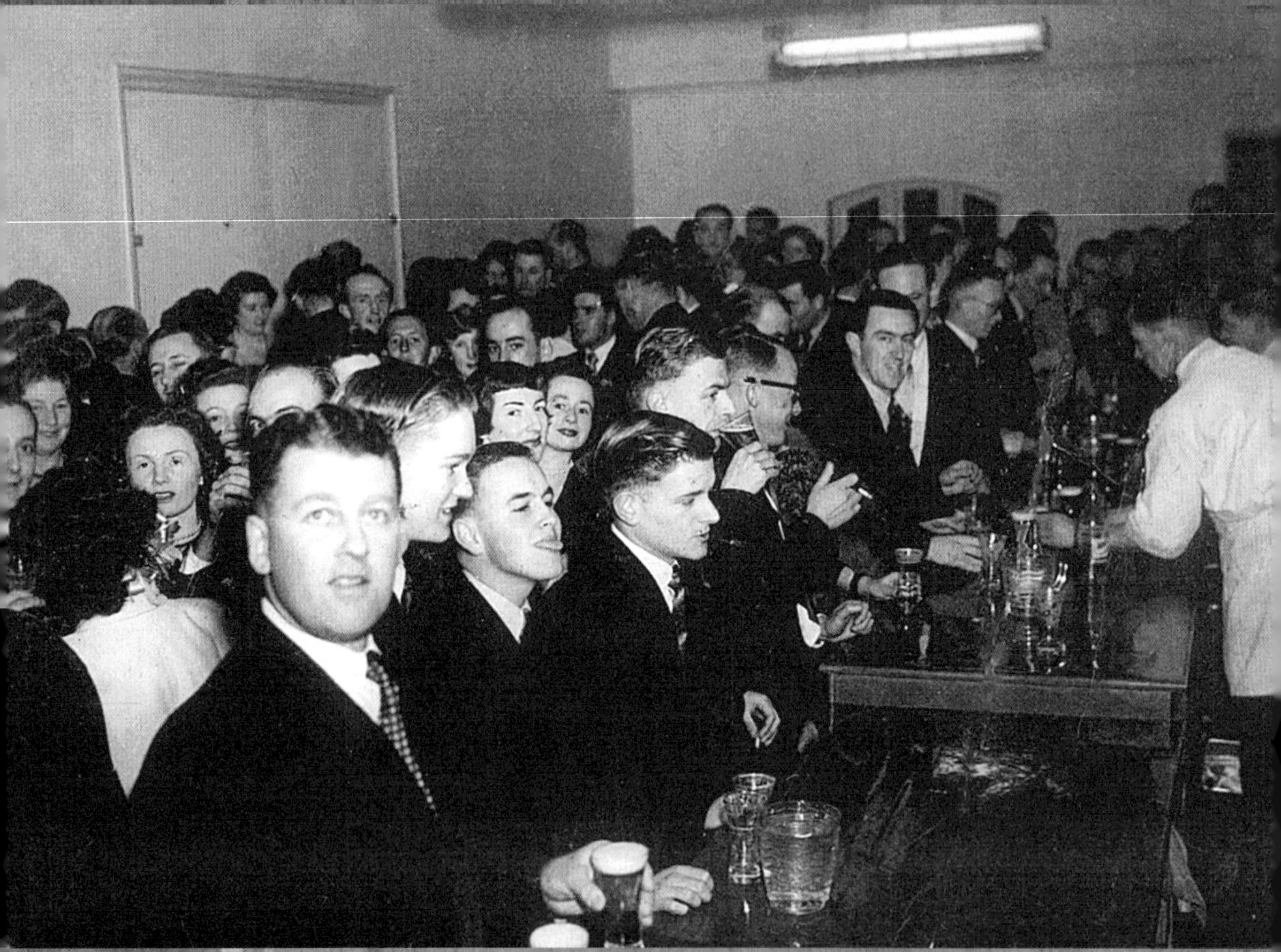

The original aim of reducing the number of hotels in Victoria had certainly been successful. From 1900 to 1950, the number of hotels was reduced from 3682 to 1665, and one-third of the licensed grocers were wiped from the business directories. But prosperity began to return to Victoria in the 1950s, and with it came growing dissatisfaction with the way alcohol was served and policed in the state.

Perhaps the chair of the Licensing Court, Judge Fraser, best summed up the mood of the time. In 1960, Fraser set off on what could only be deemed a dream gig – a tour of the hotels, restaurants and cafes of Europe and the United States, with a mission to see how Victoria's liquor licensing laws compared and could be improved. 'Drinking habits in Australia, are, from my observations in the places visited, unique. They are unique in the sense that they are deplorable,' he wrote after his return.[3]

Reg Leonard, of the *Sun News Pictorial*, expressed a similar sentiment a few years earlier:

> In the past year I have travelled thousands of miles through the United States, Britain, the Continent and Mediterranean. I will say at once that nowhere have I experienced anything as revolting and disgusting as what we call the six o'clock swill. The daily demonstration of piggery is something that no other country in the world can match.[4]

Such attitudes were expressed with more frequency in the post-war period, when the first low rumblings of social change were heard – society pushing against suddenly irritating and intrusive legal restrictions. The influence of the temperance movement had waned, with the government abandoning local option just after the war, as it offered no effective solution to the problem of liquor reform. The movement's relations with hoteliers had also chilled, as its crowd kept banging on about prohibition and closing more hotels. The attitude of government was still fiercely pro-restriction as far as the selling of alcohol was concerned, but the emphasis was now on the task of civilising Victorians' drinking habits rather than wasting any more time on futile attempts to stamp out drinking altogether.

In 1956, a referendum was held on whether to extend hotel drinking hours from 6 pm to 10 pm, in time for the Melbourne Olympic Games, which would put the city on the world stage. It failed by an emphatic 300,000 votes, even though 6 pm closing had been abandoned in New South Wales in 1955. When licensing laws were reviewed in 1960, there was still such nervousness in government about extending trading hours that it refused to make a move without the support of a successful referendum. The 1960s did see some loosening of restrictions: a Restaurant Licence was introduced, though with restrictive terms so as not to compete with hotels;

'Drinking habits in Australia, are, from my observations in the places visited, unique. They are unique in the sense that they are deplorable'

[*Opposite*] Customers vie for a position at the bar to put their orders in before the six o'clock close

[*Following pages*] Happy days at a pub in Toorak Road, 1970

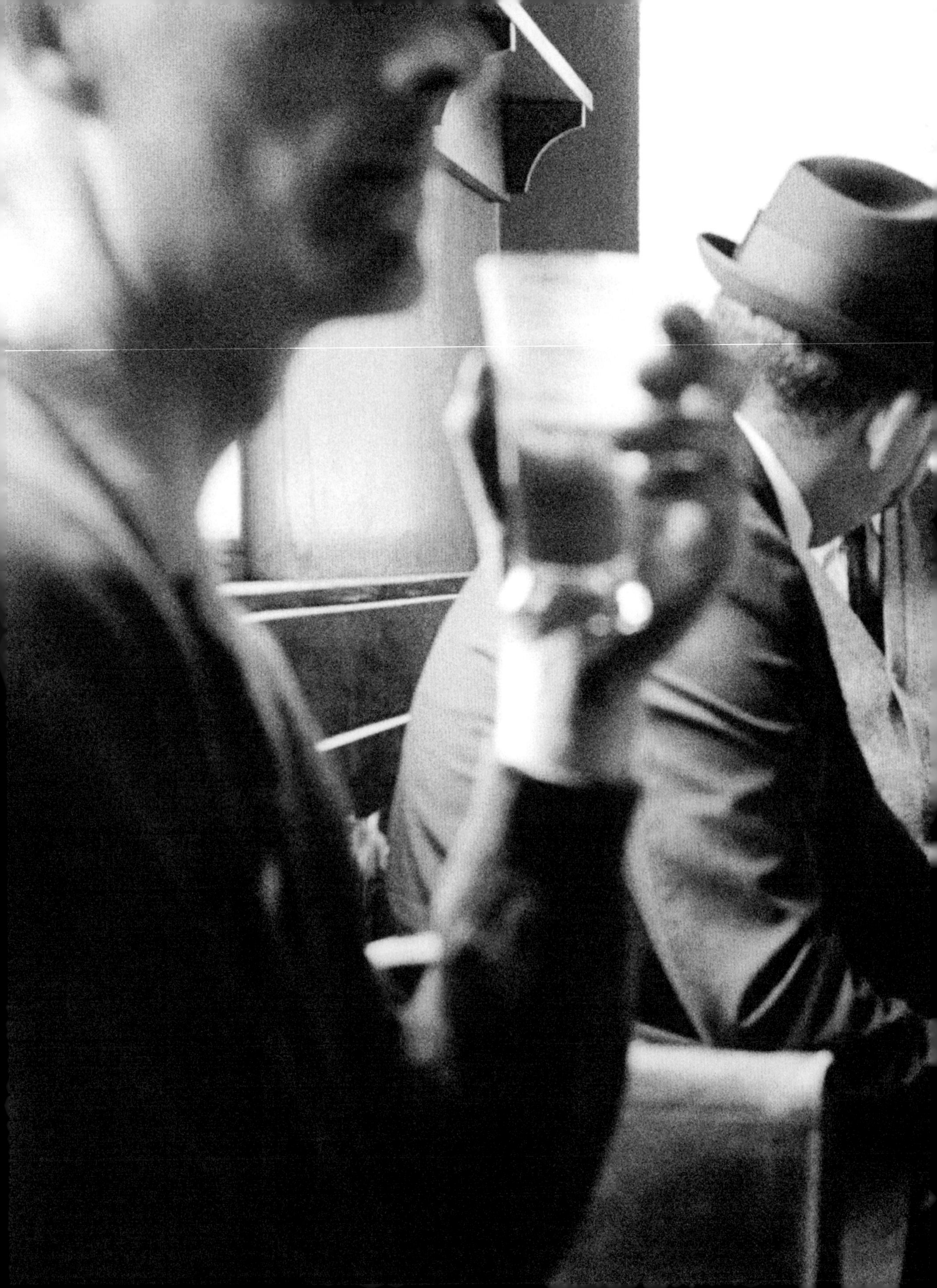

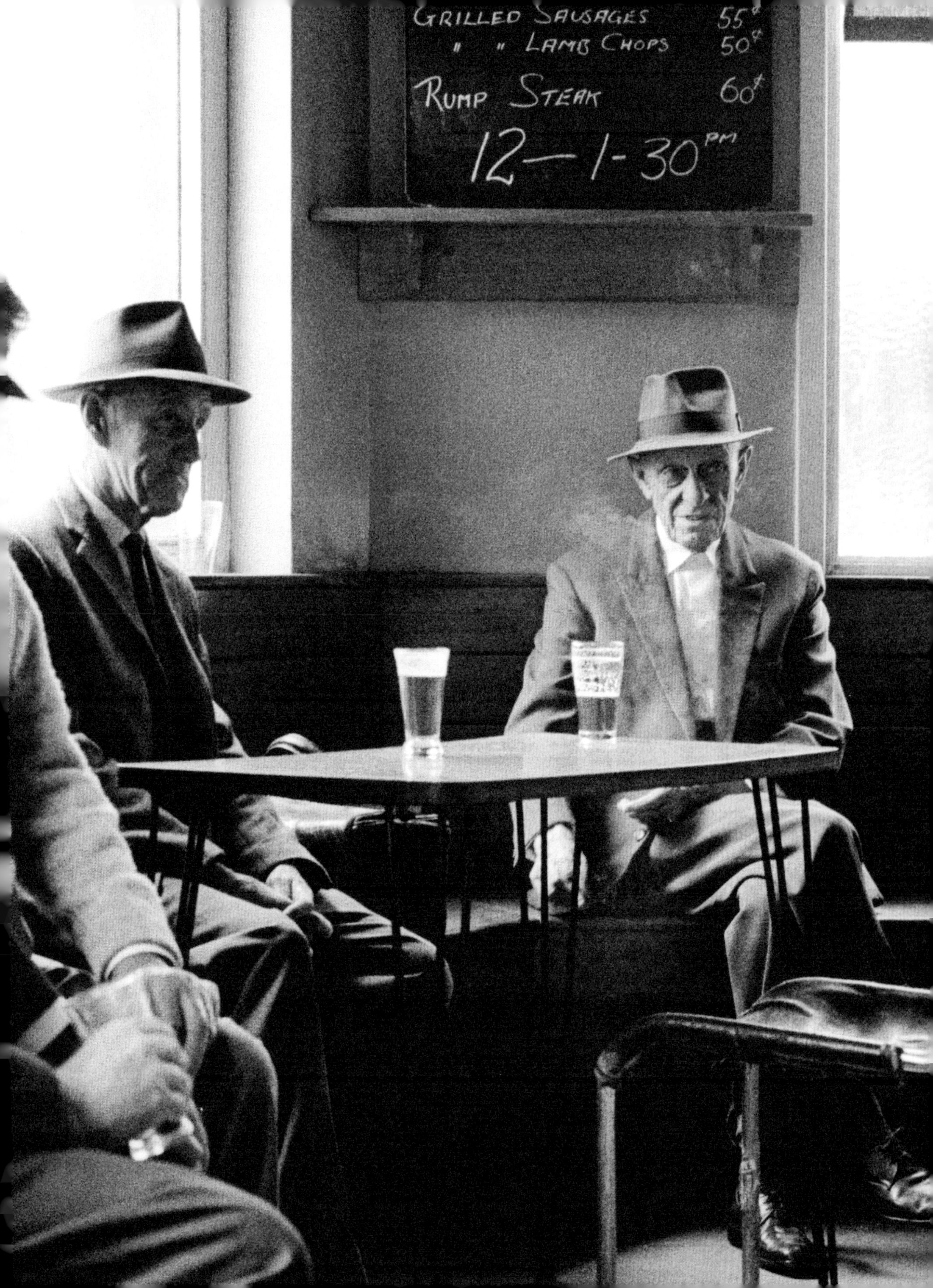
GRILLED SAUSAGES 55¢
" " LAMB CHOPS 50¢
RUMP STEAK 60¢
12—1-30PM

clubs were able to trade on Sundays; and some pub owners were allowed to serve alcohol with supper until 11.30 pm.

There was support within the government for extended trading hours, but there was not yet the political nerve to implement this. But things were changing. Mass migration after World War II, particularly from southern Europe, and the influence of a global audience descending on Melbourne for the 1956 Olympics began to broaden people's understandings of what constituted eating and drinking in the public sphere. Unsurprisingly, this, coupled with an increasing number of people travelling to Europe and seeing how the other half lived, threw institutions like the six o'clock swill into thoroughly unflattering relief. It was the time when wine consumption was on the rise, coffee was making inroads into tea's territory and beer consumption was showing signs of levelling and even dropping.

It was also a time when the existing laws were being increasingly flouted. This was not the home-brewed, sly-grog, completely inebriated flouting of the past, but (to modern eyes, at least) a more genteel and civilised breaking of the law. It was well known that you could get a glass of wine served in a coffee cup in some of the Italian-owned espresso bars and cafes that had sprung up in the city and in places like Carlton and St Kilda. Some restaurants with licences even posted lookouts after 10 pm to warn proprietors of the approach of licensing inspectors, giving them enough time to clear away telltale signs of post–10 pm wine consumption. Some restaurants without licences to serve alcohol had discovered a loophole in the law, which said patrons were not allowed to purchase alcohol on the premises but which made no mention of not being able to consume it there. It was loophole that led to the establishment of a great Victorian tradition – the BYO (bring your own) restaurant.

An increasing number of people wanted to eat out in restaurants and drink a bottle of wine without having to watch the clock. Or they wanted to have a glass or two over supper after going to the theatre, or enjoy a drink while dancing in a nightclub without having to smuggle a bottle in under their coat. What many didn't want to do was drink in hotels, which were still considered mostly masculine, often rough places of drinking in excess. These sorts of demands occur in any prosperous society, but the Victorian laws – still clinging to the basic principles that had come into being at the end of an economic crash early in the century – were not keeping pace.

Responding to societal rumblings, calls to extend hotel and restaurant trading hours and the perception that the licensing system needed more flexibility, a royal commission headed by Sir P.D. Phillips, QC was convened in 1965. Many of its findings were made into law in the *Liquor Control Act 1968*.

{*Opposite*} The timeless marriage of maraschino cherries and lobster thermidor

MENU

claret
CHATEAU MARGAUX VINTAGE 55/- (PINTS 27/6)
CHATEAU LATOUR VINTAGE 45/- CHIANTI 30/- (PINTS 15/-)
CHATEAU LAROSE, VINTAGE 1949, 45/- CHEVRON PRIVATE BIN 10/6
LINDEMAN'S CAWARRA CLARET 11/6 (PINTS 6/6)
YALUMBA, VINTAGE 1948, 12/6 CHATEAU TAHBILK 10/6 (PINTS 6/-)
PENFOLD'S ROYAL RESERVE EXTRA SPECIAL 10/-
TINTARA CABINET 10/- YALUMBA SPECIAL 10/-
CHATEAU TAHBILK CLARET 10/6 (PINTS 5/6)

burgundy
NUITS ST. GEORGES, VINTAGE 1947, 52/6
CHATEAU NEUF du PAPE 1947 45/- CHEVRON PRIVATE BIN 10/6
LINDEMAN'S ST. CORA 11/6 (PINTS 6/6)
PENFOLD'S ROYAL RESERVE EXTRA SPECIAL 10/-
SPARKLING HENKEL KARDINAL VIN 1947 47/6
GREAT WESTERN 32/6 (PINTS 17/-)

champagne
LANSON PERE ET FILS 70/- (PINTS 35/-) VEUVE CLICQUOT VINTAGE 75/-
MOET ET CHANDON VINTAGE 75/- G. H. MUMM'S CORDON ROUGE 75/-
CHAS. HEIDSIECK & CO. VINTAGE 75/-
HENKEL TROCKEN VINTAGE 1947 47/6 LINDEMAN'S PRIVATE CUVEE 27/6
MINCHINBURY WHITE LAQ 27/6 TINTARA 27/6
GREAT WESTERN IMPERIAL RESERVE 35/- (PINTS 17/6)

liqueur brandy
REMY MARTIN V.S.O.P. COGNAC 4/- HINES 5/- ORLANDO LIQUEUR 3/6
MARTELL'S CORDON BLEU 6/- MILDARA SUPREME 3/-

liqueurs
COINTREAU 3/6 D.O.M. BENEDICTINE 3/6 GRAND MARNIER 3/6
OTHER IMPORTED LIQUEURS 3/-

The Strange Attraction of 'Caffeine'

There were certainly a lot of 'coffee' drinkers after dark in Melbourne during the 1960s and 1970s. Once the pubs closed, out they would come. They'd frequent seedy, back-lane unlicensed bistros and darkened upstairs rooms of city buildings, where they'd drink 'coffee', lots of it, in luminous-orange Pyrex mugs.

These coffee haunts never advertised themselves, otherwise everyone would be in on the act, especially the coffee police. You had to know someone who knew where to go, and sometimes you also needed to know just how to get in. Take the International Club, on the first floor of the bank building on the corner of Exhibition and Lonsdale Streets, where it paid to know the system of entry. The grated gate – the kind used in old elevators – was always closed. You could see the merry coffee drinkers inside, but not a sod would acknowledge your presence or let you in. If you didn't know how to get in, you weren't meant to be there, as simple as that. (It wasn't that hard: you put your hand through the grate at the side and lifted a pin and voilà – coffee for everyone!)

Coffee lovers had their favourite haunts. In the city it was the Italian Waiter's Club. The coffee wasn't so good but, hey, there was nowhere else willing to serve it in such quantity. In St Kilda it was the Paris Nightclub, in Acland Street. It had great coffee and topnotch entertainment, making everyone thirsty for more coffee. The trouble was that every six months the coffee police would close it down. The New Paris Nightclub sprang up to replace the original, but in a different Acland Street location. When that was closed down, it became the Paris Follies Nightclub six months later. You can't keep a good coffee place down – after two years the business had just about done the block.

Richmond's Les Halles, run by Gerald, a former French Foreign Legionnaire, was a gay old place early in the mornings, once the girls from 'Les Girls' had knocked off. There was partying aplenty, but Gerald always attracted the attention of the coffee police. One day, he left the country – perhaps in search of better coffee.

The police roundsmen of the *Sun* and *Herald* newspapers were always on the lookout for good coffee, especially when working late shifts long into the night, with just the police radio for company during the 1950s and 1960s. Fortunately, coffee was always close at hand, especially after an enterprising bunch knocked a hole in the wall to the adjoining pub and supplies could simply be pulled up to the office in a wicker basket!

The Purple Cow was one of the great all-night party palaces for coffee heads, housed inside a demure Victorian terrace. Ironically, it was sold and knocked down, and in its place the coffee police headquarters was built. JENI PORT

Drinking on the Sly

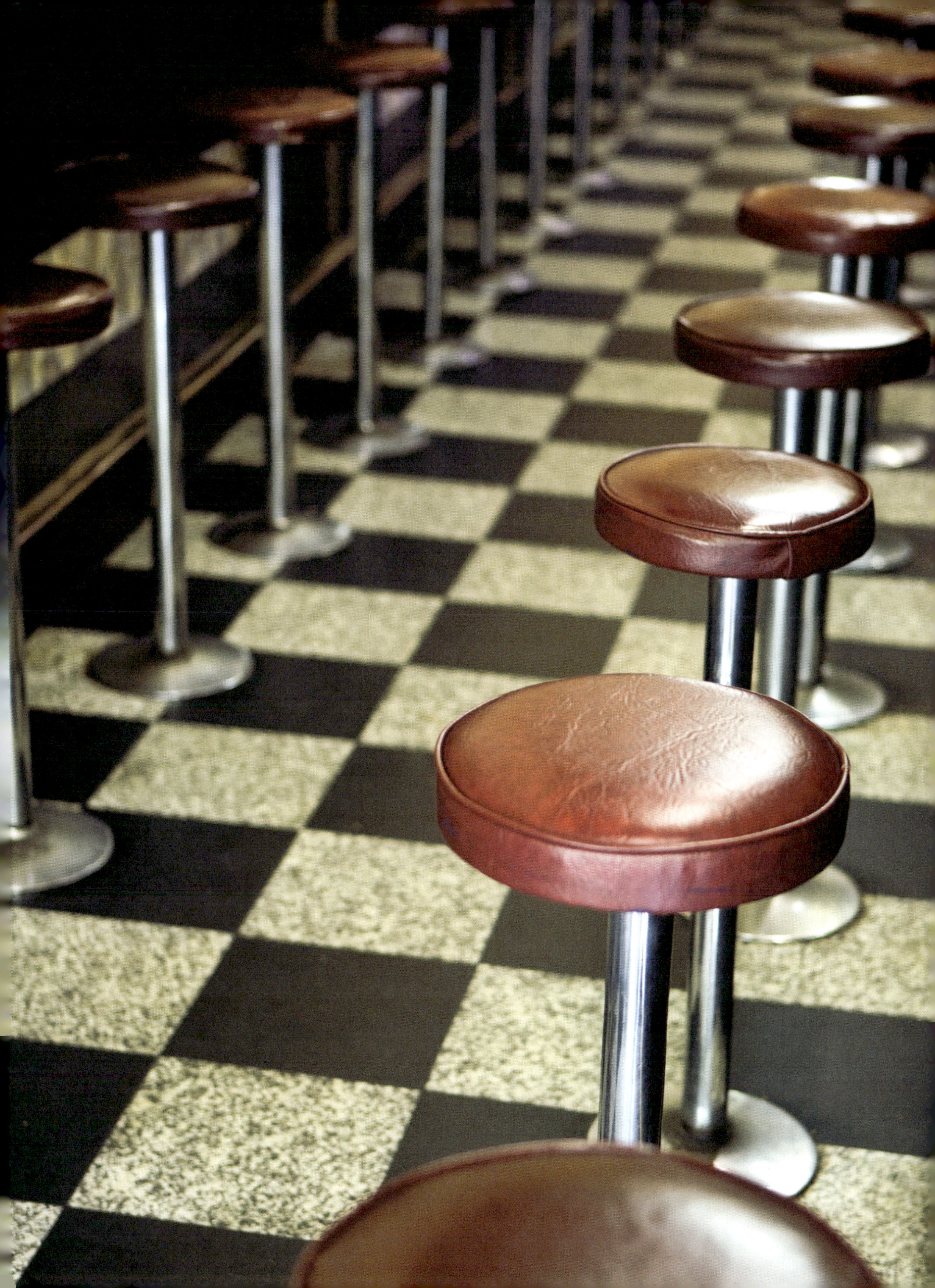

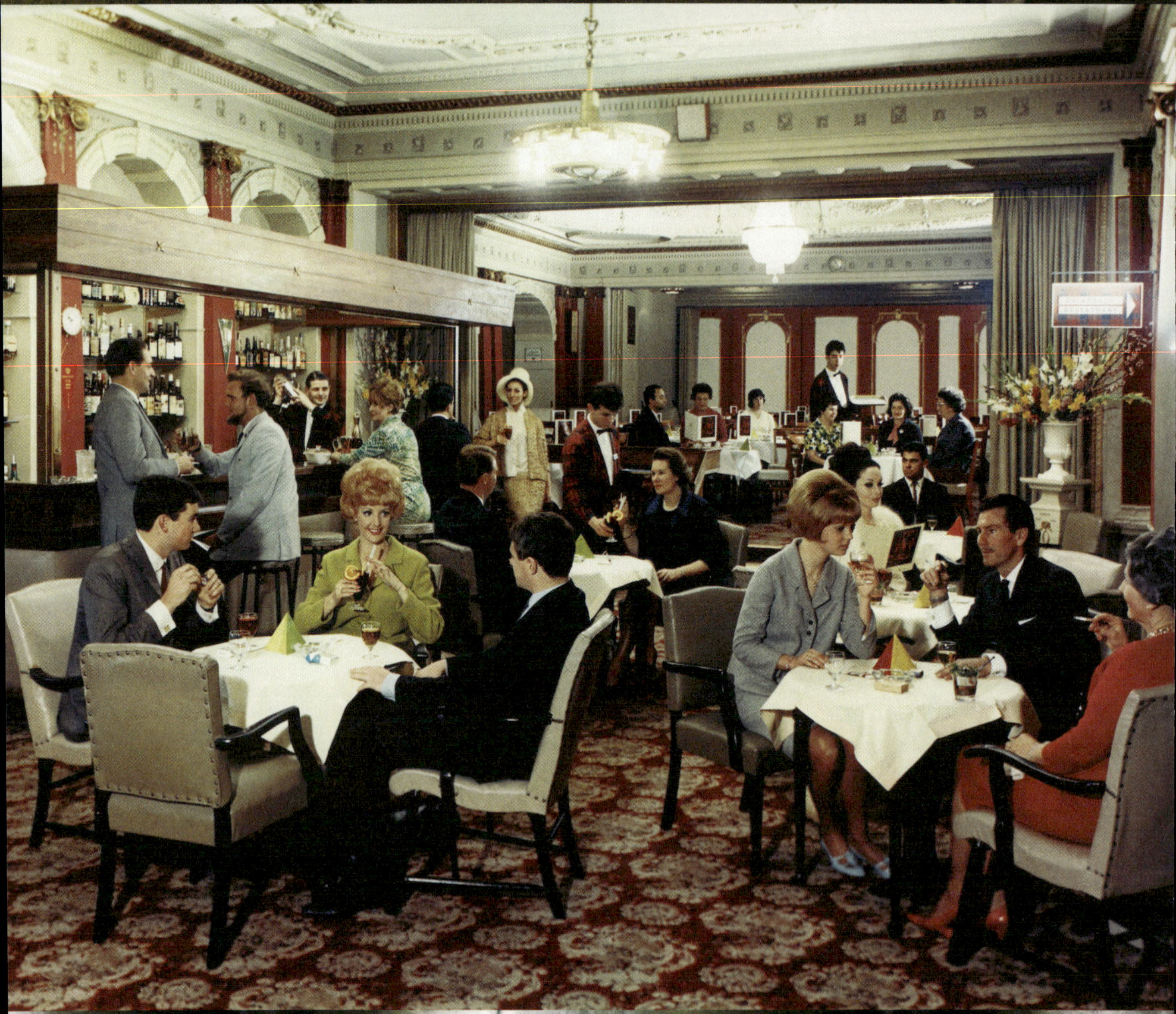

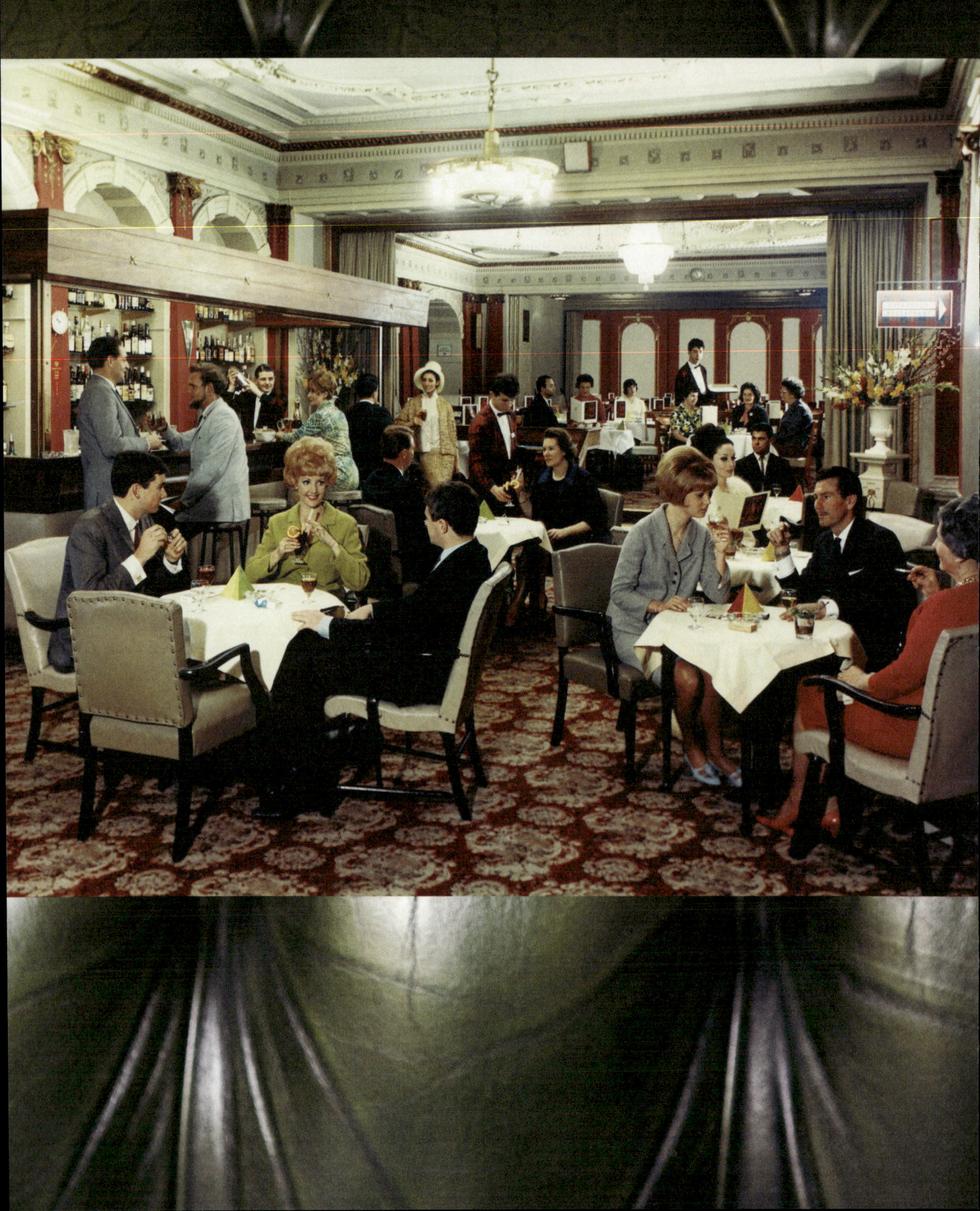

The Phillips inquiry was nothing if not thorough, hearing submissions and evidence from all who had an interest or a stake in the alcohol-related questions under scrutiny. But perhaps the most interesting, and some might suggest influential, part of the inquiry was the 'test dinner' that the royal commissioner hosted, described by M.J. Lewis in his book *A Rum State*:

> A fine dinner was provided with the usual range of drinks from aperitifs to liqueurs. No one consumed more alcohol than the equivalent of nine and a half 7-ounce glasses of beer. Norman McCallum, pathologist, and John Birrell, police surgeon, attended to the scientific assessment of the alcohol intake. The test case had a breathalyser reading of 0.053, just slightly above the level police saw as the limit for safe drinking. The whole affair seemed to indicate what Phillips was keen to show, that when consumed slowly, with food, alcohol would do no harm.[5]

The Phillips recommendations that were made into law certainly loosened things up: pubs were able to open until 10 pm, finally ending fifty years of the six o'clock swill; restaurants had their hours extended until 11.30 pm and had the restrictions lifted that prohibited them from serving beer; theatres were able to serve alcohol until 11 pm on performance nights; and nightclubs could serve alcohol with refreshments and entertainment until 3 am. There was also a host of new licences, including a new Tavern Licence that freed the holder of the obligation to provide accommodation, but which came with so many restrictions that very few of these 'bar' licences ever saw the light of day.

Aside from extending hours – including for those businesses with BYO Licences – and adding a few more licence categories to the burgeoning number already in existence, the most noteworthy parts of the new laws were the ones that spelt out how (rather than when) alcohol was to be served in Victoria.

Taking the lessons learned from Sir Phillips' 'test dinner', the new laws set up the Liquor Control Commission (LCC), a supposedly administrative body that was basically quasi-judicial and would, among other things, oversee premises serving alcohol in Victoria. It would ensure 'an orderly and continuous improvement and development of facilities and arrangements for the supply of accommodation, meals and liquor to the public'. The people carrying out these activities would have to be of 'good character and have the training skills and capacities necessary to provide an orderly and proper service'.[6] The LCC was also charged with ensuring the 'security and stability' of the industry by regulating supply and demand.

In short, the new Act opened up trading hours but entrenched a system that had been operating since the beginning of the century, effectively a monopoly for

{*Opposite*} The cocktail lounge at the Menzies Hotel

> The LCC and its seemingly didactic pronouncements on everything from wallpaper to wine lists looked like an erratic, overly powerful law unto itself

existing licence holders. The number of hotels would again be reduced by enforcing particular standards in decor, food, service and accommodation (another winnowing of the commercially vulnerable); new licences would be strictly controlled; and the hotels that complied with the often expensive demands of the LCC, all in the name of raising the tone of the place, would be protected from competition by laws that gave them the right to object to any new licences purely on commercial grounds. The industry decided who would trade and the conditions under which they did so.

In hindsight, this system of laws that so favoured the hotels and severly limited the restaurant trade's movement seems astonishingly one-eyed, unbalanced and unjust – not to mention anti-competitive. But put it into the context of its time – particularly during the 1960s – when both public and government attitudes towards alcohol were very much in favour of restricting availability and containing unruly drunkenness, the approach seems a little more understandable. In fact, under the watch of the LCC in these early days, the standards of hotels were significantly improved, with large sums of money ($5.2 million in 1968) spent on renovations and improvements. To a conservative population that liked a drink but was still slightly suspicious of it, such outward signs of civilised imbibing would have been extremely comforting.

But by the 1970s community attitudes were changing at an increasingly rapid pace and the Liquor Control Act with its multiple amendments and appendices was beginning to look very lumpy and outdated. More tinkering during the 1970s and early 1980s didn't help, as hours were further extended, more outlets of various shades were allowed and, inevitably, more licences were created as the law tried to keep up with the shifting needs and desires of the community. By the beginning of the 1980s the Act encompassed 29 licence categories: Hotelkeeper, Retail Bottled Liquor, Australian Wine, Auctioneer, Victorian Food & Wine Festival, Victorian Arts Centre, Victorian Wine Centre, Residential, Inmates, Booth, Theatre, Works, Ship, Tourist Facility, Cabaret, Cider Tavern, Cultural Centre, Canteen, Exhibition, Rutherglen Wine Festival, Club, Caterer, Tertiary Institution, Convention Facility, Ships Provedore, Vigneron, Mead Producer, Brewer and Wholesale Liquor Merchant. In addition, there were thirty-six permit categories to add further layers of bewilderment and confusion. Though there was a large industry of licensing lawyers and consultants to steer people wanting to operate a business with an alcohol component through this tangled knot of laws, no-one seemed to understand how every part of the unwieldy Act worked. The thought of trying would be enough to drive anyone to drink. And, to many restaurateurs, the LCC and its seemingly didactic pronouncements on everything from wallpaper to wine lists looked like an erratic, overly powerful law unto itself.

{*Opposite*} 'Chloe' and friends at Young and Jackson pub

{*Following pages*} Limited drinking hours at the Y&J

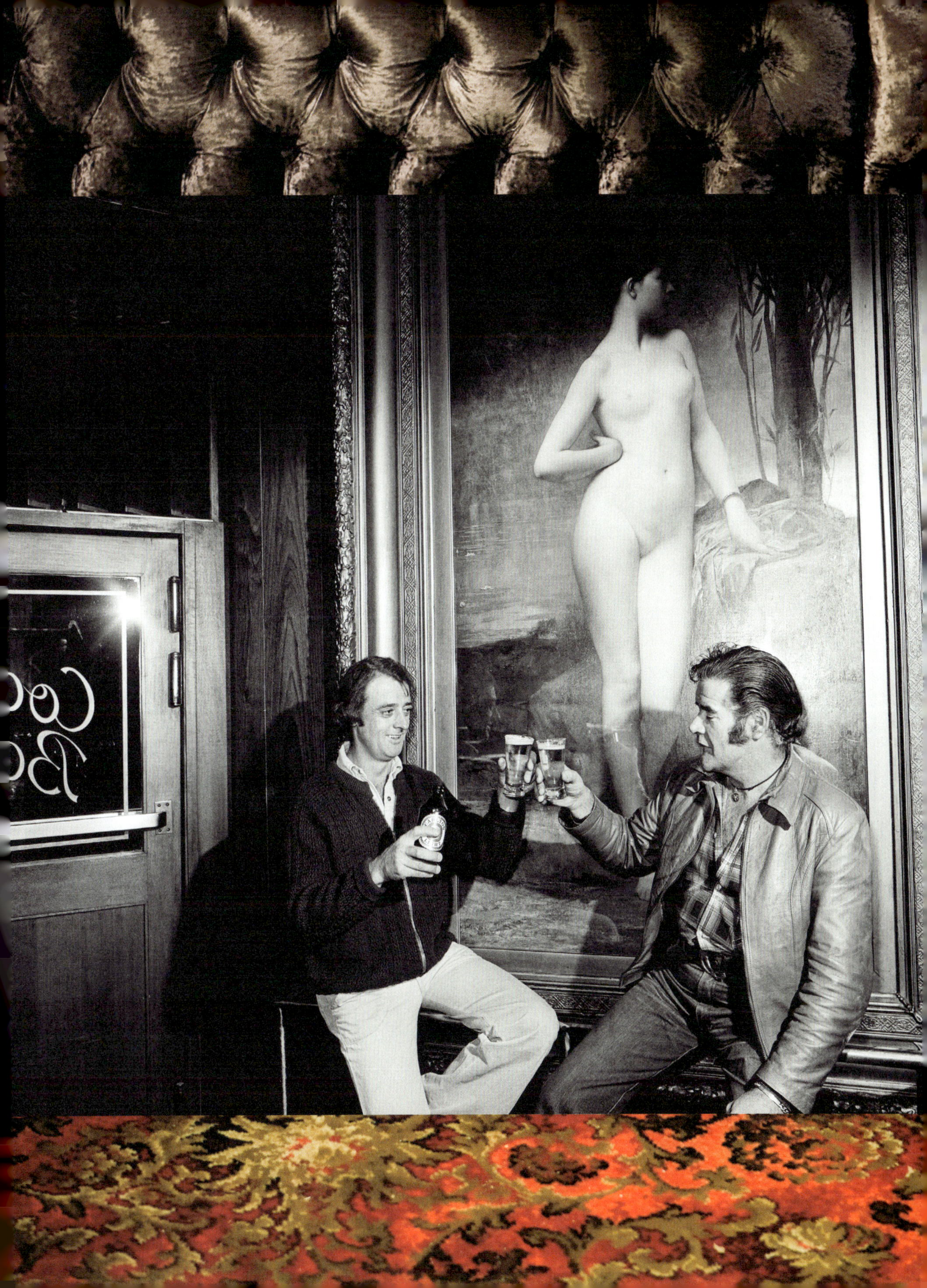

STON ST
RINCE'S BRI
OPEN
Borings Sparkling Ringolde $2.29
Morris Wine Casks
Baileys Irish Cream $12·50

OGE HOTEL.
DAY
ALL BARS
12–2
4–6
Jim Beam
Bourbon
$13.95
Stock
Gala
Spumante
$3.25
Baileys
Cream
Hardys

The Curtain-raiser

The curtain opens and you're ushered inside. There's a table in the centre of the room, with bottles of opened wine atop. The curtain is closed. A ridiculously small vessel – the size of a sherry glass – is offered, with a thimbleful of wine inside. You taste it. It's exhilarating. You'd like to tell your friends. But with your glass in hand you cannot move beyond the curtain, or indeed be seen by anyone outside the 'booth'. That's the law.

That was the law back in 1975, and it was quite specific about how a wine-tasting was conducted by wine retailers. Nick Chlebnikowski remembers putting up the curtain in his Doncaster wine shop in the mid-1970s. He even remembers the colour: orange. The curtain tracks are still in place, but the curtain has long since gone. The 1970s, he says, were different times; 'cellar door' and 'winery tourism' weren't part of the wine vocabulary, and those clever marketing temptations that today send people off for weekend getaways among vines did not exist.

What Melbourne did have was a wine-tasting circuit. A Saturday morning ritual might take you across Melbourne from Duke and Moorfield, in North Melbourne, to King and Godfree, in Carlton, or Richmond Hill Cellars, in Richmond. Alternatively, it might start at Crittenden's, in Prahran, take you over to Templestowe Cellars or Nick's Wine Merchants, in Doncaster, and finish back in Prahran at Dan Murphy's. Each retailer would hold tastings of new-release wines, and sometimes the winemaker would be there to speak on the wines – not that there was time for talk. In a period when there were no extended trading hours or Sunday trading, you only had three hours to do the circuit, from 9 am to noon. There was also no spitting. And as for 0.05, as Nick says, 'it was a different time'.

Under the licensing laws of the day, retailers could not charge for wine-tasting, so they relied heavily on the generosity of wine companies to supply samples. 'In those days the only way to create a wine market was to educate people, but they [the Liquor Licensing Commission] didn't make it easy,' says Roy Moorfield, who started Duke and Moorfield with partner Ross Duke in 1971.

By 1979, Moorfield was convinced that wine education needed to reach out to a larger audience, and so the Exhibition of Victorian Winemakers was born. It was an annual fixture for the next thirty years, at its height attracting 100 Victorian wineries and 30,000 visitors over a four-day event that included tastings, wine dinners and seminars. JENI PORT

Wine-tasting

By the 1980s, the decades-long protection of the liquor industry – particularly the hotels – was being scrutinised in a hospitality market dramatically different from the one in which the licensing laws were originally enacted. People saw the laws to be less about regulating the supply of alcohol to protect the public and more about protecting an entrenched monopoly from competition. The laws were also restricting choice and, in a time that still reeked faintly of the patchouli, pot smoke and a general anti-authoritarian questioning of the status quo, restricting choice was not part of the plan.

The times were ripe for a clean sweep. The existing laws were creaky and so overloaded that another round of amendments may make them collapse altogether. The public, looking for new ways to eat out, drink and socialise in the public arena, was beginning to notice the constraints of outdated restrictions. The restaurant scene was good and getting better, but particularly among the movers and shakers of the Melbourne scene there was a feeling that it could be a whole lot more.

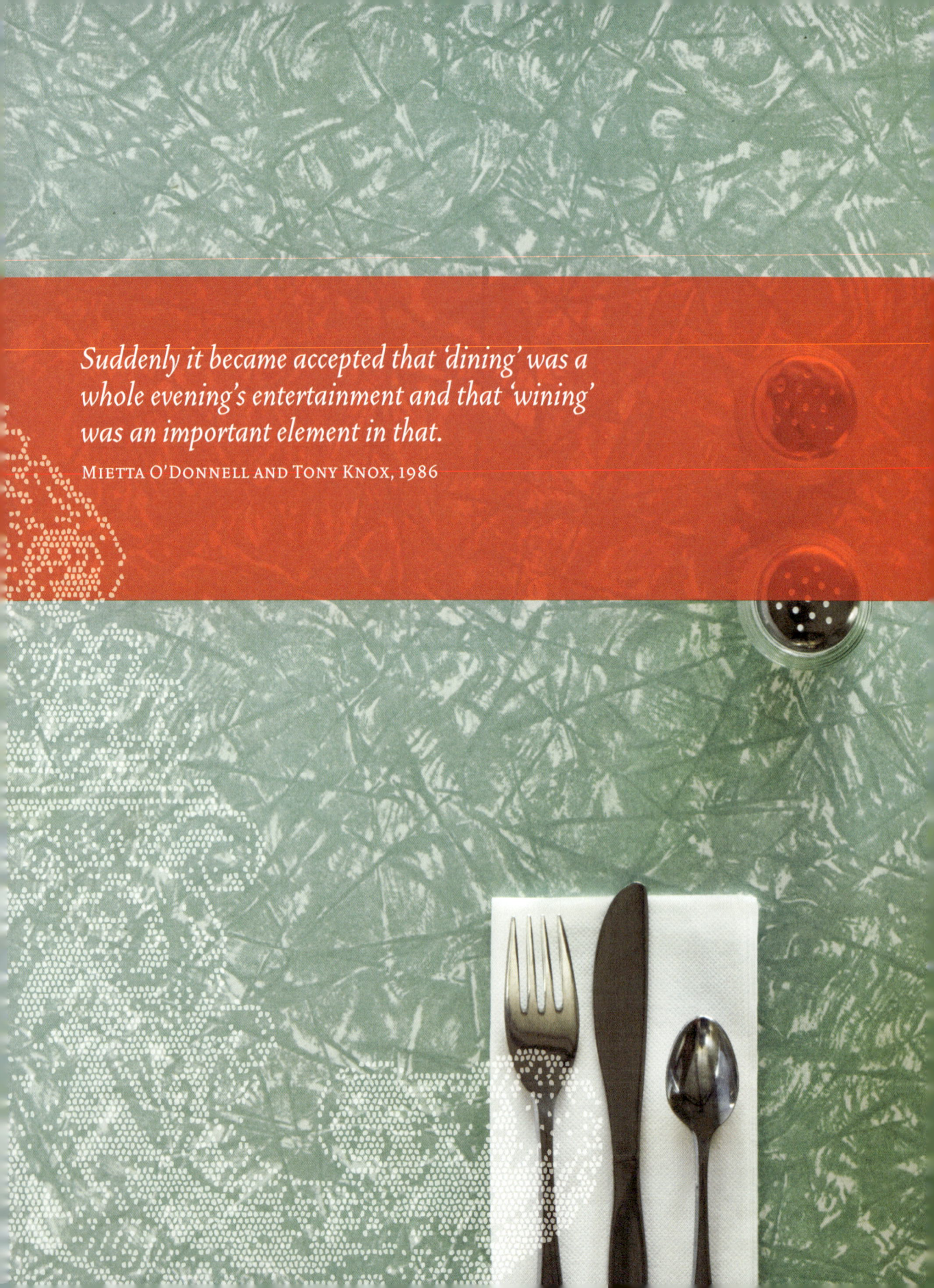

Suddenly it became accepted that 'dining' was a whole evening's entertainment and that 'wining' was an important element in that.

Mietta O'Donnell and Tony Knox, 1986

The Laws of Dining

CHANCERY HOUSE
Assure with
CITY MUTUAL LIFE
for
Bigger Bonuses

*I*t is very easy to scoff at the dining habits of those who came before us. As Michael Symons says in his gastronomic history of Australia, *One Continuous Picnic*: 'Every generation of Australians has believed that it has been the first to dine out on decent food.'[1] And while it is certainly true that modern-day Victorians have access to an array of restaurants, cafes, bars, produce and alcohol, at hours that their forebears could only dream of, a little historical context can soon turn a smug and pitying attitude into one of admiration.

Even if you put aside factors such as the vast distances and rudimentary communications that prevented outside trends, ideas and flavours from hitting the diners of the day with any immediacy, the people who were trying to supply food and drink were, for much of Victoria's history, severely hobbled by the licensing laws. These did not just govern who could supply alcohol and when, but also regulated how people could eat and drink in public. The Liquor Control Commission (LCC) became an arbiter of taste and style, as well as an administrator of laws. Hotels and restaurants, even licensed grocers, were forced to operate within exceedingly narrow parameters, and there was little impetus or scope for the industry to change its tune.

Still, Victoria's dining history is full of people who have successfully pushed against the regulations to give the market what it has increasingly craved. From a distance of years it may seem quaint that people were forced to furtively sip wine decanted into Coke bottles, or to eat dinner at 6 pm so that they could finish a bottle of wine before it was snatched from their table at 8 pm, or that a business could have its licence revoked because its carpet was not up to scratch or its menu deemed inappropriate. But before John Nieuwenhuysen's report in the mid-1980s hacked through the tangle of licensing laws, the innovative, entrepreneurial, boundary-pushing spirit that today characterises Victoria's food scene was already making its presence felt, albeit under infinitely more trying circumstances.

Even before the gold rush of the 1850s flooded Victoria with people and wealth, Melbourne had begun to develop a fashionable restaurant scene. Some of the better hotels boasted luxurious dining rooms, lists of imported wines and French-accented menus that snootily avoided the mutton, ham and plum-pudding – dishes that were

[*Opposite*] The glamorous Menzies Hotel, at the corner of William and Bourke streets, was demolished in 1969 to make way for BHP's headquarters

> Aside from the larger, more upmarket of the species, they were mostly rough places, full of men whose main purpose was to drink

the stuff of the worker and the everyday. This early distinction of 'better' types of establishment, and the elevation of French cooking to the cuisine of choice for the socially adept gourmand, set a pattern in the population's dining habits that was to continue well into the second half of the twentieth century.

But while the gold rush saw an inevitable increase in the number of these upmarket restaurants and hotel dining rooms across Melbourne's city grid, the majority of diners frequented the city's hundreds of coffee and tea houses and 'chop houses' — crowded, rudimentary places where waiters yelled orders to the kitchen from diners' tables and where mutton was served in a head-spinning number of variations (boiled, baked, roasted, stewed, curried, in pies, with eggs at breakfast etc). Chinese restaurants were also appearing in Little Bourke Street, but suspicion of the Chinese meant that, aside from a few adventurous artistic and bohemian types, most Anglo diners weren't yet ready to surrender to the joys of chicken chow mein.

Under the terms of their licences, most pubs provided food, and with the deregulation of licensing laws in 1864 they became extremely popular eating destinations. Deregulation saw an explosion in the number of licensed premises, which made competition between the hotels particularly fierce. Hotel owners hit upon a way to attract custom and so the era of the free counter lunch began.

Before the rules governing the sale of alcohol were relaxed under the 1864 Act (swiftly tightened again in 1870), many publicans' idea of providing food was plonking platters of bread and cheese, drying and hardening, on one corner of the bar. But with competition making the market more fierce, publicans had to work harder to attract a crowd. Many began serving huge roasts with piles of vegetables, which were free to any customer who bought a drink. This soon proved an expensive headache for pub owners and it attracted the wrath of the temperance movement, which saw counter meals as an insidious incentive to get poor young people onto the demon drink. It was not the first or the last time that the temperance and pub people found themselves in agreement, and the pressure of the two groups (aided by the Brewers Association) saw the free counter meal become illegal in the early twentieth century — proving once again that there is no such thing as a free lunch.

If you wanted a drink with your food at this time, the choices were very limited unless you were wealthy. If you could afford it, there were numerous oyster saloons, with curtained booths; members-only, men-only clubs, such as the Australian Club, with attached dining rooms and European chefs; and well-upholstered restaurants such as the Maison Dorée, the Crystal Café and La Mascotte. Hotels were still obliged to provide food, but aside from the larger, more upmarket of the species, they were mostly rough places, full of men whose main purpose was to drink. The food being served — aimed at the befuddled and undiscerning palate of the drunk — was produced accordingly.

{*Opposite*} The classical facade of the gentlemen's club the Australian

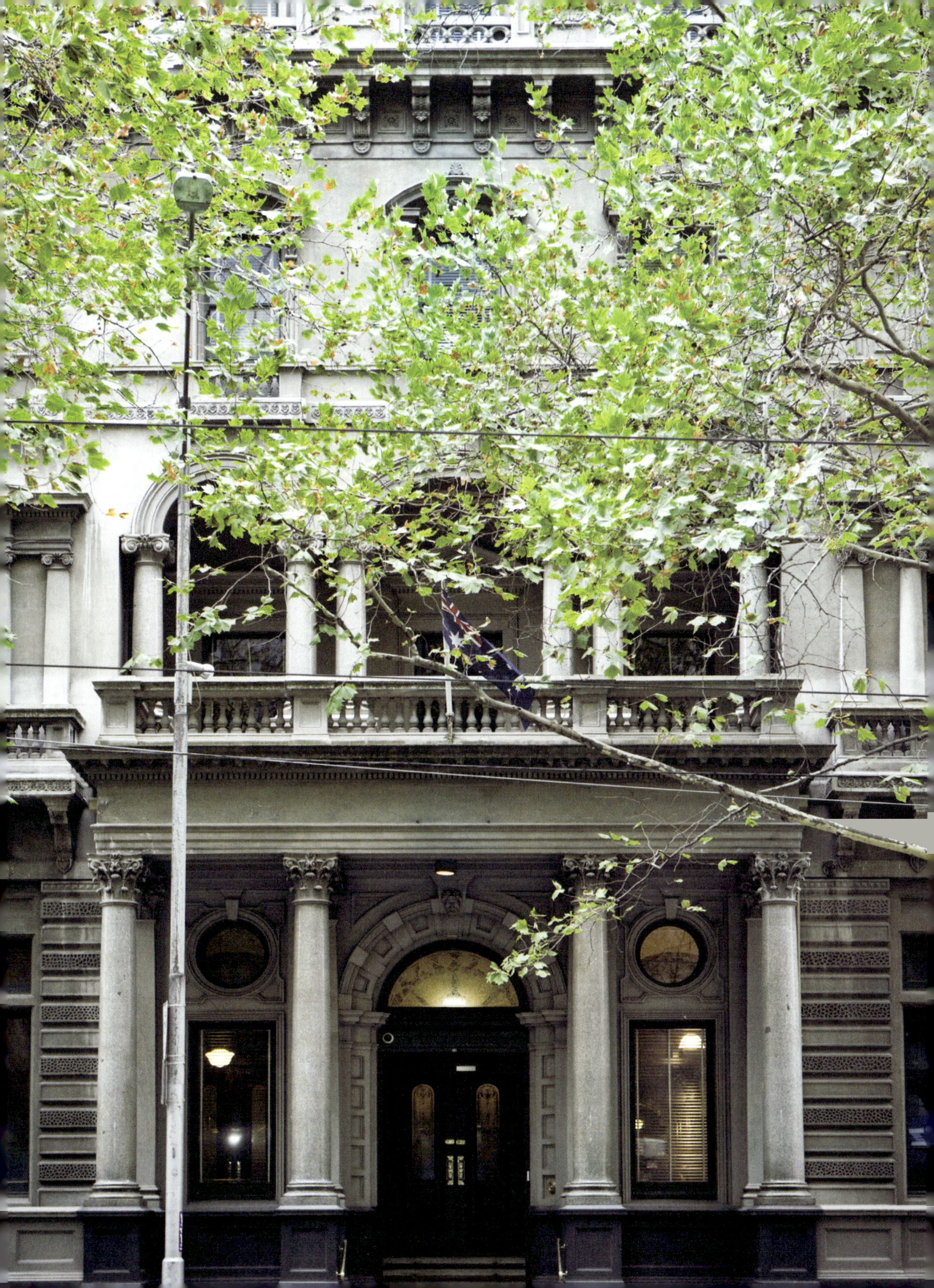

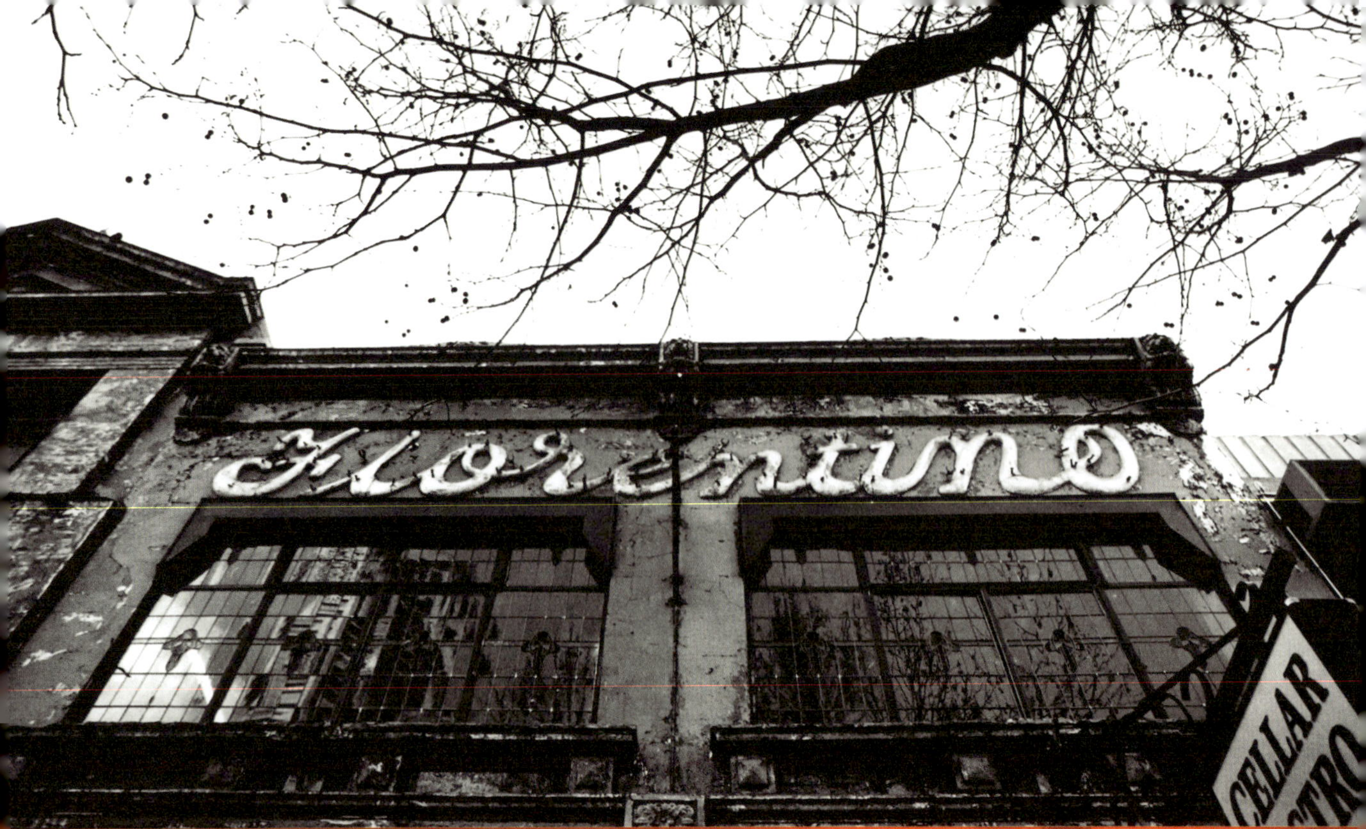
Florentino
CELLAR
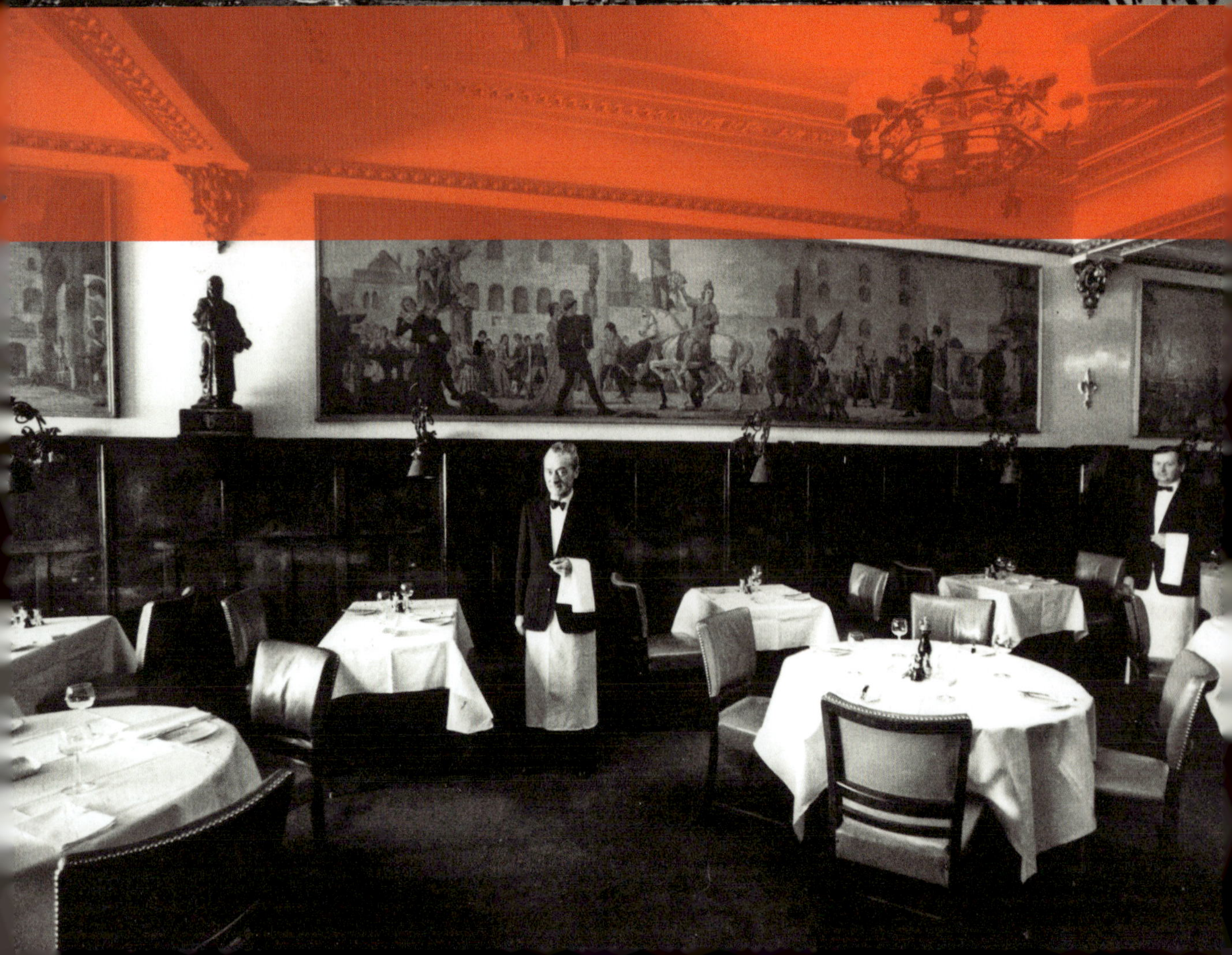

By the early twentieth century, then, dining out, particularly where alcohol was involved, was an activity mainly reserved for the upper end of the economic spectrum. This was in no small way due to the licensing laws of the time, which allowed little room for any kind of business model that wasn't either top end or bottom end. For most people at this time who couldn't afford the expensive hotel dining rooms and didn't want to spend time in pubs, the best option was to drink with a meal in the privacy of their own homes.

Despite rigid legal barriers seeming to prevent other styles of eating and drinking, there were some savvy individuals who discovered the cracks in the foundations and the loopholes in the fine print. Many were Italian immigrants, a group that even in the early 1900s played a significant part in expanding Melburnians' perceptions of what it was to eat and drink in public.

The earliest of the Italian-run places were probably Fasoli's and Rinaldi's Wine Hall, which both operated around the turn of the century on Lonsdale Street. Rinaldi's Wine Hall – which later became The Latin – started off as a wine shop operating with an Australian Wine Licence (AWL).

This licence was a curiously specific document that inadvertently did wonders for the restaurant industry. It allowed the holder to sell only Australian wine – no beer, no spirits, no cider, no imported wine – for consumption on the premises or to be taken away (in bottles) between the hours of 9 am and 6 pm. Businesses associated with AWLs were traditionally the decrepit haunts of glazed-eyed, port-swilling alcoholics. In fact, wine itself was a largely discredited drink at this time, aside from some of the sweetened fortified stuff, and drinking red wine would have polite company looking at you sideways. But the Italians, used to drinking table wine with their meals, saw in these wine saloons the potential to operate businesses that more closely resembled their own cultural traditions. The Rinaldis took over an existing wine shop in 1901, and shortly afterwards began serving simple meals accompanied by table wine, establishing something of a minor trend. With AWLs there was the potential to run a licensed restaurant in Victoria, albeit a restricted one.

Over the next couple of decades some of the most famous Italian names on the Melbourne dining scene – the 'spaghetti mafia' as they were later termed – set up shop, mostly in former wine saloons but also taking over pubs. They gradually morphed from humble trattoria-style establishments like Fasoli's and Rinaldi's, where diners shared a central table in humble back rooms and were served a series of dishes and glasses of wine for a set payment (two shillings in the 1920s), to some of the most renowned and fashionable eating establishments in Melbourne.

Cafe Florentino, still operating today as Grossi Florentino, was opened on the site of Melbourne's first licensed wine bar, and by the 1930s it had been joined at

{*Opposite*} The Mural Room at Florentino's

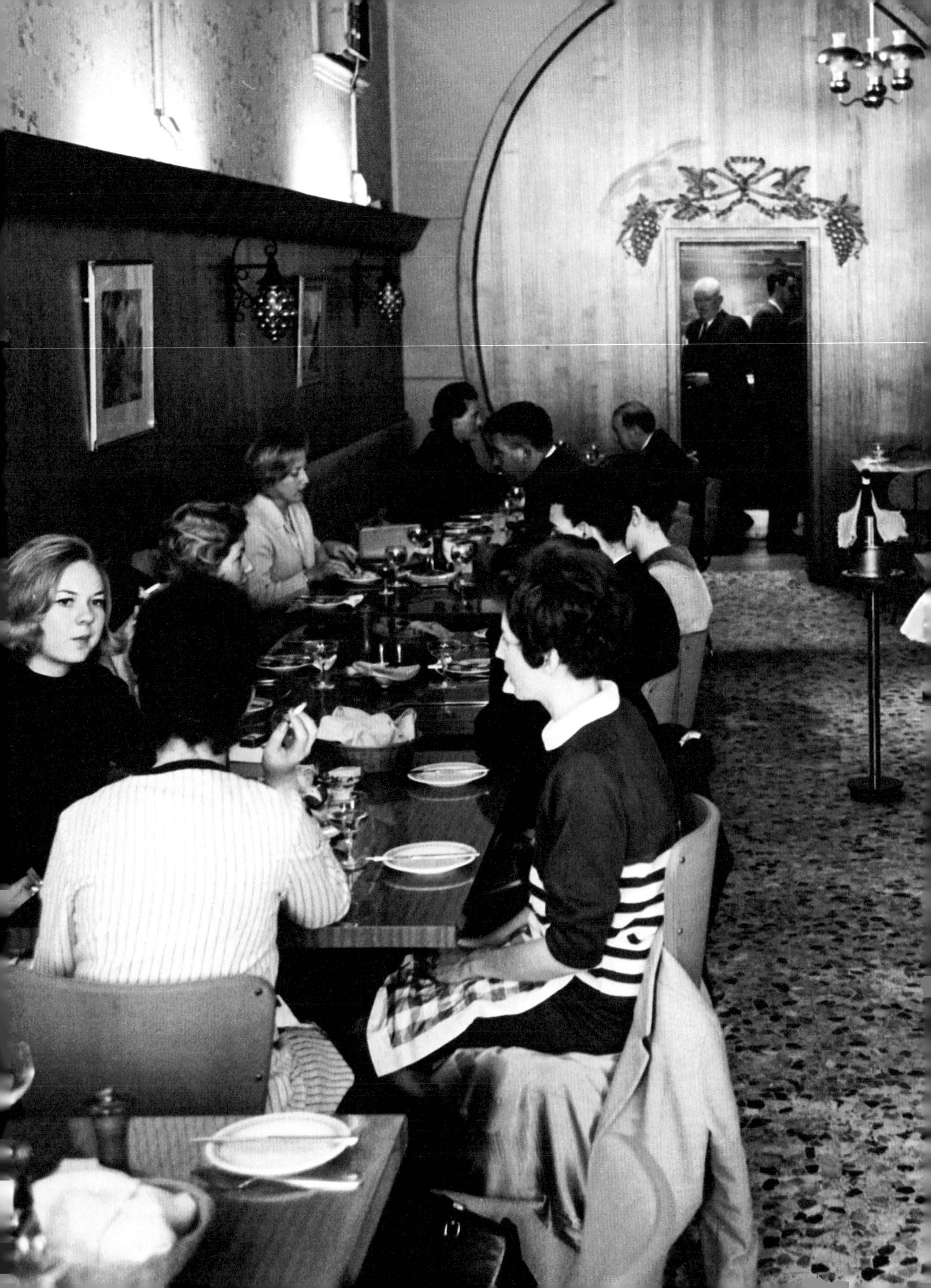

{*Left*} European fare was on the menu at Casa Virgona in Fitzroy

the parliament and theatre end of the Melbourne city grid by a fashionable group of Italian-run businesses – Molina's, Cafe D'Italia, The Society and Mario's. Combined with the many upmarket dining rooms of hotels like the Australia, Menzies and Windsor, this group of restaurants constituted Melbourne's most visible, fashionable and concentrated dining scene for many years.

These city restaurants mainly catered to the well heeled, but wine bar/trattorias began opening in the inner suburbs around this time, which provided a limited but real alternative for those who wanted to drink wine with their food. The most famous of these were Virgona's, in Brunswick Street, Fitzroy, and the still-operating Jimmy Watson's, in Lygon Street, Carlton. Both defied the seedy, alcoholic-infested wine-bar stereotypes by offering a more casual, affordable and thrillingly sophisticated imbibing to the academic, bohemian and artist populations that congregated in those suburbs.

The first real stirrings of change began to be felt in the 1950s, despite restrictive licensing laws continuing to hold the hotel and restaurant industry in their rigid grasp. The lean times of the Depression, World War II and the post-war recovery were replaced by increasing affluence, and combined with a surge of migration from southern Europe this produced a dining scene offering more alternatives. In the city, Carlton, Fitzroy, North Melbourne and St Kilda, espresso bars with the latest Gaggias, La Cimbalis and Faemas started something of a coffee craze that attracted a young crowd that mixed with the new immigrants. Citizens and media alike often regarded these places as hotbeds of illegal activity – and many of them were. Illegal card games and sneaky booze were part of the attraction. But mainly what drew people was that these places offered an alternative to pubs, which were still under the sway of the six o'clock swill.

Mirka and Georges Mora opened a French-style cafe in Exhibition Street in 1954 and later that year successfully applied to have streetside tables, among the first in the city to do so. At around the same time Cafe Florentino opened Il Bistro (now the Cellar Bar) in a former wine shop, with an AWL. Il Bistro's formula of fast, simple Italian food and cheap wine was so popular that the lunch-only crowd queued to get in and diners often spilled out onto the streets with their pasta and wine.

One of Melbourne's most famous espresso icons, Pellegrini's, also opened in 1954, in a former tailor's shop in Bourke Street. Run by brothers Leon and Vildo Pellegrini, who had worked as waiters at the nearby Cafe Florentino, Pellegrini's curved bar, mirrored walls, timber-grained laminex and state-of-the-art Gaggia epitomised the edgy Italian cool that young, style-famished Melburnians embraced

{Opposite} Fine dining at the Savoy Plaza Hotel

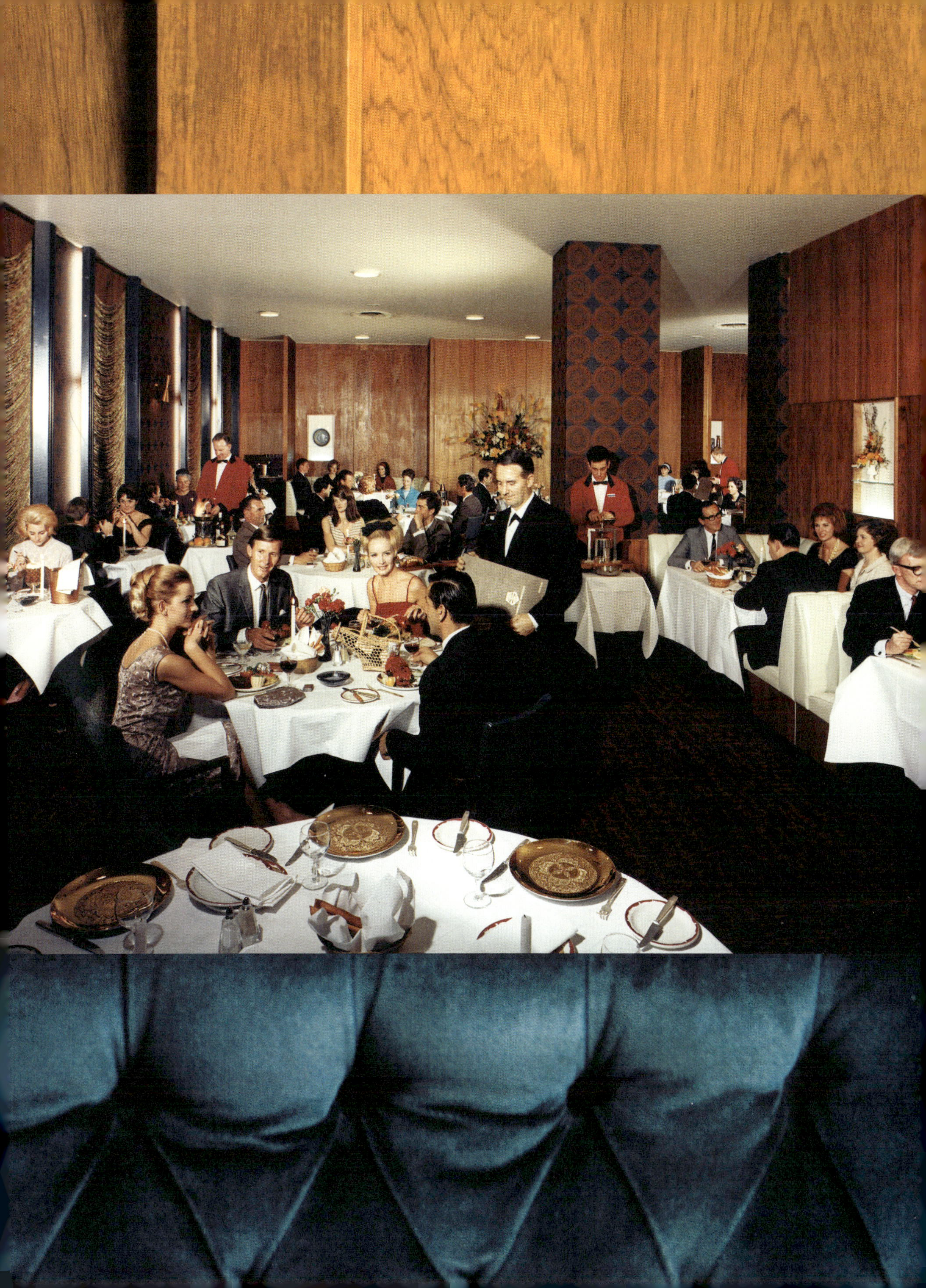

N TAILORS
andre's
PELLEGRINIS BAR ESPRESSO
RESTAURANT
Pellegrini's

CHEVRON
CHEVRON
GHX 430
BAM 659

in droves. Largely unchanged, Pellegrini's continues to inspire new generations of fledgling espresso drinkers with its innate, raffish sense of style.

The 1956 Olympic Games also brought change to Melbourne. The presence of so many foreigners, used to a more relaxed dining scene with longer opening hours, showed the home crowd just how limited their options for eating really were. Nando Donnini, an owner of Lygon Street's University Café, remembers one of the top Italian sports journalists banging on the door of the cafe at 9.30 pm, after covering a night of Olympic boxing: 'What sort of place is this?' he asked, 'I can't get a meal because everything is closed.'[2]

One of the most important impacts of the Olympic Games on the Melbourne dining scene was the recruitment of 160 foreign chefs by the organising committee. There simply were not enough chefs in Melbourne to cater for the crowd and the only solution was to import them. Many returned home after the Games, but a significant number stayed on. One of these was Swiss chef Hermann Schneider, who was bemused by Melbourne's tripartite restaurant scene:

> There were the Italian restaurants like Mario's and the Florentino that were well established and popular, and then there were the hotel dining rooms in hotels like the Menzies, the Chevron and the Savoy Plaza. There were also the Chinese restaurants in Little Bourke Street and the suburbs, and these were the places that the average Australian would go because they would feel intimidated by the more upmarket restaurants. The people who dined in the Italian places and the hotels would never go to the Chinese restaurants.
>
> In the hotel restaurants they all served basically the same menu of French International cuisine. There would be *coq au vin*, whiting Caprice [pan-fried whiting with crumbed bananas on top], steak Diane, steak *au poivre*. It was very red-meat dominated, but they didn't serve lamb. Lamb was what you had at home, the roast on Sunday, so the idea was that when you ate out you wanted something sophisticated.[3]

After finishing his Olympic Games stint, Schneider worked in a series of kitchens, including at hotels such as the Chevron and in private clubs catering to ex-servicemen and golfers, but he soon became disillusioned with the type of food being served and how it always played second fiddle to the alcohol. A corner was turned when he started cooking at Maxim's, one of the few restaurants in Melbourne attempting to serve a more classic French cuisine.

Maxim's opened in time for the Olympic Games, in premises with an AWL. It was places like Maxim's and Il Bistro that saw the LCC begin to take an interest in businesses operating with AWLs. Amendments to the laws in 1960 removed the option for an establishment with an AWL to sell wine for consumption on

Doyen and Doyenne

A classically trained perfectionist chef and wine connoisseur with an impeccable palate, Hermann Schneider's influence has been profound. This is not only for setting the highest standards of European professionalism with his original restaurant, Two Faces, but for training a succession of young protégés who went on to make their mark.

Hermann Schneider

The ambience of the South Yarra basement restaurant may have been rather austere, but the food was superb, the wine cellar outstanding and the service exemplary. Schneider personally visited the markets to select the best ingredients and was master of matching textures and flavours with wine. His menus maintained a nice balance between proven favourites, such as his Swiss-style veal Geschnetzelles, and more creative offerings.

After twenty-eight years at Two Faces, Schneider took charge of the new Delgany Country House in Portsea in 1988, and later the Arthurs Seat restaurant–reception-centre complex. The commercial success of these did not match their critical esteem. In the intervening years he revitalised the long-established wine merchant Seabrooks, and for three years also ran the admirable Roesti Bistro in the city. He retired in 2003, having won numerous awards and respect as one of Melbourne's food and wine icons.

Her trendsetting restaurants rating as highly in the 1970s and 1980s as Hermann Schneider's, Gloria Staley was the improbable proof that you don't need to be a celebrity chef to be an acclaimed restaurateur. Indeed, she would say that when she became a teenage bride after a spell on the stage, she couldn't boil an egg. What made Gloria Staley the grande dame of the restaurant scene were her gifts as an inspired impresario, a flair for design, a sense of style and an intuitive feeling for exquisite food.

Fanny's was the serious elder-sister city restaurant, dignified and discreetly opulent upstairs, with a smartly casual bistro and wine bar at street level. Staley's accountant husband Blyth looked after the business, her son Daniel supervised the splendid cellar and talented chefs came and went; meanwhile she devised the innovative seasonal menus, which were never repeated – except for the signature grilled whiting with fat chips. Often she would sit by the kitchen door, an eagle-eyed quality controller, to ensure that each dish going out was perfect.

Not content with Fanny's pre-eminence, Mrs Staley created Glo Glo's (the family pet name for Gloria) in Toorak. 'Sophisticated', 'chic', 'glamorous' and 'romantic' were the adjectives applied to this younger-sister restaurant. Against a black background and without ambient lighting, waiters flitted unobtrusively among the tables bathed in round pools of light directed down from translucent shades of shocking pink. And the food? It was elegant and refined, partly inspired by the Staleys' regular visits to top restaurants in Europe and America. CLAUDE FORELL

Gloria Staley

CAFE BALZAC
62 Wellington Parade,
East Melbourne, 3002
Phone (03) 419 6599

Luncheon: Monday to Friday
Dinner: Monday to Saturday

the premises, effectively making it a form of takeaway licence, but gave the licence holder the option to convert their existing permit to the new Restaurant Licence. This allowed on-premises consumption if the restaurant met certain criteria. It was a case of the laws playing catch-up with the restaurants, adding to existing legislation in order to keep the restaurants reined in.

Maxim's would have been the proud owner of the first Restaurant Licence in Victoria, but in an ominous portent of things to come it was denied the licence at the last minute because the sign outside was, according to Judge Archie Fraser of the Licensing Court, too small. The honour of the first Restaurant Licence went instead to Georges and Mirka Mora, who had moved from their cafe in the city to open Café Balzac in a former wine shop in East Melbourne.

There were indications that restaurant owners and the public who frequented these businesses were beginning to look at ways around the restrictive laws. Some of these tactics legally exploited loopholes, while others simply defied the law.

Richard Frank, an immigrant from Poland, opened his first restaurant, Rick's, in Queen Street after owning a city cafe for several years. There was little chance that he would be able to get a licence for Rick's, but he blanched at the idea that he could not serve his customers the way he wanted to. Shortly after he opened, the owner of the Rhine Castle Cellars bottle shop, two doors down, paid Richard a visit to ask why he didn't sell wine:

{*Below, right*} The interior of Fanny's

{*Opposite*} The holders of the first Restaurant Licence, Georges and Mirka Mora

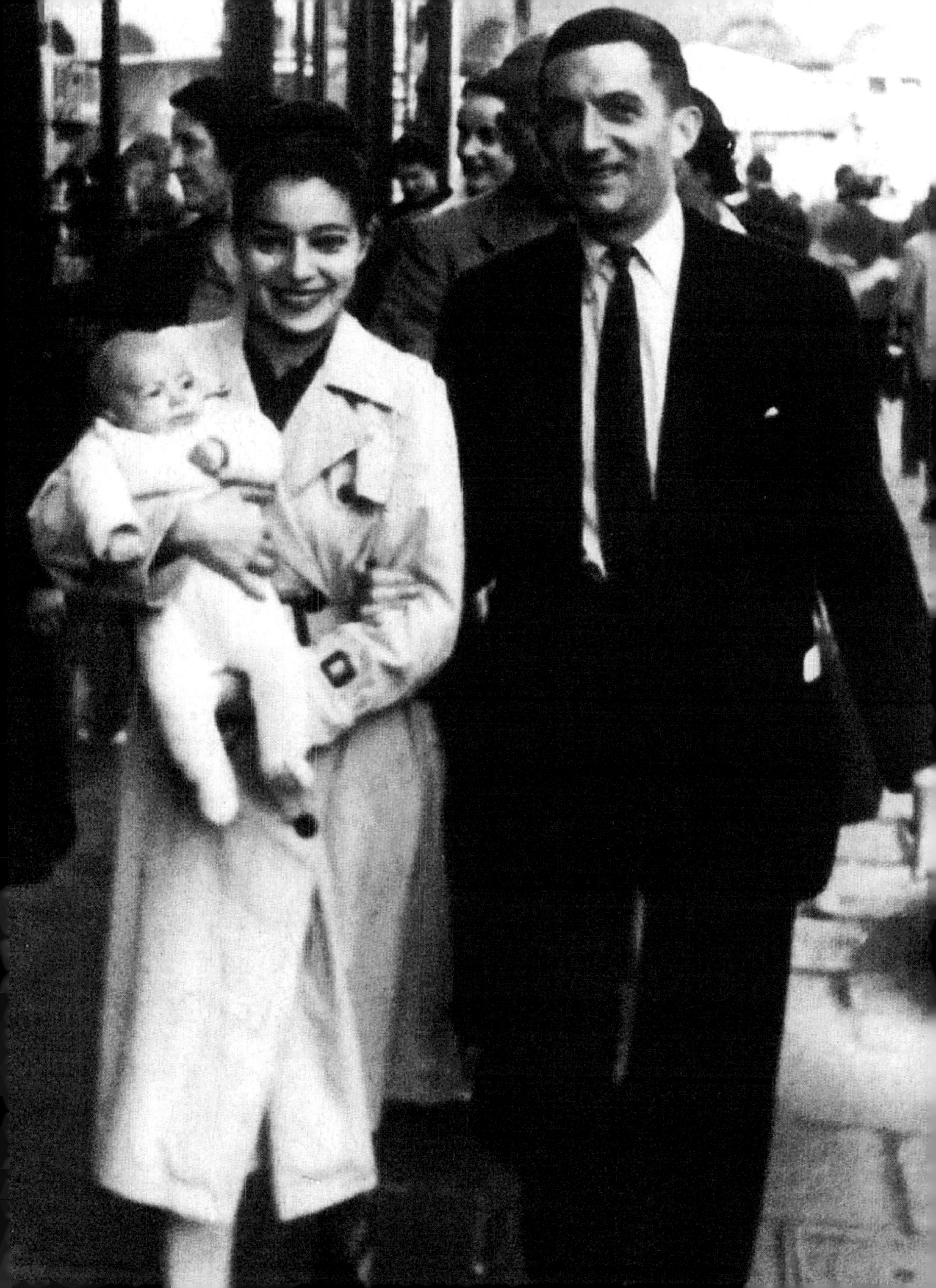

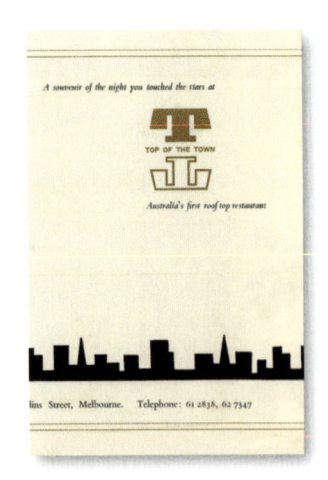

He told me that I might not be able to sell wine but I could serve it because the law said nothing about customers consuming wine they had brought with them. It was perfectly legal. So we set up a system. I would have a list of wines that I would show my customers when they sat down. The customer would then select the wine and give money to one of the waiters who would go to Rhine Castle, buy the bottle and bring it back to the customer in a brown paper bag. I never charged for the service and it was something that made my customers very happy. It was the first BYO restaurant.[4]

Mietta O'Donnell's family, the Viganos, owned Mario's in a hotel in the city. As renowned for its music and dancing as it was for its food, Mario's found a way to circumvent the laws that would have forced it to stop serving alcohol by 8 pm. The Viganos became regulars at the Licensing Court, where they would apply for special occasion permits that would allow liquor to be served until 10 pm to the parties mentioned on the permit. In 1986, Mietta O'Donnell wrote:

I find it amazing to consider that a highly respected and popular business such as my grandfather's hotel was continually forced to operate outside of the law. This was an establishment which saw the whole of Melbourne society come through its doors — including former prime ministers Menzies and Holt, the governor of the day Sir Dallas Brookes and all visiting celebrities. It's hard to believe that it was a fact of life that such a hotel dining room would be 'raided' to check on diners drinking with a meal after 8 pm.[5]

In 1964, Richard Frank was able to install what was ostensibly a bar in his highly fashionable restaurant, Top of the Town. His lawyer ducked and weaved around the restrictions by calling the bar an 'hors d'oeuvre area'. 'The licence', says Richard, 'wasn't all that expensive but the lawyer certainly was.'[6]

Most restaurants simply turned a blind eye to their patrons clinking into their dining rooms with bags full of bottles, which were placed under tables and delved into during the night. It could be a risky business, however, because if restaurants were sprung allowing alcohol to be drunk after 8 pm they could face a fine or lose their licence. But there were ways around this, too.

Hermann Schneider left Maxim's to work at a restaurant owned by an English woman and her Italian husband in Greville Street, Prahran, called Antonio's. The restaurant was not licensed, but diners — including lawyers and business people and judges — would come with bottles in their bags:

Once a month or once a fortnight, the police would come and knock on the back door and ask to speak to the owner. So Mrs Paul would go out the back and have a chat with them. The place was never raided so you knew quite well that there was some sort of arrangement that had been reached with the police.[7]

There was certainly a whiff of corruption around the way the laws were applied, with many stories of backdoor visits and restaurants operating beyond closing time with the tacit approval of the authorities, the representatives of which were seen in these places openly enjoying the rule-flaunting. It seemed that if you were in favour with the LCC, paid your licence fees on time and were friendly to inspectors you were cut a certain amount of slack. But it was this sort of arbitrary approach that got up people's noses.

When Schneider opened his groundbreaking restaurant Two Faces in late 1960, he was told he would never get a licence because his restaurant was in a basement. He applied anyway, but it took nearly two years before it was granted. It was a particularly difficult time for his fledgling business because he had been warned by his lawyer not to let diners bring alcohol to his restaurant; if he was sprung even once by the licensing inspectors he would never get his licence. People complained when they weren't allowed to drink, but as Schneider says, 'They [the LCC] had us over a barrel.'

The LCC was adhering to law, but there appeared to be a fair amount of personal taste and judgement in many of its rulings. Some of the reasons for denying licences can come from a stance that today is more the domain of restaurant critic or interior designer than a legally sanctioned licensing authority. For example, there was confusion about what constituted a 'bona-fide meal' in a case before the commission in the late 1960s. A large pizza house in South Yarra applying for a licence to sell alcohol spent a whole day at the Licensing Court, arguing whether or not pizza constituted a bona-fide meal. (It did after pizzas were delivered to the court as proof, though the licence was rejected on other grounds.) In another case, the commissioners' judgement included a quite specific list of what constituted 'light refreshments' suitable for the business in question: 'at least six oysters natural, hot roast beef roll or garlic bread, or Continental sausage salad or Danish open sandwiches or at least 50g of house paté or cheese and biscuits or fresh fruit platter or soup'.[8]

In another judgement during the 1970s, on the application for a Restaurant Licence in Geelong, the commissioner said of the applicant:

> I think he showed a lot of courage in breaking away from the established format of a licensed restaurant in a sort of starched napery, Oysters Kilpatrick, Garlic Prawns, Filet Mignon and Crepe Suzette syndrome. He has developed a menu which is quite unusual and might be a great success.[9]

> There was certainly a whiff of corruption around the way the laws were applied

ROSATI
TOTO PIZZA
FULLY LICENSED
WE WERE THE FIRST WE SHALL REMAIN THE BEST
120-122 Little Bourke Street, Melbourne, 3000
FULLY AIR CONDITIONED
TOLARNO
French Bistro
&
Two Brochettes
42 Fitzroy St., St. Kilda, 3182
Lunch & Dinner seven days a week
Telephone (03) 534 0521
THE BRYSON
LOWER PLAZA
OPEN 7·00
Phone 63
OCIETY
ESTAURANT
Bourke Street, Melbourne.
Flower Drum
LICENSED RESTAURANT
FIRENZE
Florentino
Pellegrini's
66 Bourke St, Melbourne
329 9344
Old Melbourne
ORIENTAL GOURMET
NESE RESTAURANT
114 Little Bourke Street, Melbourne 3000 Australia
OOKINGS 663 1991
Fax 663 5648
fully licensed
SOUTHERN CROSS
INTER·CONTINENTAL HOTEL
EXHIBITION ST. MELBOURNE
63 0221
Tel. 347 4471
Chalky's
B.Y.O. AND LICENSED
Italian & French Cu
中僑大酒家
Leo's Spaghetti Bar
CASABLANCA
RESTAURANT DISCOTEQUE
61 Fitzroy Street, St.Kilda.
ROWEE'S
TAVERN
BAR
RESTAURANT
7 COLLINS STREET
CAFÉ CAPRICE
LICENSED RESTAURANT
63 3818
THE WALNUT TREE
RESTAURANT
458 WILLIAM STREET
MELBOURNE
INDIAN RESTAURANT
Fairy Sto
RESTAURANT
仙鶴樓
LICENSED TO BR
YOUR OWN LIQUO
La Cacciatora Restaurant
Two Faces
LICENSED RESTAURANT
MAXIMS
Il Vicolo
Phone 94 2425 94 2426
TIENTSIN
Licenced Restaurant
The doorway to the
Lynch

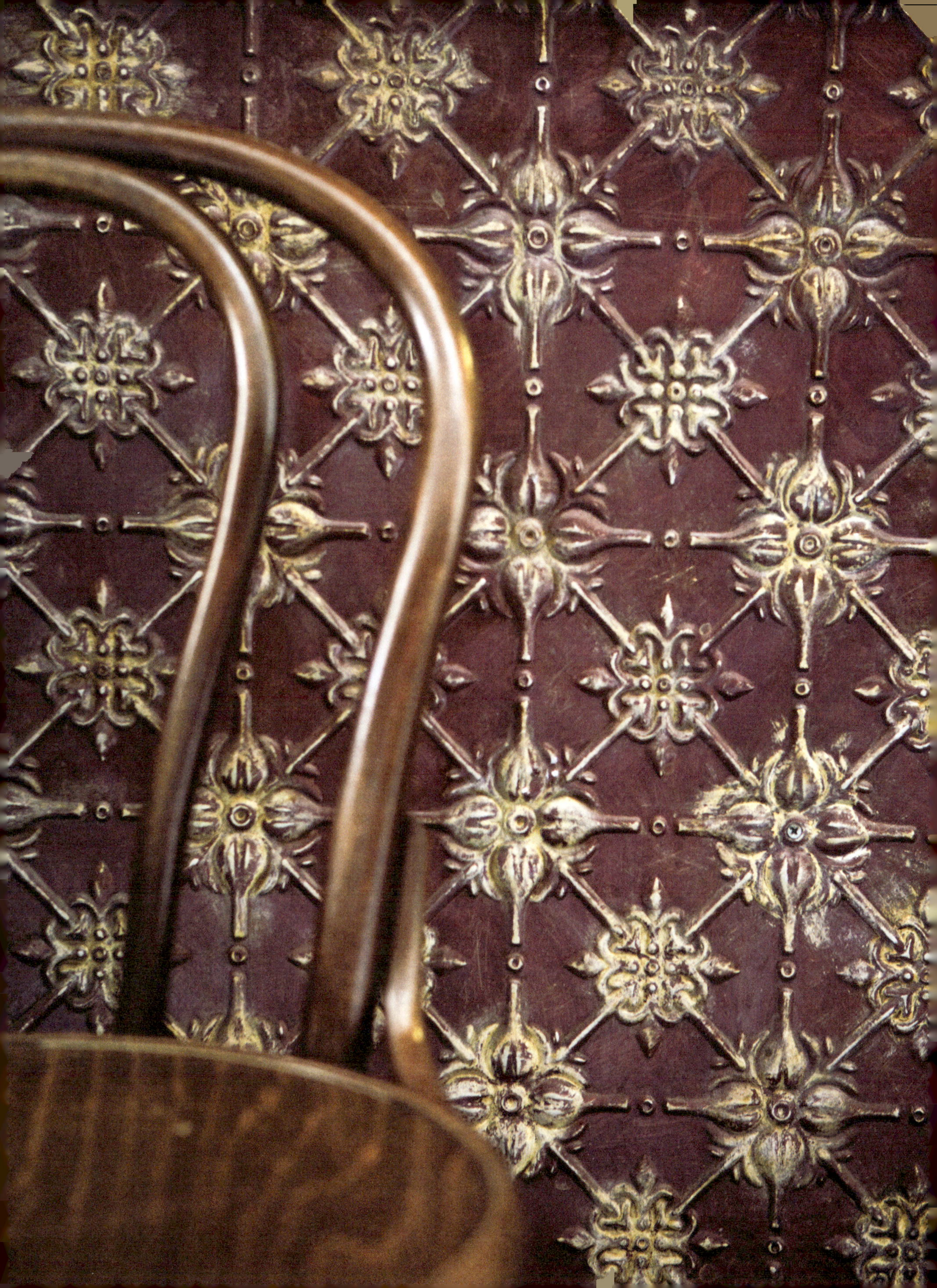

The Epicurean Emperor of Chinatown

There is nothing imperious about the man dubbed the epicurean emperor of Melbourne's Chinatown. His smooth face, wrinkled only by a benign smile, his soft voice accented with ever-courteous charm, Gilbert Lau epitomises the essence of hostmanship.

For nearly twenty-eight years he reigned over his Flower Drum restaurant, with unparalleled success. Acclaimed by food critics and courted by celebrities, the Flower Drum has been acknowledged as one of Australia's very best restaurants. A *New York Times* reviewer declared: 'It may well be the best Chinese restaurant anywhere, as its partisans believe.' At the age of sixty in 2003, the 'emperor' abdicated, selling his illustrious business to three trusted long-term employees, but remaining as a consultant and devoting himself to a humbler Lau's Family Kitchen, opened by his well-trained sons in St Kilda.

It has been a long journey for Gilbert Lau, first seduced as a boy by the pork buns in his grandfather's huge restaurant in southern China. Coming to Melbourne as a teenager, he began work in the kitchen of Chinatown's Wing Sun. He opened the Empress of China with a group of partners in 1971, before establishing the Flower Drum in its original location in Little Bourke Street.

The Flower Drum's pre-eminence is due to Lau's careful selection of skilled cooks, his insistence on the best procurable ingredients, his regular trips to Hong Kong and Singapore for culinary inspiration, his emphasis on impeccable service and, of course, his flair for hospitality. His influence has spread beyond the Flower Drum, as former staff used their training to open restaurants of their own, and as Lau's brilliant example raised the status of Asian restaurants in general. CLAUDE FORELL

But the application was refused in part because the owner wanted to stock only local wine. The commissioner wrote:

> I don't altogether go along with him on his wine list ... if he confines his wine list to the two local vignerons the majority of irregular diners-out are likely to get completely flummoxed. I am not saying that it's not a good thing. I think it is highly admirable for him to be promoting the local district wines but he could do that as well as having a wine list with a much larger range.

There were other instances where restaurateurs were questioned over their ability to make a whisky sour, and in the case of a restaurant called the Great Australian Bite concerns were expressed that the name 'might conceal some off-colour double entendre'.

But it was not just the choice of food and wine (or even name) that could stop a licence application in its tracks. The provision of toilets was also a thorny and much-deliberated issue. There were concerns raised about male and female toilets being too close together, about people having to walk too far to the toilet, about having to share toilets with other businesses, about toilets having the right dimensions and door widths, about how many toilets a business might need so patrons' waiting time would be minimised, and whether or not it was ever appropriate for men and women to share the same toilet facilities. An *Age* journalist commented at the time that 'the Bench's constant grave preoccupation with matters lavatorial could suggest some early oddity in potty training'.[10] And John Nieuwenhuysen remembers that 'the toilet responsibility of the commission was highlighted in its absurdity by the adventure of Judge Kim in riding the tram car restaurant to count the incidence of usage as evidence for his decision on whether joint male/female facilities were acceptable'.[11]

There are other tales of licences being refused because the inspector didn't like the colour of the ceiling or the pattern of wallpaper, but many may more likely be attributed to folklore. The fact that they started to circulate in the first place, however, shows just how arbitrary and often high-handed the LCC was perceived to be. Both Richard Frank and Hermann Schneider talk of the fear that pervaded the industry when dealing with the commission during the 1960s, and this persisted into the 1970s and 1980s. The law had become so convoluted that no-one really knew what they were and were not allowed to do.

Confusion breeds fear, and the way the LCC hearings were run didn't help, particularly as the clock ticked into the 1970s, when many of the traditional foundations of society were so colourfully questioned. In this context, the LCC began to look positively Dickensian. The Licensing Court was packed every day with hopeful

> The law had become so convoluted that no-one really knew what they were and were not allowed to do

applicants surrounded by legal teams and supporters. It looked like and was run along the lines of a regular court of law, complete with battalions of expensive barristers and specialist licensing lawyers, who cross-examined licence applicants and required police checks and character witnesses. Alongside was all the other paperwork (profit statements, menus and wine lists for approval), the obligatory course that licence applicants had to undertake and the hours they had to spend behind a bar pulling beers (even if pulling beers was never part of their business plan). There is little wonder people feared their licences being taken away, if only because of the horrific prospect of having to go through it all again.

The other obstacle for businesses applying for Restaurant Licences was the inevitable objections from the hotels. One part of the licensing laws that had not changed since the earliest days was that in return for the privilege of serving alcohol, hotels were required to continually upgrade their facilities and to supply food and accommodation. In return for this often-expensive investment, hotels were able to object to any new liquor licence application in their area, purely on the grounds of increased competition. And object they did.

John Chalker, who fought his own battles with the LCC over the licence for his Lygon Street restaurant, Chalkies, during the 1980s, was the lessee of the Commercial Club Hotel, in Fitzroy, in the late 1970s. He was also the local council representative for the Victorian branch of the Australian Hotels Association – the go-to man for the thirty-five hotels in Fitzroy at the time. When Mietta O'Donnell and Tony Knox decided to apply for a licence for their Brunswick Street BYO restaurant, Mietta's, in 1979, Chalker received a phone call from the chief executive of the Australian Hotels Association, telling him about the application and to 'get your guys organised to get their objections into the Liquor Commission'. Objecting to any new Restaurant Licences, Chalker says, 'was policy for the hotels'.[12] Though he didn't object to the Mietta's application himself, others in the area obviously did, and it was not until 1982 that a licence was granted.

{*Below, left*} Jacques Reymond; {*right*} Gilbert Lau

By the beginning of the 1980s the restaurant scene in Melbourne was a very different animal from the one around which the 1968 Liquor Control Act had wrapped its legal tendrils. Beer sales had dropped, wine sales were soaring and the desire of the public to drink wine with their meals was obvious from the 396 licensed restaurants and 1914 BYO permits that existed in 1982 (compared with ninety restaurant licences and no BYO permits in 1966). Restaurant-listing guides had started to appear, most of them with sections dedicated to theatre restaurants and nightclubs. *Herald* journalist Eric Page's 1977 guide, which sold 15,000 copies in three weeks, listed a whole thirteen places where you could get something to eat after 10.30 pm. The first of the twenty-four-hour coffee shops had begun operating on Lygon Street; Melbourne's first Vietnamese restaurant, Vietnam Kinh Do, had opened in Hartwell; and restaurants such as Two Faces, Fanny's and Glo Glos continued to define fine dining in Melbourne. There were new operators, too; innovators such as Stephanie Alexander, Mietta O'Donnell, Tony Bilson, Gilbert Lau, Jacques Reymond and Sigmund Jorgensen were throwing down the gauntlet to the older, more formal generation of restaurateurs.

There was much creative energy in the industry and a public increasingly hungry not just for good food but also for knowledge about food and wine. The feeling of being shackled was turning, as *Age* journalist Rod Usher put it in a 1984 article, to a mood of 'anger and bitterness'.[13] Restaurateurs were sick of battling unwieldy laws and of an entrenched system that gave hotels an unfair commercial advantage and the power to tell them how they were to run their businesses. Something had to give.

> Beer sales had dropped, wine sales were soaring and the desire of the public to drink wine with their meals was obvious

It can, I think, be said that it may have been more comfortable and secure for us to have left the whole thing alone or at best have given the liquor laws another fine tuning. That would have been the safe course.

JOHN CAIN, PREMIER OF VICTORIA 1982–1990

Revolution Not Evolution

WYNDHAM ES
Wine Selection
Ryland River
Dry White
Fontana di Papa
Woodley
Sauvignon
Dewar's

On 12 June 1984, the *Age* newspaper ran a full-page story in its Melbourne Living section entitled 'Licence lunacy'. It started like this:

> Victoria's liquor laws are a mess. For many they are killjoy and repressive, antiquated, over-restrictive and uncivilised. People in the tourism and hospitality industries say the laws alone can dissuade visitors from holidaying in the Garden State. The 136 pages of the Liquor Control Act and its 82 amendments are imprecise and ad hoc, the instrument of seemingly whimsical and arbitrary management by a Liquor Control Commission presided over by two judges, a former hotelier and a former radio personality. But the most alarming aspect of alcohol in Victoria is that many of those whose livelihoods depend on retaining their licences are frightened to talk about the commission. Rod Usher, in 20 years as a journalist, some of them investigating major crime, has never met a group of people so afraid. Here is his report.

And so it had started. The first mad-as-hell-and-not-going-to-take-it-anymore shot had been publicly fired, and though the fall was still several years away, Victoria's 1968 Liquor Control Act was doomed.

Rod Usher's article was by no means the first volley of the revolution – since 1982 the Hospitality Industry Association's president, Gerd Kratzner, had been calling quietly, politely but insistently on behalf of his 2000 members for 'consistent standards' and an overhaul of the existing 'stifling' system. But it was the first attack on the system and the perceived absurdities of the Liquor Control Commission (LCC) that was launched with any real vigour and outrage. Usher suggested that the LCC should be more accurately called 'the Liquor, Lavatories, Carpets, Wallpaper, Plumbing and Shiny-Paint Commission', and he wrote that such was the ill-defined nature of its powers that 'in theory it could decide that all restaurants be painted blue, have three-legged chairs and serve poached haddock on Wednesdays'. He railed against the culture of fear that was stifling the industry and, by calling the 1968 Act 'a giant legislative hangover', made it clear that Victoria's licensing laws were ready for a much-needed overhaul.

[*Opposite*] Dr John Nieuwenhuysen, reader in economics at Melbourne University

> In many ways Nieuwenhuysen was the ideal person to tackle the hellishly complicated licensing laws

He was not alone. Two months later, in August 1984, Dr John Nieuwenhuysen, a reader in economics at Melbourne University, was in his office presiding over a tutorial in labour economics when his phone rang. The caller was Bill Cushing from the Department of Industry, phoning on behalf of the minister, Ian Cathie. After some perfunctory preliminaries, Cushing got to the point and asked if Dr Nieuwenhuysen would be interested in looking at the liquor laws, with a view to investigating an alternative model of licensing. Though the call was, according to Nieuwenhuysen, 'out of the blue', as he had no expertise or even knowledge of the area, his immediate response was that he would be happy to serve.

On 11 October 1984, just four months after the appearance of Usher's 'Licence lunacy' article, Minister Cathie, with Nieuwenhuysen at his side, announced that the government was commissioning a report into the state's licensing laws. Of the announcement, Nieuwenhuysen says:

> I remember that I flew down from Canberra that morning, having been at the CEDA State of the Nation Conference at Noah's Hotel the day and night before. The custom there was for revelry to conclude the conference but, despite lack of sleep, I managed, I hope, to speak appropriately at the launch, responding to questions about my drinking habits without mentioning the night before.[1]

Despite Nieuwenhuysen's professed surprise, he was by no means an 'out of the blue' choice, having already chaired an inquiry into state revenue raising for the newly elected Cain Labor (ALP) government in 1982. While many of the recommendations of that fifteen-month investigation into taxes didn't translate into policy, the direction of its findings – simplifying the enormously complicated state tax system by imposing one broad-based consumption tax – showed that Nieuwenhuysen had a talent and a predisposition for cutting through unnecessary legislative tangle. In many ways he was the ideal person to tackle the hellishly complicated licensing laws, particularly when the Cain government had liquor licensing in its sights as one part of a broader plan.

The Cain government was the first Labor government to come to power in Victoria for twenty-seven years. During his time as premier, John Cain spoke openly and idealistically of the ALP's goals, including 'progress towards a fairer, more enlightened and enlivened society where the basic principle is the wellbeing of all its people'.[2] There were some symbolic changes early in his rule, such as the removal of restrictions barring women from entering some areas of major sporting venues, signalling a particular modernising social agenda. Outdated restrictions on the sale of alcohol were certainly not part of the Cain government's social plan:

{*Opposite*} Premier – and teetotaller – John Cain

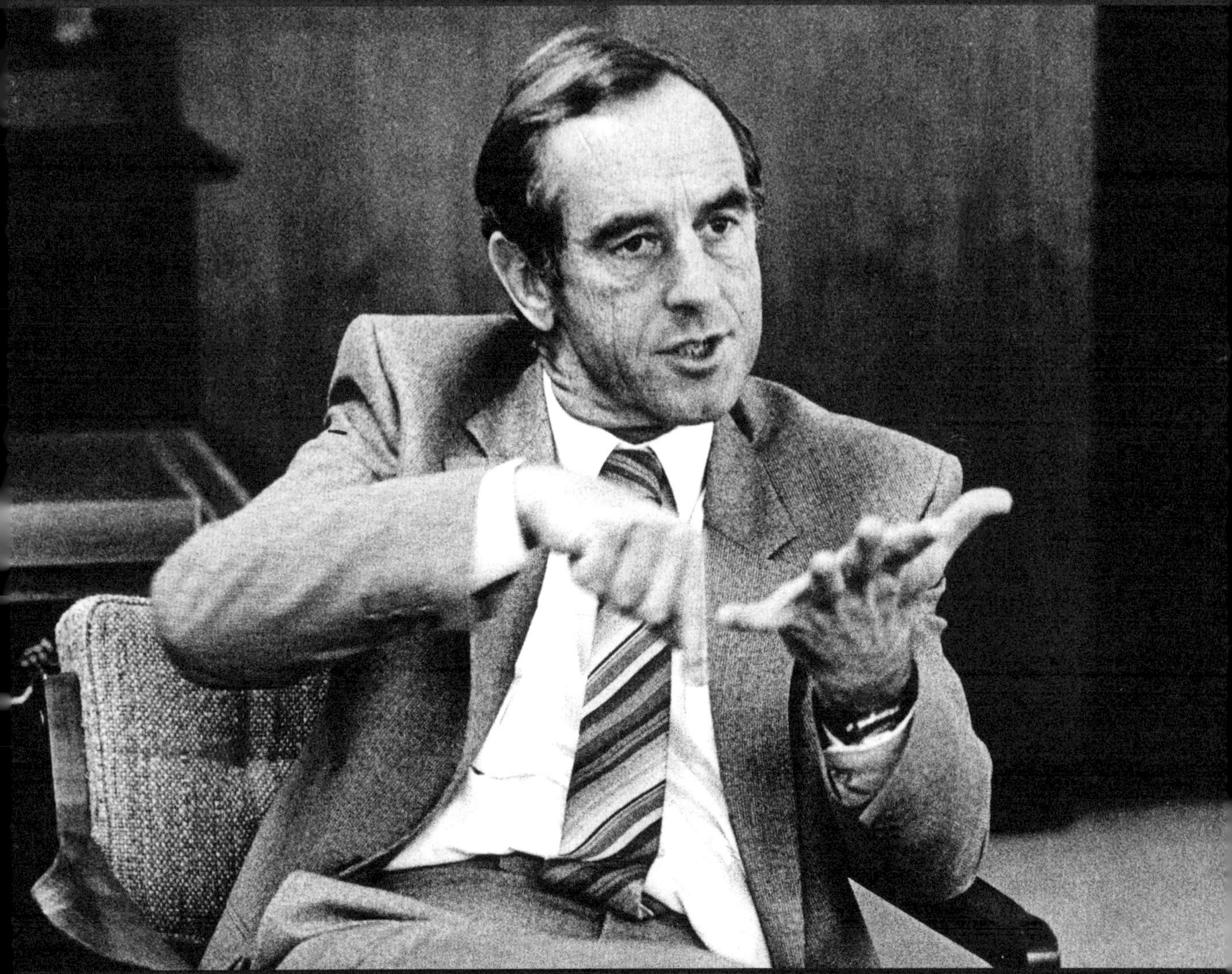

> This was a government led by a man who rarely touched alcohol – an immediate cause for suspicion

We saw Melbourne as a fairly European-style city. And the liquor laws were part of that view we had of what the city could be. We wanted to see Melbourne as a place you could go after dark, with good theatres and entertainment in the city complemented by eating houses and European-style bars … We wanted to provide an alternative to the big beer barns that were out in the suburbs, on the highways, and were considered the worst face of the modern liquor industry … We wanted to use Melbourne's predominantly European style of buildings and lanes to create a cafe society and provide something better than the beer barns. We were also conscious of the self-interest and domination of the liquor industry, [which] had been able to write the legislation as [it] saw fit.[3]

These goals arrived when the hospitality and tourism industries were becoming increasingly restless under the constraints of outdated legislation and sections of the media had jumped on board with full-throttle support, which suggests a serendipitous coming together of like-minded forces. But on closer inspection these concurrent stirrings appear more like carefully constructed foundations created to support a push being organised at the top. Change was by no means inevitable. There was no broad clamour from the wider public, no mass marches demanding the right to enjoy European-style cafes or not to be force-fed in nightclubs. And there were substantial, even formidable, forces both within and without the government that were perfectly content with the status quo. But those driving the government agenda were determined to press on, giving change its best shot in decades.

Liquor was just one of the 'social' items looked at by the new Victorian government. Before Nieuwenhuysen was contacted in 1984, there had already been reviews into the introduction of poker machines and the possibility of establishing a casino in Melbourne. Both of these reviews had slapped down the possibility of pokies and casinos appearing in Victoria any time soon. Whatever the reasons for denying Victorians access to these forms of gambling, the double negative had left the Cain government with the faint stain of wowserism. This, after all, was a government led by a man who rarely touched alcohol – an immediate cause for suspicion in a country where, it has been said, the right to drink has a place analogous to that of the right to carry a gun in America. Cain had been lampooned in the press as someone whose idea of an exciting night was to stay home and rearrange his sock drawer.

This supposed wowserism on the part of government saw the announcement of the liquor review being taken in two ways: that the government would surely quash another attempt at allowing the population a bit of potentially harmful fun; or that making some widespread changes to the Liquor Control Act would help the party (and Cain in particular) shed its image of being a humourless killjoy.

A less obvious motive, but one that went deeper than any concerns about image, was the resentment felt in some sections of the government towards an industry that, according to Cain, 'had told governments ... how they should regulate it [the industry] for more than 140 years ... and [who] took government support and compliance for granted'.[4] Wielding the ideological broom is common to any political party that has been out of power for decades, and this was a government willing to sweep aside any of the entrenched systems from the past to make way for their clearly stated modernising agenda.

In its choice of review chair – and in the terms in which the review was couched – the government seemed to be pushing the liquor inquiry in a certain direction. Most if not all reviews of the liquor laws in the past – by Davies, Phillips, Fraser and others – had been undertaken by men with legal backgrounds and with connections to the industry. Their instructions had been to take the existing legislation and improve it, or, at the very least, bring it into line with current social practice. By commissioning an economist to look at the legislation, the government had taken a substantially different slant. This was a man with no investment in prior legal process and no experience of the industry other than as a patron, so he was, essentially, able to start with a clean slate. Nieuwenhuysen was being given the opportunity to imagine what the best liquor laws would be for Victoria – as if no liquor laws had existed previously.

Cain knew that Nieuwenhuysen was a radical choice, independent, academically trained and beholden to nobody, nor to the legislation of the past. He was also a man with an antenna finely tuned for injustice, something that had been learned from growing up white and privileged in apartheid-era South Africa.

Nieuwenhuysen's grandparents were wealthy farmers and landowners in the Orange Free State in central South Africa. He says that many of his ideas were formed on his grandparents' farm because 'it showed some of the worst aspects of the apartheid system'.[5] As a child he didn't realise there was anything wrong with living in a beautiful home with 'lots of servants – seven or eight for the house and garden alone', but after he went to university in Durban and enrolled in a course in African government taught by the daughter of a Swiss missionary his perceptions began to change.

The teacher applied for and received permission to hold mixed-race classes in the subject, and so for the first time Nieuwenhuysen interacted with indigenous African students and Indian students on something other than a master–servant level. Making friends and listening to other points of view threw his life and the attitudes of his family – and most of white society – into stark relief:

> Cain knew that Nieuwenhuysen was a radical choice, independent, academically trained and beholden to nobody

I realised we were like kings. My grandfather and [grand]mother had absolute authority over their employees. They could order them off the farm at any time, but if the servants wanted to leave they needed to have permission in writing. Wages were not fixed but were at the behest of the employer, and they lived with their children in huts with no electricity, one tap to service the whole community and no toilets. And there we were, my brother was driving a sportscar, there were overseas trips, big Christmas parties and so on. It was a really uncomfortable conjunction of wealth and poverty.

It was also, at the beginning of the 1960s, very uncomfortable to be a white liberal moving in white circles: 'every day there would be issues of major morality, about the way a white person would treat a black person, the way in which my family would treat the servants'. This, combined with the fact that several of his friends had been imprisoned for supposedly subversive activities and that he could not think of himself as a martyr, led Nieuwenhuysen to leave South Africa for London in 1961. 'I could no longer live in that racist country,' he says.

After completing his PhD at the London School of Economics he was faced with the prospect of having to return to South Africa. He couldn't countenance that and so looked to moving to Canada or Australia. The offer of a position at the University of Melbourne sealed his fate and he came to Australia in 1963. Though he at first found Melbourne 'depressing and parochial', he stayed on, marrying an Australian and coming to appreciate an approach to life that was several rungs up the ladder of egalitarianism from the life he had been born into. He has never again lived in South Africa, but still bristles with anger when he describes what it was like living in a racist police state. Small wonder that he is a man sensitive to injustice and entrenched privilege.

When he was first sounded out about new ways to approach liquor licensing in Victoria, Nieuwenhuysen assumed the review would be run along similar lines to his 1982 review of revenue raising; that is, he would be the head of a government-appointed committee. But in this case, the government decided he would be the committee, the frontman and the spokesperson for the review, and would have to handpick staff to help him through the licensing labyrinth. The review was to take a little under twelve months (subsequently extended by four months) and was given a budget of $600,000 to cover six full-time staff and eight part-time consultants. Nieuwenhuysen himself had his university salary covered, with a $30,000 fee on top. In comparison to other inquiries, it was something of a bare-bones budget. As Nieuwenhuysen points out, the entire cost of the liquor licensing review was similar just to the barristers' fees in the casino inquiry, and his salary as chair was one-third of that paid to that inquiry's leading counsel. The relatively tight deadline

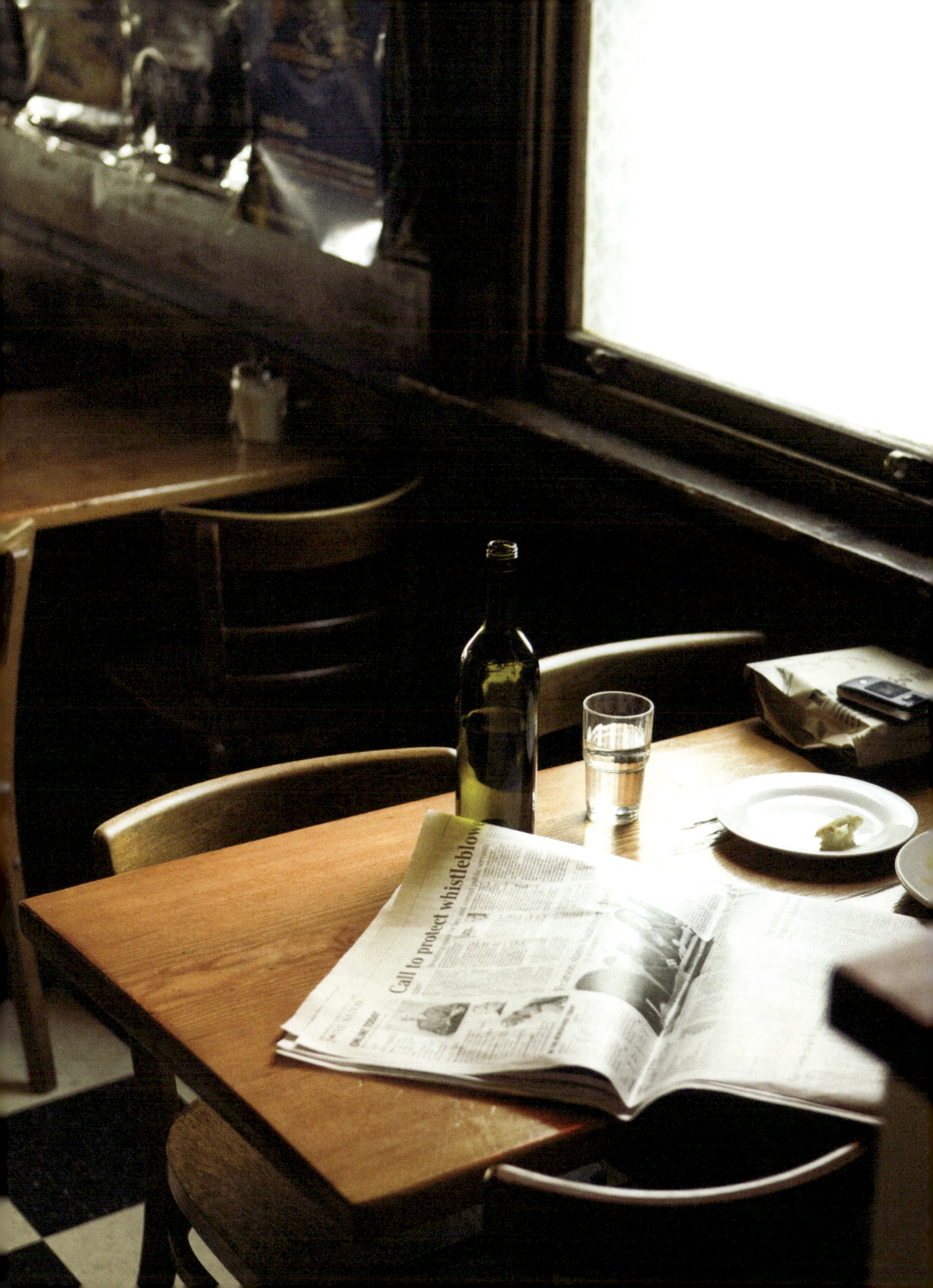
Call to protect whistleblow

The Wine Wars

Nick Chlebnikowski was once labelled the 'buccaneer' of Melbourne's retail wine scene. Well, it was back in the 1980s and things were a little different then.

The hard-nosed Irishman Dan Murphy was pushing for the title of 'discount wine king', but Nick and his brother Vic, of Nick's Wine Merchants, were giving Murphy a real fight. They went into battle with everyday Australian drinking wines, slashing wildly at margins. Melburnians from all over the city were attracted by the whiff of a bargain, and Saturday-morning tastings at Nick's, in Doncaster, were mad affairs. 'It would be packed with people; shopping trolleys would be loaded with bottles and in the midst of this buying pandemonium, Nick would stand … cross between a symphony conductor and a traffic cop, issuing directions and orchestrating sales,' wrote Mark Shield in the *Age*. 'The lasting impression is that they sell a power of wine at Nick's.' And so they did, with Nick eventually expanding his empire to four stores.

They were heady times. Nick went uptown in search of the lucrative corporate dollar, and there was certainly plenty of money to be made supplying wine to cashed-up legal, advertising and big-end businesses. There was also heartache: he is still owed money from convicted corporate crooks George Herscu and Christopher Skase.

If Nick chased the bargain hunter through the 1980s and the corporate tie in the early 1990s, these days he's got his eye on grander and broader horizons: the world. Nick's Wine Merchants was one of the first, if not *the* first, Australian wine retailer to see value in marketing and selling wine through the internet – that was back in 1994. Now, his Vintage Direct is probably one of the biggest online wine retail businesses. He has five staff dedicated to running the website and processing orders, which he says is run like a military machine.

He also provides wine education on the net, with *The Wineman* series of wine talks featuring on YouTube. In fact, wine education today – or the lack of it – is something that he claims to miss under the changes to the industry over the past twenty years: 'The whole industry was [once] much more education orientated than it is today. It was full of people who were wine lovers and not accountants and not people from other industries.' Nick puts part of the blame at the feet of liquor licence reform: 'It opened up the industry and it made it far more competitive. Margins were eroded and it became less viable to run all of these things for free.' JENI PORT

and small budget, combined with the government's stated wish for recommendations 'on ways of de-regulating the industry, while serving and protecting the interests of the community', seemed to show that quite particular outcomes were being sought. Nieuwenhuysen was the figurehead who would have to make those outcomes not just clear, but palatable to the wider community. He would also be the focal point – some might even say target – for those people and organisations that were averse to change.

This target-like part of the job description became clear very early on in the piece. Not long after the review had been announced, Nieuwenhuysen was in the office in East Melbourne assigned to him by the Department of Industry, Commerce and Technology when there was a knock on the door. His unexpected visitors were the Victorian president of the Australian Hotels Association (AHA) and a solicitor with ties to the AHA and former ties to the LCC. Nieuwenhuysen says that it was, perhaps, the most important meeting of the whole review:

I invited them into the office and they said, 'We see you have a big place here and lots of money for this inquiry, but we were just wondering how you are going to go about it.' And so I told them it was going to be research based. And they told me that I had to provide evidence and that I had to give them scope within the inquiry to challenge any evidence that was being brought to me by the other people. They were wanting to have hearings and so on where they could cross-examine witnesses.

> I immediately got the impression that they were used to getting their own way and that they were surprised that this was happening with an economist as the sole person. I didn't appreciate their attitude and it fired me up, you see. Because I thought they might have always had their way with the government but they're not going to bully me. It was an important meeting because it was not long after that when I started to form the view that this was an industry that was being regulated for the sake of the people who were in it rather than for the purposes of the people who were using it or for the prevention of the abuse of alcohol.[6]

It was the start of what would, over the coming years, prove to be a combative relationship between Nieuwenhuysen and the AHA.

The work of understanding and unravelling the Liquor Control Act began in earnest. The team picked for what was widely referred to as the Nieuwenhuysen Review, were chosen on the basis of skills that would enable them to take on particular areas of the review's sizeable scope. The main researchers were Allan Tunstall, another economist who would concentrate on hotels and analysing the myriad licences and permits in Victoria; Louise Clayton, a lawyer assigned to study the

'I thought they might have always had their way with the government but they're not going to bully me'

procedures of the LCC; Dr David Cousins, who was to look at the history, logic and administration of the existing laws; Will Foster, a labour economist assigned to research the impact on employment of any changes to the existing laws and to coordinate the public and industry opinion surveys; Catherine James, who would review the relationship between alcohol controls and alcohol abuse; and Gary Max, another economist with liquor industry experience, who would look specifically at retail bottle outlets. This was the core team, but there were also many others involved: several administrative staff laboriously gathering and typing information; legal counsel from Brian Bourke (author of *Bourke's Liquor Laws of Victoria*); a small battalion of other consultants, who were accountants, academics, lawyers and research experts; and still more people from government departments – Employment and Industrial Affairs; Industry, Technology and Resources; Economic and Budget Review; and Health.

It was a review that was nothing if not thorough. Though the terms of reference allowed it to 'inform itself as it saw fit', the review did not take short cuts or refuse to listen to any opinions. Submissions were invited and 176 were received from individuals, including a 'John Citizen', city councils, churches (Baptist, Presbyterian, Uniting), hotel groups and individual hotels, temperance groups, unions, sporting clubs, retailers, cinema owners, winemakers and winemaking groups, distilleries, brewers, universities, social clubs, government departments, the Tourism Commission, the Road Traffic Authority, the National Trust and the Country Women's Association.

The committee visited well over 200 licensed and other premises in Melbourne and country Victoria, and conducted surveys with both industry and the general public. There were also trips to several states in Australia to study licensing laws in other parts of the country. If there were stones left unturned, it was not through lack of trying.

Most of the submissions received fell into fairly predictable 'for' and 'against' camps. Restaurants and wineries argued for change and deregulation; hotels, churches and temperance societies pushed for maintaining, even strengthening, the status quo. Probably the most accurate gauge of how the general population felt about Victoria's liquor laws – particularly the confusion about what was and was not allowed – is found in the survey of public opinion, one of the mandatory requirements that the government included in the terms of reference.

The review's survey (conducted by an independent research group) polled 702 people above the age of eighteen and was weighted to ensure a representative spread of Victorians in terms of age and gender in both country and metropolitan areas. Though there were very few absolute responses, negative or positive, towards the

{*Above, top*} The late Catherine James was largely responsible for the authorship of two key chapters dealing with alcohol abuse; {*below*} Brian Bourke, legal counsel for the review

{*Opposite*} The liquor laws review panel: {*from left*} Sarmita Demetry, David Cousins, Jean Dunn, Gary Max, Allan Tunstall, Louise Clayton and Will Foster. Seated is John Nieuwenhuysen

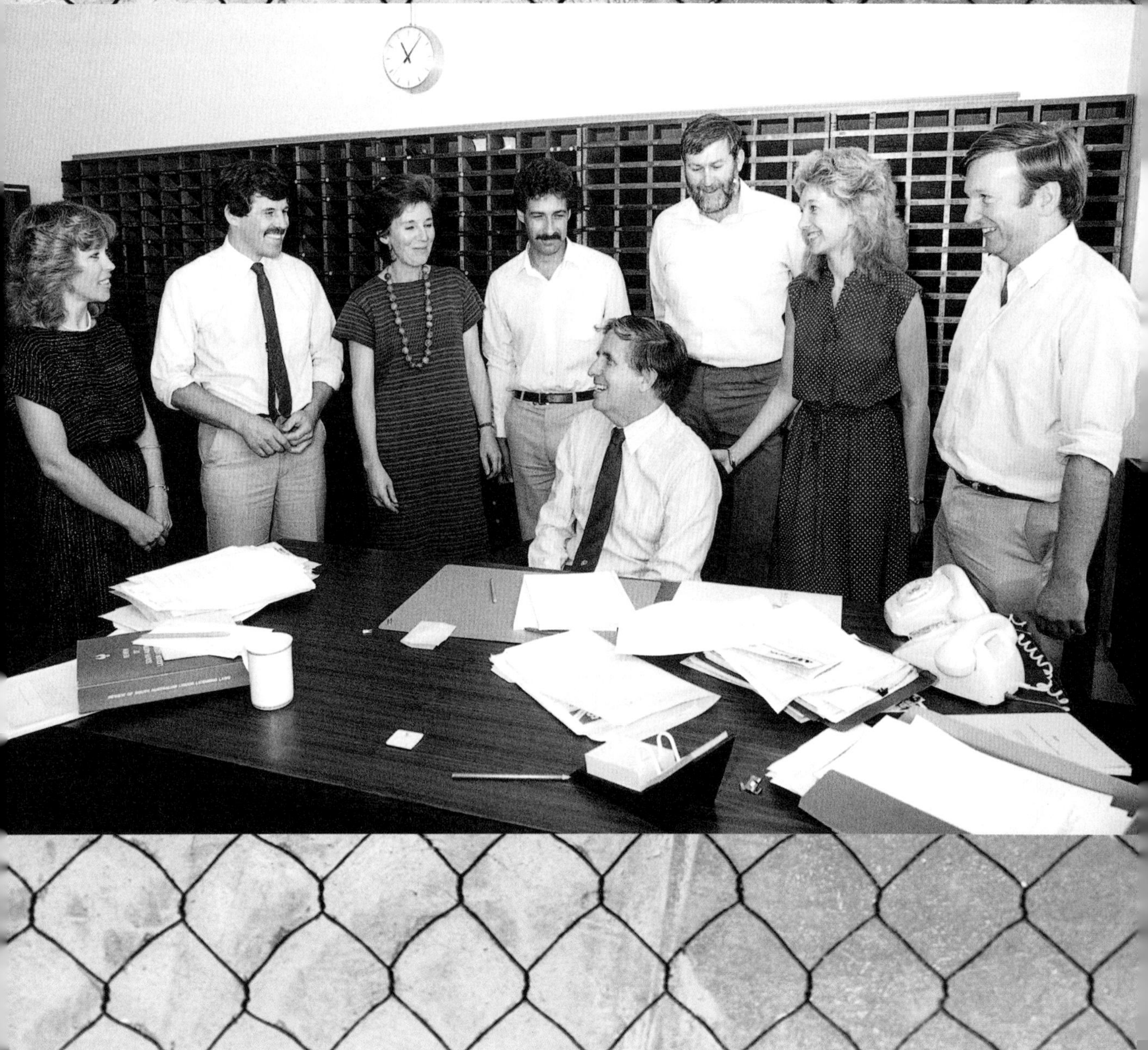

Tale of Two Cities

What's the difference between Melbourne and Sydney restaurants? At least $10 a main course, according to one critic. Another observed: 'Melbourne diners look at the food on their plate; Sydneysiders look to see who's at the next table.' What does this tell us?

First, prices tend to be higher in Sydney, a reflection of higher rents and other costs, and possibly of slightly more affluent clientele. Second, Sydney's socially conscious diners are perhaps more eager to see and be seen, and more fickle in their choice of restaurant – flitting from one voguish venue to the next 'in' place.

Melburnians may be a little more conservative – and perhaps discerning – in their tastes, but tend to be more loyal to their favourite eating places. And as Melbourne attracts fewer international and interstate visitors than Sydney – though it is catching up – restaurants here have to be more responsive to their local market, both in the quality of food and the hospitality of their service. These are, of course, generalisations, but they contain an element of truth.

Another question that constantly springs from the well of inter-city rivalry is which has the better restaurants. According to one critic, Sydney has flashes of brilliance but Melbourne has a more solid core of first-class restaurants. International observers are divided. American celebrity chef Anthony Bourdain and *New York Times* reviewer Patricia Wells have expressed a preference for Melbourne, a *Los Angeles Times* critic for Sydney.

Melburnians do take their food seriously: witness the success of the Melbourne Food and Wine Festival, regular ethnic food festivals and the fresh-food and farmers' markets that have proliferated around the city.

Another striking difference – a direct result of the liberalised drinking laws – is Melbourne's exciting cafe, bar and nightlife culture, which has helped to revitalise the central business district, especially in its little alleys and laneways. Sydney seems more attached to its traditional pub and club patronage. CLAUDE FORELL

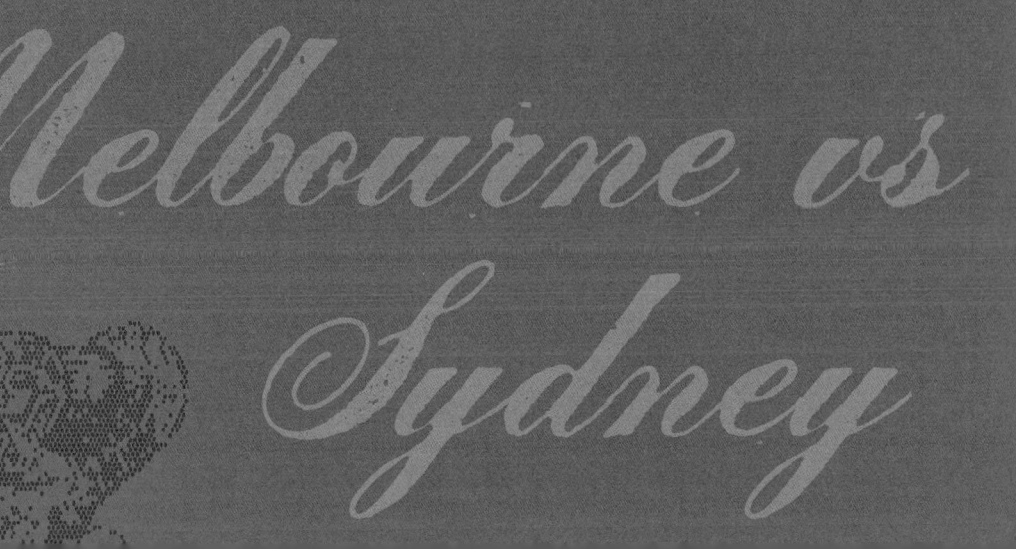

Melbourne vs Sydney

REMOULADE
PARMESAN SALAD
POTATO GNOCCHI
SWEET PEPPERS
ZUCCHINI
RISOTTO
RABBIT,
2000

> There was certainly the feeling that change and choice would be more welcomed than opposed

status of alcohol sale and consumption in the state, there were many instances in which more than half of the surveyed group welcomed a change of approach.

It is interesting to note that while the vast majority of respondents (95 per cent) trusted themselves not to go wild should the laws be loosened up, more than half thought that there would be increased alcohol abuse if liquor became more readily available. It was, obviously, other people who could not be trusted to control themselves and who would cause the problems that two-thirds of those polled said they had concerns about.

Though there was no sign of overt resentment towards hotels and how they were conducting their business, more than half of those polled liked the idea of European-style cafes, of being able to buy a bottle of wine in a BYO restaurant, of not having to eat a meal when they went out dancing late at night, and of having an alternative to pubs for a late-night drink. Sunday trading, late-opening bottle shops and drinking in restaurants without having to eat were looked upon with suspicion by more than half of the crowd, but half also agreed that licensed premises – restaurants, clubs and hotels – should be able to choose their own hours of operation. The poll seemed to prove that while there was no simmering outrage in the community about liquor laws, there was certainly the feeling that change and choice would be more welcomed than opposed.

In many ways it would have been easier to do nothing. No-one but a few irate restaurant owners, 'trendies' and journalists would have raised much of a fuss. But for a newly elected government full of newly elected energy and plans to revitalise and modernise the state, the easy way was completely unattractive. The government was actively seeking hard work, as its reforms on nude bathing and prostitution seemed to show. A heavy workload was something that those working on the Nieuwenhuysen Review experienced firsthand, not least Nieuwenhuysen himself:

> I doubt whether I have worked so hard in all my life. It was very complex writing it up – I spent all those fifteen months writing and writing, trying to get the script right and the message correct, trying to understand the law. I was blessed with having a good team and it was such an interesting subject and was given so much attention that the team became enthused. We used to have debates about certain aspects of what we were looking at, but in the end we all agreed on the recommendations and on the changes that needed to be made.[7]

It seemed to this logical economist that not only was the system and the law unwieldy, obtuse and protectionist, but it was also failing spectacularly in achieving what it was put in place to do – minimise the effects of alcohol consumption on the

Dump liquor laws — says report to Govt

SUN FEATURES

Sober approach on liquor laws

By KEN MERRIGAN

IT is the sober judgment of the man trying to blow the froth off Victoria's drinking laws that much of the reaction against his report has been intemperate.

Intemperate, perhaps, but not totally surprising.

Dr John Nieuwenhuysen wants, after all, to convince the community there is nothing contradictory about freeing up our drinking laws while also cultivating greater social responsibility toward alcohol.

This notion, that wider availability of drink will not lead to a boost in consumption, has emerged at the core of the debate over Dr Nieuwenhuysen's proposals.

It has, among other things, spawned an unlikely alliance between the Australian Hotels Association and the temperance movement, both of which claim the Melbourne University academic has produced a strategy for a giant boost in consumption.

This strange cocktail of vested interest and altruism appears to bemuse Dr Nieuwenhuysen, an enthusiastic reformer.

But he is not at all persuaded by the arguments that have been mounted against him since his report was released three months ago.

He gauges his recommendations have received an enthuiastic response. His confidence in his blueprint to demolish part of our wowser tradition is unshaken.

"I think it is an excellent report," he says, somewhat immodestly. "I believe the balance struck between acknowledging the problem of abuse, and saying how it can be solved, and then talking about deregulation is exactly the right road."

Those who believe there is a link to limiting drinking hours and the number of outlets only have to look backwards to see

● Dr Nieuwenhuysen

you were required to finish your drink by 8 o'clock."

Yet the more liberal conditions introduced cautiously since the demise of the six o'clock swill have not led to a upsurge in consumption. Nor has the emergence of 450 licensed restraunts and 700 retail bottleshops since 1968 decimated the hotels.

Dr Nieuwenhuysen says the changes have produced greater civilisation in Melbourne, a process he would like to prod along.

"The only place you can go to have a drink in Victoria in a public premise where you don't have to have a meal is the public bar of a hotel," he explains.

"Now, I say if more people can have a drink in public places where they can buy it on the spot, even if liquor consumption doesn't go up — and I don't believe it will go up on a per capita basis — more of it that is purchased will be drunk in public.

"But there will be more incentive if there are more smaller, convivial places for people to go to drink it there rather than go home.

"I mean, the hotels dislike intensely some of the findings of the report about the opinions of the public on hotels. The one I keep quoting, which they dislike most of all, is that 70 per cent of

He believes that trend will lead to extra employment, contradicting claims by the liquor trades union that his reforms will jeopardise jobs.

Those jobs might not be in hotels, but he sees no reason why they should be protected. The only ground for caution would be a fear of greater alcohol abuse.

"And I don't believe it will lead to greater alcohol abuse," he says emphatically. "On the contrary, I believe that would civilise the drinking standards in Victoria."

Dr Nieuwenhuysen says the AHA has gone about protecting its interests in a rough and tumble way. "Minimal" weight should be given to its views.

As for the union, its views on job security and standards were best addressed by industrial legislation, not laws governing liquor controls.

"I feel they are protected people who have no right to further protection," he says. "I think they should be grateful they have been protected for so long."

He is equally dismissive of an internal police report, disclosed last week but disowned by the police, which warned of underworld figures being enticed to Melbourne to take advantage of more liberal liquor laws.

"Canberra is now deregulated," Dr Nieuwenhuysen said. "Is Canberra now a great centre for laundering money? Is it a great centre for crime? It's a great centre for vacuuming our money, but that's not laundering it.

"No one can say the rise of restaurants and bottleshops has produced a Melbourne where you see a great deal of drunkedness or where drinking conditions are much less civilised than they used to be."

As it is, the problem of underage drinking has emerged despite the controls. He recommends stronger drink-driving laws, more police and a co-

public. As Nieuwenhuysen saw it, the object of the law was to control the abuse of alcohol. The extensive study into alcohol abuse, under-age drinking, drink driving, disorderly behaviour and other alcohol-related social problems that was undertaken during the course of the review made it clear to all concerned that alcohol was a dangerous drug that did need some form of control over its sale. But it also found that much of the existing Act was totally unrelated to the rationale behind the law. The Act was protecting certain parts of the community, but it wasn't doing much to help the community as a whole.

The other thing that became clear was that the community had outpaced the law, and that constant, normalised, low-level law breaking was occurring across Victoria. 'It was like prohibition', says Nieuwenhuysen:

> In doing my report I came across a lot of people who were not observing the law. There was a man who had a little pub up near Rutherglen where he was required to provide food as part of holding a hotel licence. We ended up there around lunchtime one day and went in for lunch and he said, 'Oh yes, I do provide lunch, but I need 24 hours notice.' Another time I went to a friend's engagement party and we wanted to drink beyond a certain hour but were only able to do so if we were having a meal. So we were ushered into this room where the tables were laid with knives and forks and chequered cloths and they said, 'I know you've had your dinner and we don't want you to eat again, but if the police come then tell them you are waiting for the meal.' In fact, my first drink of alcohol in Australia was with a Melbourne University student in an unlicensed Lygon Street cafe – warm Porphyry Pearl in a cracked teacup.[8]

As the time for submitting the report drew near, it became obvious that, contrary to what liquor reviews in the past had recommended, the Nieuwenhuysen Review was going to be more about revolution than evolution.

As Erik Hopkinson, a consultant to the review and who later became the founding chief executive of the body that replaced the LCC, says:

> What John Nieuwenhuysen's report recommended was a fundamental change in the direction of liquor laws in Victoria, the moving from a regulated to a de-regulated system … It was about facilitating change and responding to the needs of the marketplace; it was about allowing operators to give the market the sort of places it wanted.[9]

On 31 January 1986, twenty years to the day since the six o'clock swill had been banished, Nieuwenhuysen signed off on his 846-page *Review of the Liquor Control Act*

[Above] Erik Hopkinson

1968, handing it over to the new minister for Industry, Technology and Resources, Robert Fordham. He was exhausted, but pleased with the work he and his team had done. Little did he know that his part in overhauling Victoria's licensing laws was only just beginning.

There is no conceptual reason why milk bars, take-away food premises, delicatessens, corner stores, and petrol stations should not be eligible for a general licence which would permit trading as a hotel ... This conceptually would mean that the number of Victorian hotels and clubs could jump from 2000 to around 10,000.

AHA BROCHURE ARGUING AGAINST CHANGE, 1986

Hopes, Fears and the Word Made Law

"TIME GENTLEMEN, PLEASE"

If it was the Cain government's plan to heighten tensions around the reshaping of Victorian liquor laws by resorting to delaying tactics, the ploy certainly worked. From the moment the Nieuwenhuysen Review was commissioned until nearly four years later when parts of it were made into law the process seemed to consist of brief, publicity-surrounded flurries of activity – followed by long periods of loaded government silence. For those whose lives and businesses would be affected by the report's outcome, the government's apparent dithering and indecision was the source of enormous frustration and resentment.

The report had taken fifteen months to complete – four months longer than anticipated – and even before it landed with a thud on Minister Fordham's desk in early 1986, speculation about what it might contain was rife, within both the industry and the press. The hospitality industry has never been averse to a bit of rumour and innuendo, so it is hardly surprising that word began to circulate that the unseen report contained recommendations for a radical reshaping of liquor laws in Victoria and would unleash a tsunami of newly licensed venues, overwhelming an unsuspecting public with a vast ocean of liquor. What is more surprising is that some sections of the press, particularly the regional press, had already begun railing against 'a totally unnecessary step towards young people, the nation's leaders of tomorrow, being further exposed to a great and dangerous social evil which must be effectively and swiftly contained, not expanded'.[1] The fact that these sentiments surfaced before even the government had seen its commissioned report illustrates the nervousness with which some sections of the industry were awaiting the report.

Much of the credit for the pre-emptive strike on potential challenges to the licensing status quo must be attributed to the Australian Hotels Association (AHA). Taking up the mantle of protector of the public good, the AHA speculated in letters to the editor and statements released to the media that should John Nieuwenhuysen's recommendations be made law they would be disastrous for under-age drinking and the road toll. The new laws, they said, could see alcohol being sold in milk bars, service stations and convenience stores, a situation that could only lead to an increase in teenage drinking and an inevitable tearing of society's fabric.

> Why would the government be acting so evasively if there were no political dynamite lurking within the report's pages?

Given the economic advantages existing laws gave to hotels and the economic burden those same laws placed upon them, it is understandable that the AHA would come out swinging. Attack had, after all, always been its default setting in the past. But sniffing a change in attitude with the new Cain government, the hotel industry was perhaps more amped up and it wasn't going to sit around and wait for the report to be released before starting a campaign against it.

When the government finally received the Nieuwenhuysen Review, news of this did little to dampen the feverish speculation, particularly as weeks and then a month drifted by with no word on when the public would see it, other than a vague fob-off by Premier Cain that the report would not be made public 'for some time'. This evasiveness confirmed the worst fears of those who felt threatened by its potential implications: why would the government be acting so evasively if there were no political dynamite lurking within the report's pages? The reluctance to release the report so frustrated Opposition frontbencher Phil Gude that he declared it was being deliberately suppressed and he applied to see the document under the *Freedom of Information Act*.

The delay also infuriated those calling for an overhaul of the existing Liquor Control Act. The *Age* in particular had kept up a steady stream of columns, opinion pieces and editorials welcoming the commissioning of the Nieuwenhuysen Review, but as time and silence wore on it began prodding the government to release its findings. According to Claude Forell, well-known food critic, columnist and co-editor of influential restaurant guide *The Age Good Food Guide*, the newspaper had made a decision to back the reforms very early on and he had been assigned the task of expressing its views. There was, he says, no sense of confidence that the government would do what the *Age* was calling for: 'scrap the Liquor Control Act and the Liquor Control Commission and start afresh'.[2]

On 11 March 1986, six weeks after the government had received Nieuwenhuysen's report, the *Age* ran an editorial entitled 'Why is Cain so coy on liquor?'

> When a government asks an independent and intelligent person to conduct an inquiry into questions of public controversy, it runs the grave risk of receiving a report full of independent and intelligent answers. These are not necessarily what the government, ever mindful of sectional interests and political sensitivities, wants to hear. In the absence of any more meaningful explanation from the Premier, Mr Cain, we wonder whether this is the reason for his strange reluctance to publish the Nieuwenhuysen report on the liquor industry and licensing laws.

With timing that was strangely similar to when the *Age* started campaigning for licensing reform – just before the government announced a review into liquor

{*Opposite*} The Nieuwenhuysen Review team celebrate submitting their recommendations, not knowing that these will be kept from the public for months.

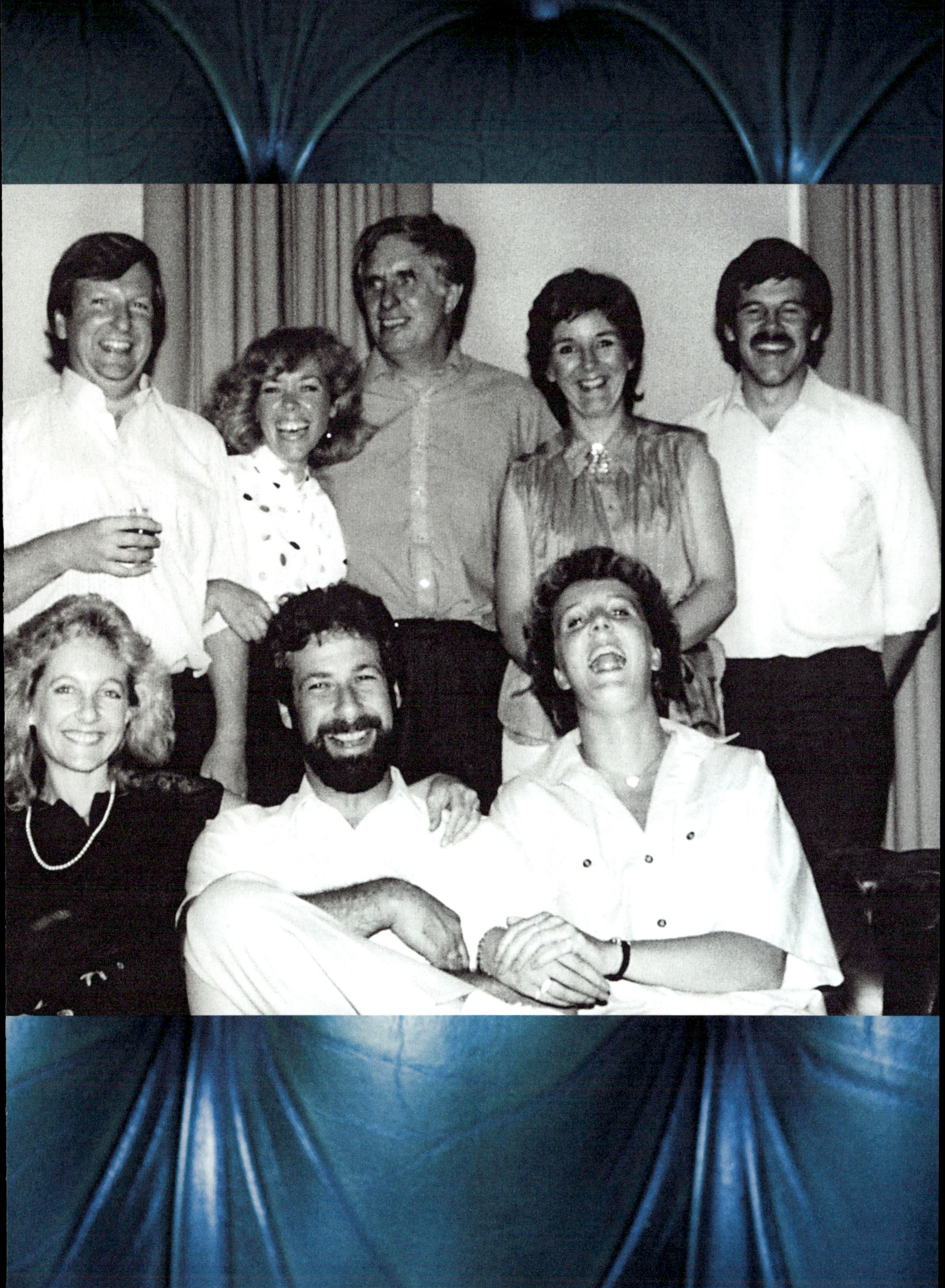

licensing – word arrived that the Nieuwenhuysen Review would be released on 19 March. It was finally time for the gloves to come off.

At the press conference that signalled the release of the report, John Nieuwenhuysen found himself with Minister Fordham sitting on a podium in a room in State Parliament, 'chock a block with television cameras and reporters' and facing a capacity crowd.[3] He was, he says, all worded up on the subject, and he spoke for some time, even managing to haul in some Greek mythology to help explain why the current system needed a major overhaul.

Quoting one of his licensing law review predecessors, Sir Philip Phillips, Nieuwenhuysen likened the 1968 Liquor Control Act to the procrustean bed. Responding to what one reporter described as the mostly blank stares and dead silence that greeted this classical reference, he went on to explain that the Greek legend of Procrustes, who made people fit his iron bed by stretching those who were too short and cutting off the legs of those who were too tall, was an ideal analogy for the current laws. New ideas and good intentions could not work in a system where they were constantly being stretched out of shape or chopped down to size to fit the requirements of the existing rigid laws. They were, in fact, stifling the industry that they were supposedly regulating.

That night and the next day the television and the newspapers were filled with news of the report and its audacious suggestions to completely overhaul and liberalise the current system. It was, says John Nieuwenhuysen, 'very unusual for an academic to be on the front page of the paper', let alone on the front page of every paper and on every local television news service. It was also unusual that, at this early stage, the reaction to the report across the board was either cautiously or enthusiastically positive. Admittedly, having less than a day to read an 800-plus-page, two-volume document that was fifteen months in the making, and then to make a reasoned response that did any more than skim the surface was probably stretching things. But the report – aided by John Nieuwenhuysen's comments at the press conference – did go some way to address and alleviate the major fears that had been circulating in the community in the weeks prior to its release.

Most widely reported was the explicit rejection, both in the report and by Minister Fordham, of the rumour that booze would become available in service stations, milk bars and convenience stores. Also well covered was the way the report crunched the figures to negate the direct relationship between the availability of alcohol and alcohol abuse. The report pointed out that while Victoria had the most restrictive and regulated liquor industry in the country – 994 people per licence compared with 679 in New South Wales, 547 in the Australian Capital Territory and 457 in the Northern Territory – its consumption of liquor was on a par with the

> That night and the next day the television and the newspapers were filled with news of the report and its audacious suggestions

national average. It was also pointed out that although hours had been extended and outlets had increased over the previous twenty years, Victorians' consumption habits had remained almost static. On first viewing, people seemed to be soothed by these reassuring figures.

There was also much attention paid to the report's emphasis on combating the problems of alcohol abuse, which the existing laws had obviously failed to stem. Recommendations such as extra resources to combat drink driving, the wider use of breathalysers and increased penalties and stricter laws concerning underage drinking seemed to many commentators, on their first reading, to underline a sensible, rational approach to a quite radical proposition.

The *Age*'s editorial on 20 March 1986 said it was 'so clear-headed in its approach and analysis, and so firmly founded on common sense, public interest and the changing social ethos, that it is difficult to understand why the State Government should have hesitated to release the report'. The editorial in the *Herald* on the same day said that there was 'a great deal of commonsense in Dr Nieuwenhuysen's report' and that it was 'a sensible examination of the licensing laws [that] deserves a better fate than gathering dust in a pigeonhole', while the *Sun*, also favourable, concluded that 'sweeping reform has been in the wind before – only to be knocked down faster than a pot of draught in a drought'.

Despite this initial reaction, and the cautiously encouraging remarks about the report that were coming from the government, it did not take too long for the doubts and the fears to emerge. With a good percentage of the population concerned about the effects of alcohol on the community, and with no overt desire to have the current licensing situation completely revamped, those who were opposed to the Nieuwenhuysen recommendations found it relatively easy to score some telling blows on the initial positive spin.

The government had set a two-month period during which people could respond to the report and respond they did. The AHA led the charge of those opposed to the report, taking the line that while it agreed that the 1968 Act needed to be updated, it should, as it pointed out in the 20,000 pamphlets distributed to hotels, MPs, local councils and other interest groups, be along the lines of an evolution rather than a revolution.

The main thrust of the AHA's argument was that the reforms proposed could see an immediate five-fold increase (from 2000 to 10,000) in the number of places allowed to sell alcohol. This would not only lead to an increased number of underage drinkers, but would also require more police to deal with the greater liquor consumption. The AHA disagreed with the report's findings that increased availability does not lead to increased consumption (quoting a 1983 study conducted in the United States that contradicted the report's conclusions); disputed the opinion that a change in laws would have any effect on tourism; claimed that there would be a drop in employment levels under the changes and an increase in bureaucracy, with myriad local councils taking on the job of the centralised Liquor Control Commission (LCC); and declared the new laws would probably lead to an increased financial burden on the Victorian taxpayer. It also hinted that John Nieuwenhuysen was arrogant, out of touch, 'highly emotional and defensive' and imposing his own personal desire for deregulation on a public that had shown it was in no hurry for any such change and was not 'knocking on [its] MPs' doors demanding the right to turn Melbourne into Paris'.[4]

Of course the AHA made little mention by of the economic benefits that its members stood to lose should the report become law, other than a slightly feeble defence that the 'hotel industry "cake" has been available to an increasing number of Victorians over the years', quoting a 25 per cent increase in the number of licences since 1968. This may have seemed like an impressive figure in percentage terms, but it was decidedly less so when you consider that there were only around 100 Restaurant Licences in existence in 1968. The 'cake' was still mostly on the hotel's plate.

Among the other main groups that first joined the AHA in the fight against the reforms was the Retail Liquor Merchants' Association of Victoria, which argued that alcohol abuse would increase with deregulation. The National Party said it could not support changes that would dismantle a well-controlled industry and might only encourage an increase in the incidence of under-age drinking, and the Victorian Temperance Alliance maintained its age-old opposition to any relaxation of liquor laws. In joining with the AHA in this campaign, the temperance groups resurrected the strange alliance between pubs and temperance that had first come together in the late 1800s. The Federated Liquor and Allied Industries Employees' Union of Australia also became part of this rather misshapen group of lobbyists that had one goal uniting many disparate aims, but it joined the fray a little later in the piece.

Another interesting submission received by the government was from Judge John Campton, who was chairman of the LCC and one of its four commissioners. Not surprisingly, Judge Campton made a detailed critique of the Nieuwenhuysen Review, rejecting outright the claim that availability of alcohol did not bring about an increase in consumption. Judge Campton was also vocal in his opposition to John Nieuwenhuysen being the one to publicly defend the report he had been commissioned to deliver. He believed it was up to the public to decide and that the government should sell the initiative themselves. To some extent, the author of the report agreed with him. But the government seemed to like having him

> Judge Campton made a detailed critique rejecting outright the claim that availability of alcohol did not bring about an increase in consumption

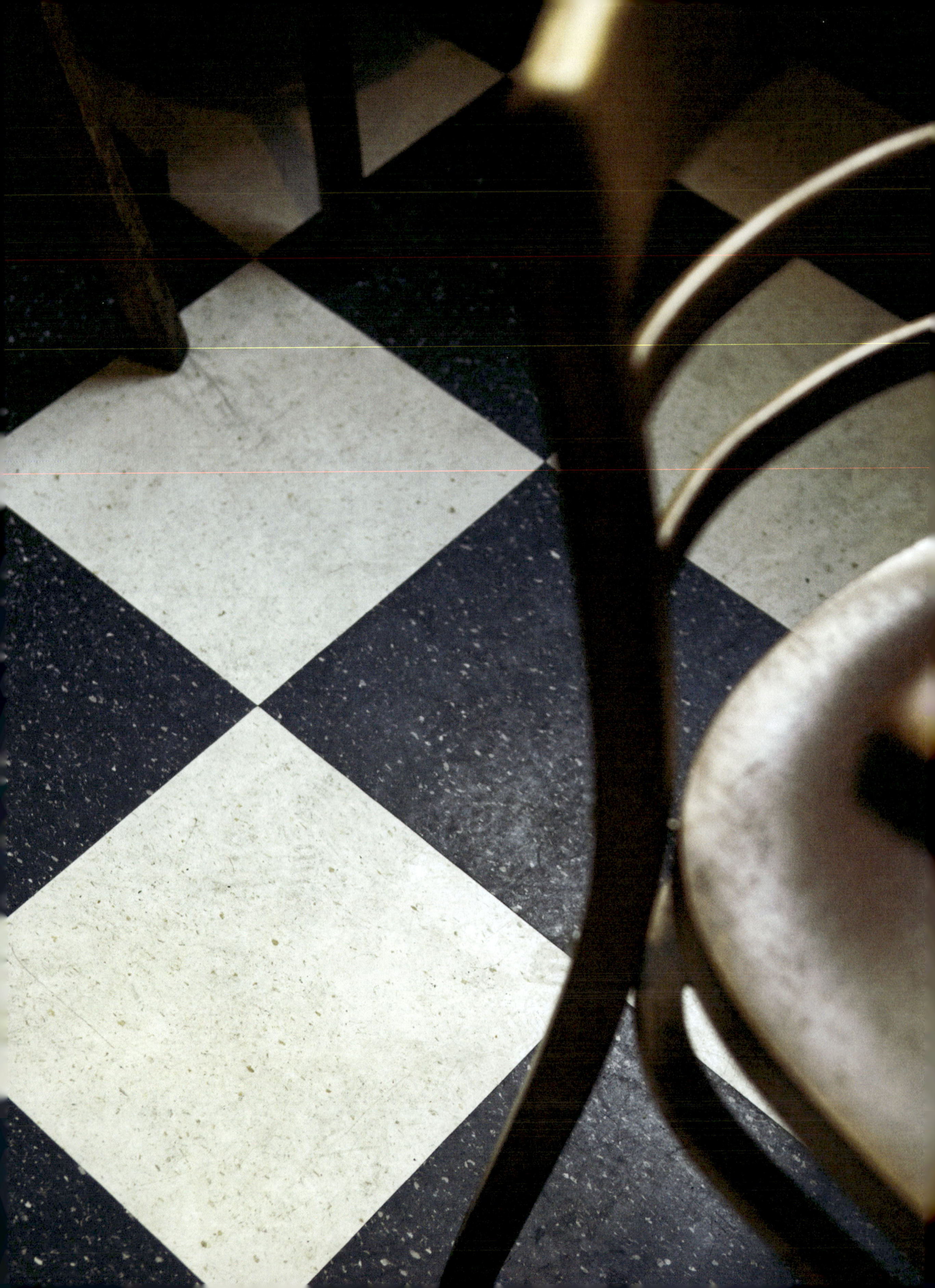

FOCUS

What the doctor orders is a dash of bitters for some

Victoria
PAUL AUSTIN

TWENTY years after the abolition of the notorious "six o'clock swill", Victoria at last has a practical and reasoned blueprint for a more enlightened future in which it will be easier to get a drink, harder to abuse the privilege.

Dr John Nieuwenhuysen, the highly respected reader in economics at the University of Melbourne, who was seconded by the Cain Government 18 months ago to drag the State's drinking laws out of the Victorian age, this week outlined his vision for a new society centred on what he calls the European-style of socialising.

He sees industry regulations reduced to the point where Victorians would be able to enjoy a glass of port with coffee on street cafes at any time of the day or night; where they could join friends at a restaurant and order a drink without being obliged under law to purchase a meal; and where they could visit corner bottle shops whenever they wanted an extra bottle of wine.

The Government, often portrayed by the Opposition as a "wowser" administration, appears to be rather proud of the 900-page report.

However, before the Nieuwenhuysen theory becomes the Victorian experience, the Government must overcome the predictable but forceful objections of the guardians of everything good and sober, and of the hotel industry which is protected under the presented Liquor Control Act from direct competition from licensed restaurants, BYOs, cafes and cinemas.

Within hours of the Nieuwenhuysen document being made public, the National Party — which despite winning only a minority of the votes is quick to claim it speaks on behalf of the moral majority — was warning that the evils of deregulation were such that the required legislative changes were likely to be blocked in the Opposition-dominated Upper House.

Dr Nieuwenhuysen . . . a reasoned blueprint

The Nationals' message was clear: 24-hour liquor trading was out, and so were any reforms that would "dismantle a well-controlled industry and might only encourage an increase in the incidence under age drinking".

The Australian Hotels Association, the vested interest with the most to lose if the Nieuwenhuysen vision were become a reality, picked up the teenage drinking boge warning the proposals wou result in a doubling of liqu outlets with potential "tragic" consequences for th young.

The good doctor is at pain in his report to question th logic of such reactions. H points out that despite the fact Victoria's liquor laws ar the most restricted in the country, it is up with the bes of the other States in terms o alcohol consumed per head o population. And Dr Nieuwen huysen urges the Governmen to couple deregulation with a vigorous attack on alcohol-related road accidents, underage drinking and anti-social behavior.

Hoteliers might never admit it, but Dr Nieuwenhuysen's report offers Victorians the best of both worlds — more civilised drinking arrangements for the majority who act responsibly, and harsher penalties for the few who don't.

> Nieuwenhuysen described the feeling following its completion and handing over as 'a bit like post-natal depression'

there as a spokesperson and focal point, as if using him as a buffer to keep government slightly distanced from the reforms and any potential fallout until it made its final decision.

John Nieuwenhuysen was very much the figurehead for the new approach to licensing, a position he had never imagined when he first took on the review. In an interview with Rod Usher in the *Age* shortly after the release of the report, Nieuwenhuysen talked of the long hours he had worked on the report, the weight of responsibility and the need to give the report a style, a sense of logic. Most tellingly, though, he described the feeling following its completion and handing over as 'a bit like post-natal depression'. It may be that he was still enjoying the unusual ride of being a public figure and so, when the government asked him to hit the road to sell the reforms, there was not too much hesitation before he agreed:

> I had to go out on a speaking tour. The government said to me, 'We would like you to go out and defend your report now.' And I said, 'Well why don't you make up your mind about it and go out and defend it yourself,' but they wanted me to do it. I was like a champion fighting on their behalf.[5]

It was arranged for him to first speak to the caucuses of the Labor, Liberal and National Parties and then embark on a tour of Victoria, speaking to various interest groups and at public meetings. The Labor Party meeting was, not surprisingly, mostly supportive (though not without its dissenters), while the Nationals were dubious but polite. His biggest surprise came with the Liberal Party, whom he assumed would be all for any reform that spruiked deregulation. If he presumed that speaking gig would be one of the easiest, he was mistaken:

> After I had spoken to the Liberal Party caucus, one of the shadow ministers came up to me and said, 'You've been telling us that this is like a Liberal Party report, and not just because the cover is blue but because what's inside it. Let me tell you, we are not like Pavlov's dogs – we don't salivate every time someone mentions the words "free market" to us.' And so I knew that there was opposition being fostered in the party by the hotels and small business.

From there the speaking and the spruiking of the report never stopped, and Nieuwenhuysen was pretty much on call for the whole year. Every time there was any newsworthy, alcohol-related happening – under-age drinking, binge drinking, unruly drunken behaviour at a sporting match – he would be contacted for his opinion and how he thought the reforms he was proposing would have affected the outcome. His photo became a familiar sight in the press. His position as spokesperson and defender also saw him under constant pressure from the AHA, as it kept the heat on the government to abandon or dilute the deregulation parts of the reforms. The pressure might have been constant but it was, perhaps surprisingly by current standards, not personal. Other than a couple of subtle jibes about him being a 'Toorak academic', it was a fairly civilised campaign.

But the campaign – particularly between Nieuwenhuysen and the AHA – was certainly not all sweetness and light. There were numerous instances of what Nieuwenhuysen refers to as 'bullying tactics' in the form of solicitors' letters that caused him to seek the assistance of the Crown solicitor because they 'bordered on an attempt at intimidation'. There was also the instance of a Mata Hari–like AHA plant.

> I remember I had to go and give a talk in Melbourne and there was a very attractive lady there who came up and spoke to me afterwards and I didn't know until later that she was from the AHA. She phoned me the next day and asked if she could come and see me and have a talk. I asked her why and what she wanted to talk to me about and she said, 'Well, I really want to know where you are coming from' and I thought, oh right, and so I told her she should just read my report and she could find out where I was coming from in that.[6]

So constant was the pressure on Nieuwenhuysen in the year following the release of the report that he developed tinnitus, a constant, often stress-induced ringing in the ears. It was not helped any by the government's constant delay and a noticeable decline in the number of outright positive noises they were making about the proposed recommendations.

Of course, the tales of potential doom and destruction were the ones that made for the best headlines. Banners proclaiming that 'Publicans warn of tragic consequences', 'Fears over drink-drive surge' and 'Little support for "free for all" approach' packed more of a punch than those announcing that 'Recommendations are in line with public opinion'. But there was, nonetheless, a good deal of support for the recommendations of the report to be adopted, from both within the industry and the community, even if this support was less well organised and less vocal than those that opposed the changes.

The Restaurant and Catering Association (RCA) was naturally in wholehearted agreement with the report, saying that liberalised licensing laws would create opportunities for restaurant owners and their employees, that profits would increase and that tourism would be boosted, as would Victoria's wine industry. It also suggested that more civilised and responsible drinking habits would ensue with a more European-style approach to drinking and dining out. Richard Frank says that within the ranks of the RCA Nieuwenhuysen was looked upon as 'sort of a god, really'.[7]

Support also came from the Victorian Tourism Commission, the Municipal Association of Victoria and the Law Institute of Victoria. Victoria Police also cautiously backed the report, despite an article in the *Herald*, claimed to be the official police response, warning that a relaxing of liquor laws would see a rise in organised crime, alcohol abuse, family breakdowns, ill-health, the road toll and crime generally. It was later found that this was the submission of one policeman to the government, and Victoria Police quickly clarified its position, commending the attempt to formulate a simpler and more flexible licensing system that would aid in more efficient policing.

But probably the best arguments for change came from people who were struggling under the outdated 1968 Act. Despite the position of the AHA, there were just as many hoteliers as restaurateurs, both licensed and BYO, who found the law too proscriptive and restrictive. This had become especially apparent to the restaurant industry, with the proliferation of BYO restaurants in the 1980s. These business owners began to see that the restrictions on them selling alcohol, coupled with the expectation they would supply glasses, ice and refrigeration gratis for the alcohol their customers lugged in from pubs and bottle shops, was costing them money and limiting their capacity to operate in the way they wanted to. The BYO culture was also increasingly seen as encouraging excessive drinking, with people coming

[*Above*] Queenscliff Hotel

Restaurateur Extraordinaire

No other Melburnian can match Richard Frank's remarkable record as an innovative serial entrepreneur in the hospitality industry for more than fifty years. And few were such determined campaigners as this former president of the Restaurant and Caterering Association for the reform of the liquor licensing laws.

The son of a Polish refugee and having grown up in Shanghai, Frank came to Melbourne as a lad in 1948, first working as a waiter in the old Victoria Coffee Palace. Three years later he and a partner opened a coffee lounge, the Fan Court, in Little Collins Street, serving toasted sandwiches and raisin bread.

In 1957, trading on the popularity of the film *Casablanca*, he opened Rick's in a Queen Street basement, next door to the Rhine Castle Cellars. Due to a legal loophole and business canniness, Rick's became Melbourne's first BYO.

While still running Rick's, the young entrepreneur seized on the boom in suburban bowling alleys to set up restaurants in six of them. Then came a string of upmarket restaurants that he either opened or took over – Top of the Town, on top of the old National Mutual Centre in Collins Street; Petty Sessions, in William Street; The Walnut Tree, leased to Louis Fleyfel; Lazar's, in the historic bluestone building on the corner of King and Lonsdale streets; and Quarter Sessions, in a Collins Street basement. In more recent years Frank and partner Erik Hopkinson had Windows on the Bay, on the Mordialloc foreshore, and Carter's, in Toorak.

In 1983, Frank enticed a brilliant young chef from Normandy to Melbourne; Jacques Reymond's eponymous restaurant is now among Melbourne's elite.

There is no denying Richard Frank's long-established eminence and influence in the Melbourne's hospitality industry. JENI PORT

Richard Frank

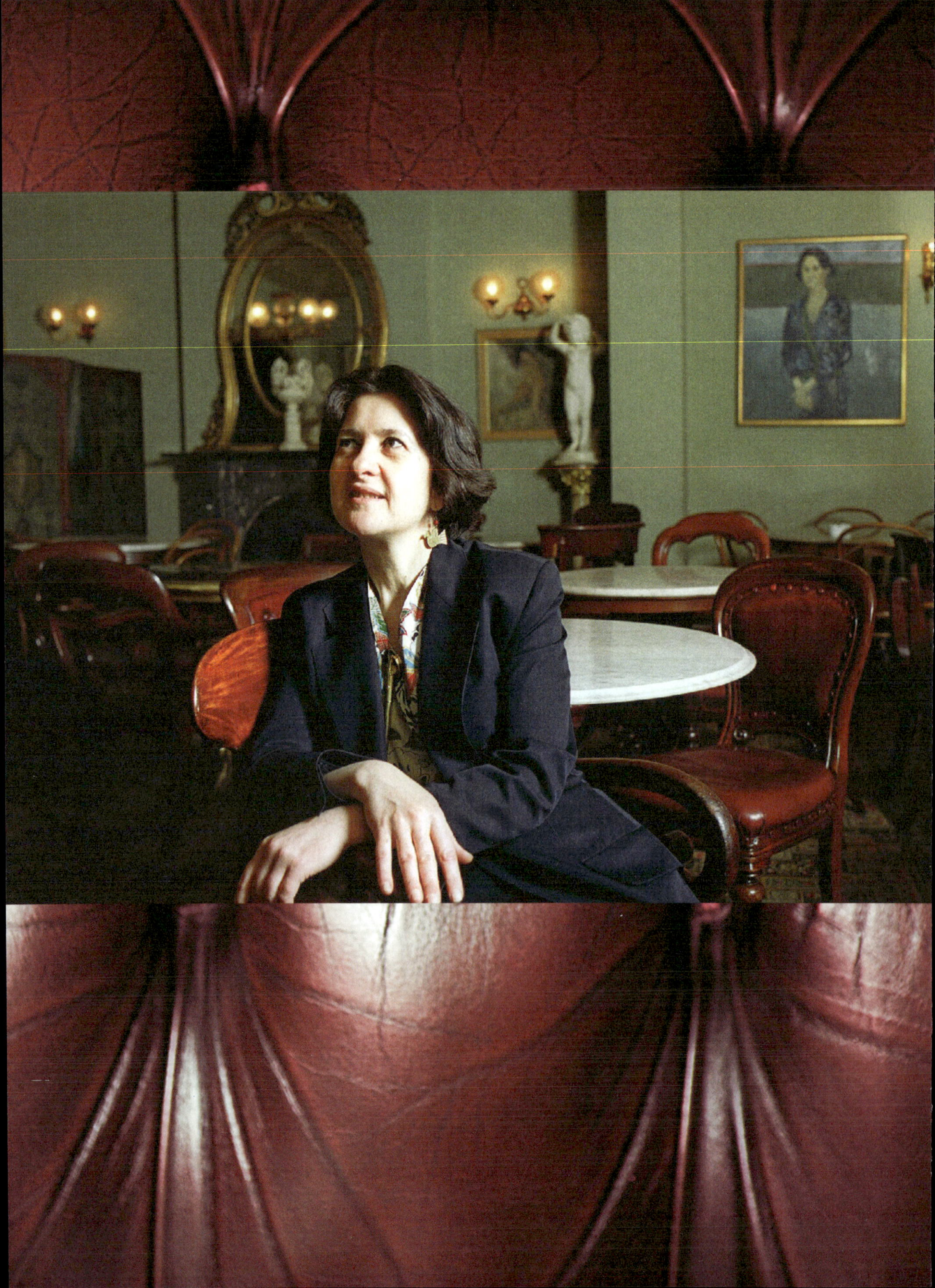

to restaurants with Eskies full of alcohol, and not leaving until they were empty. As many restaurateurs began pointing out, when people were paying for their drinks as they went, they would usually be more circumspect in their consumption habits.

One of the submissions received by the government on the Nieuwenhuysen Review came from Mietta O'Donnell and her partner Tony Knox. The couple was in a particularly good position to understand how the laws were affecting the industry as a whole, as they had started with a BYO restaurant – Mietta's in North Fitzroy – before going through the lengthy and expensive process of applying for a Restaurant Licence. The submission made it clear that applying for a Restaurant Licence was a somewhat traumatic process and one that had cost them an estimated $250,000 and 'months of bureaucratic agony to acquire ... this scrap of paper that overnight transformed our business from an Esky infected BYO to one of Melbourne's "nicest" restaurants'.[8] They were also hotel owners, having bought the Queenscliff Hotel in 1978 and, the year before their submission, sold their North Fitzroy restaurant and moved to the former Naval and Military Club in the city, a building that came with a hotel licence. They point out in their submission that as hoteliers:

> It is not in our immediate interests to support the recommendation ... that only one licence should apply in Victoria, however, we feel that it is essential for the health of our industry and the well being of the community at large that not only this, but the whole of the report should be adopted. A breath of fresh air is needed in the liquor industry to dispel the odour of cigarette smoke, the deep fryers and stale beer overlaid by the ubiquitous smell of toilet deodorant. We think it is essential that large numbers of new people should be able to enter this closeted industry and that new groups of businesses, more in line with community needs, should be able to be established. We believe that the short term financial loss this may cause us will be more than compensated for by a surge of community interest in the rejuvenated liquor industry.

They went on to talk of how, under the existing laws and the rule of the LCC, their business was only able to get a licence by becoming more formal – something that could only be achieved by an enormous monetary outlay. They mention restaurateurs trying to achieve something different – Iain Hewitson and Sigmund Jorgenson at Clichy in Collingwood, for example – whose businesses failed under the imposed pressure.

So, among those who welcomed the report's recommendations there was initially real hope that things might change. Some were more hopeful than others. At the University Cafe on Lygon Street, Giancarlo and Beverly Caprioli installed fridges and made alterations that would enable the transition from cafe and

{*Opposite*} Mietta O'Donnell at her city establishment Mietta's

{*Above, top*} Sigmund Jorgenson; {*below*} John Chalker

restaurant to cafe, bar and restaurant. On the front cover of the menu it stated: 'BYO until state government liquor licensing laws are amended or changed as in the Nieuwenhuysen report'. But as the months wore on and there was no word from government about which, if any, of the recommendations they were thinking of adopting, or when they would make a move, the mood became gloomier and some became resigned to the fact that this could well be an opportunity lost. John Chalker, who owned Lygon Street restaurant Chalkies at the time, says: 'There was real apprehension that the report was being put into the government's too-hard basket; that they were folding to powerful lobby groups and that we had probably lost the whole thing.'[9]

The sense of gloom was heightened after the ALP Victorian Conference in June 1986 debated and then voted to express firm opposition to the recommendations put forward in the Nieuwenhuysen Review. This opposition was the result of strong lobbying on the part of the Federated Liquor and Allied Industries Employees' Union of Australia, known more simply as the Liquor Union.

The Liquor Union was the second-largest union in Victoria, with 33,000 members, 60 per cent of whom worked in the hotel sector. Though much of the union's rhetoric on opposing the laws was on the moral issues of reducing alcohol abuse and under-age drinking, its opposition had more to do with union power being undermined by deregulated restaurants, which, they believed, already breached awards, offered unstable employment and were fanatically anti-union.

In the diary he kept at the time, John Cain writes about a 1987 meeting he had with Linda Rubenstein, one of the Liquor Union's officials who was responsible for looking at the recommendations:

> I raised with her the question of the Nieuwenhuysen recommendations and then she told me that she was generally opposed to them ... In summary she opposes the proposals on the social and moral grounds about liquor abuse and young people, all the other well known arguments about the Liquor industry. At the same time she acknowledges she's really on about retaining a system where it's reasonably easy to organise membership in the large hotels and large organizations and very difficult in the small restaurants and other small liquor outlets. This is what the union is concerned about.
>
> She's an interesting person though and qualifies all she says by putting to me that if we can demonstrate or say to her that the next election will be won if we amended the liquor laws as suggested then they wouldn't hesitate in supporting it. She says the union wants to support Labor governments and will do all it can to see they remain in office.[10]

Though it may have seemed like a significant blow to the fortunes of the Nieuwenhuysen Review from the outside, the union opposition was not that fierce.

{*Opposite*} Restaurateurs grew impatient with the delays to the Act

Lygon St toasts liquor law reform

By PETER GAME

COCA-COLA will give way to Cinzano on the umbrellas shading Lygon Street's pavement cafes if the Government accepts Dr John Niewenhuysen's suggestion.

Overwhelmingly, owners of the little coffee bars of Melbourne's most international of streets say they will seek to sell liquor if the laws are liberalised as the doctor suggests.

Some of them already have BYO licences, but they say that the ability to sell alcoholic drinks with coffee would bring Australia into line with the relaxed international attitude to liquor.

They say they are repeatedly turning away overseas tourists who ask for a beer or a glass of wine.

Anyone who has enjoyed a relaxed hour sipping a beer, or a glass of chianti as they watch the passing parade from, for example, an Italian pavement cafe, will know the frustration these tourists must feel.

But, already, regular local customers at the Lygon St. coffee bars are licking their lips at the prospect that things might change and that they will be allowed to lace their short black coffees with grappa or sambuca as their cousins can in any coffee bar in Italy.

The only opposition seems to come from fully licensed restaurants that would face competition from the cheaper prices at the coffee bars.

At the Universita Bar Ristorante, Giancarlo Caprioli has a $34,000 marble bar complete with refrigerated bottle-coolers.

He imported the elaborate bar in the hope that one day the law would permit him to serve liquor with the coffee. At present, instead of campari and other aperitifs, the bottle-coolers are occupied by innocuous aqua minerale.

His bar will swing into action if the government accepts Dr Niewenhuysen's suggestion that there should be a move towards European-style cafe outlets offering coffee, meals and snacks, with or without alcohol, any time during the day and night.

Mr Caprioli said: "It would raise Australia to the standard of other countries. There would be less drunkenness.

"Coffee bars can do this overseas: we get many tourists, Italians, Americans, who come here and ask for an alcoholic drink. We have to send them to the pub."

Mr Caprioli's patrons, seated around a pavement table, agreed.

One said: "Most of us don't like pubs. We would rather drink here socially."

At the Caffe Sport the proprietor, Napoleon Marretta, said: "I think it would be lovely. I am just back from Los Angeles and all the coffee lounges there can serve liquor.

The Cafe Notturno's Jim Mastroianni says he would begin selling liquor if the law relaxed: "This street is a perfect place to start. We get a lot of tourists.

"If people could buy a drink at any time they wouldn't abuse it. When the pubs close, people buy half a dozen bottles of beer and get drunk at home."

At the Cafe L'Alba, Toni Princi feels the same way: he says he's always sending overseas visitors next door to the hotel when they ask him to sell them a beer.

Piero Brunetti runs Piero's Cafe. He said: "It would be beautiful for this business. People come in to order cakes and rolls and ask for beer and wine.

"If this was Italy we could serve them."

At the Tiamo trattoria, proprietor Bibbi Succi said: "We would like to be able to sell beer and wine, not for the profit but to give people more enjoyment with their meals.

"If people could buy drinks for 24 hours there would be fewer drunks because they would drink a lot slower.

"With a BYO licence people are forced to bring in a whole bottle when all they may want is a glass of wine."

Giancarlo Caprioli with a bottle of mineral water, behind his $34,000 marble bar ... hoping for the day.

The Rise and Decline of the BYO

It was a canny Italian restaurateur who discovered, some seventy years ago, a loophole in Victoria's antiquated liquor laws. That was when hotels and clubs had a virtual – and jealously guarded – monopoly of liquor service.

Only a lucky handful of restaurants were legally able to offer Australian wine (but no beer, spirits or imported wines) under a limited Australian Wine Licence. The law prohibited the provision of alcoholic drinks in all other restaurants – but not the consumption. Therein lay the loophole, through which emerged the happy birth and proliferation of the BYO (Bring Your Own) restaurant.

It was a concept Victorians eagerly embraced, and the law eventually recognised by issuing BYO permits that were much easier, quicker and cheaper to obtain than a full Restaurant Licence. The first Restaurant Licence was not granted until 1952, and when John Nieuwenhuysen began his inquiry in 1984 there were still only 427 licensed restaurants in Victoria, compared with 2100 with BYO permits.

Wine buffs welcomed the rise of the BYO restaurant because they could bring better vintages from their own cellars than all but some of the most elite (and expensive) licensed places could offer. The mass of diners loved the BYO because it was so much cheaper to pop into the local pub or bottle shop than to order from a restaurant wine list with an average 100 per cent mark-up on retail.

The 1987 liquor law reform has changed the equation. Fully licensed restaurants and cafes now predominate in a greatly expanded market. Those with BYO-only permits are mostly small or ethnic eateries at the lower end of the market. Most Victorians have welcomed the enhanced freedom of choice. But many people regret, or even resent, the decline of the once-ubiquitous BYO, even though this peculiar phenomenon – almost incomprehensible to many international visitors – arose as an anomaly of restrictive liquor licensing, even though restaurants make their living from providing food *and* drink. (Who would dream of bringing their own drinks to a pub?)

Some licensed restaurants allow BYO wine (less willingly, slabs of beer or large bottles of fizzy drinks). It's at their discretion, not a legal obligation. But it is common for such restaurants to charge 'corkage', either as a deterrent or to cover costs of service and possible breakage. This is another cause of contention. The late wine merchant Dan Murphy ruefully recalled paying $30 a bottle corkage on nine bottles of rare wine he took a top city restaurant for a dinner he hosted. But he accepted the $270 charge and its justification as legitimate. CLAUDE FORELL

B.Y.O.
UNTIL STATE GOVERNMENT LIQUOR LICENSING
LAWS ARE AMENDED OR CHANGED AS IN THE
NIEUWENHUYSEN REPORT

Universita BAR Ristorante

DRINKS

IMPORTED ITALIAN SOFT DRINKS	$1.50
IMPORTED MINERAL WATERS (500 ml)	$2.00
(1 litre)	$3.50
COKE, FANTA, LEMONADE	$1.20
CAFFE (Coffee)	$1.50

MENU

257 Lygon Street, Carlton
Telephone: 347 2142

> Cain's diary entries show his mounting sense of anger and frustration that there had been so little movement on the recommendations

As Cain says, 'they realised that their political or industrial strength was insufficient for them to go to the wall on the main direction of the legislation'.[11]

The government also seemed to realise that despite a fairly vocal opposition that now included church groups and a significant number of people working in the areas of drug and alcohol abuse, the sentiment in the community had remained about the same as indicated in the polls conducted for the Nieuwenhuysen Review; that is, more than half of the community remained cautiously supportive of change.

Cain's diary entries in March 1987 show his mounting sense of anger and frustration that there had been so little movement on the recommendations. His position, he writes, was 'we should seize the opportunity to have it passed quickly'.

In April 1987, an announcement was made that the government had decided to incorporate in full 141 and in part 26 of the 184 recommendations made by the Nieuwenhuysen Review. It had accepted the report's three main recommendations – deregulation, a new means of countering abuse other than through regulation of the industry, and administrative reform. Licence numbers would be reduced from twenty-nine to six, restaurants would be allowed to serve alcohol without meals and hotels were no longer under the obligation to provide accommodation and meals.

Nieuwenhuysen was, of course, extremely pleased, not to mention surprised that such a large percentage of his report had been accepted. Again he went into full-on interview mode, discussing the ramifications of the government's decision. But he was not yet ready to celebrate fully. The Liberal Party was the formal opposition in the upper house in Victoria and had, so far, refused to make any noise of support for or opposition to the recommendations before seeing the government's legislation.

Don Hayward was the shadow minister for Economic Development and, as such, was the man who had 'the carriage of legislation' within the Liberal Party. It was he who had to recommend whether or not the party should support the legislation. He had a meeting with Nieuwenhuysen and was attracted by his arguments and reasoning, though he didn't need too much persuasion, as he had 'always thought that our approach to liquor consumption in Victoria was quite uncivilised and had the effect of encouraging bad drinking habits'.[12]

Convincing the shadow cabinet to support the legislation was a relatively straightforward task, but Hayward also had to get support from the party room generally. This was more difficult than he had expected:

> Based on the Liberal Party's general political philosophy, you'd think that they would have been in favour of the legislation but the vested interests – the hotel keepers and the people who had the licensed bottle shops and that

sort of thing – were extremely well organised and they were good at putting pressure on members of parliament at a local level … In the weeks leading up to the party room meeting there were attempts to put a great deal of pressure on me personally, some of which got very close to blackmail. There were threats that people would work against me in my seat, that I was allowing people's livelihoods to be destroyed, putting children and families at risk.

Still, believing the legislation to be in the best interest of Victoria, he pressed ahead. The debate in the party room was robust, with, he says, 'some quite vicious attacks by two or three members'. But in the end, helped no doubt by support from Liberal Party leader Jeff Kennett and the shadow cabinet, it was resolved that the party would support the legislation.

Nieuwenhuysen had just finished debating some of the points of the proposed *Liquor Control Act 1987* with an AHA representative on ABC TV's *The 7.30 Report*, when he was told there was a call for him. Don Hayward had called to deliver the good news: 'I knew then that everything was going to go through. It was a great moment for me.'[13]

And so the long and laborious passage of making word law was almost over. But there were more delays, this time more to do with democratic process and politicking. Finally, in May 1988, nearly a year after the government had accepted 167 of the recommendations, the *Liquor Control Act 1987* came into being. The old way was gone and everything had changed. Drinking and eating in Victoria would never be the same again.

> And so the long and laborious passage of making word law was almost over

If it is permitted to proceed the Act could herald the most important changes in the style of drinking premises in Victoria for many years.

JENI PORT, 1988

The Taste of Freedom

Delice
Stilton
garrotxa
Occelli B

Anyone expecting the new Liquor Control Act to instantly create a cataclysmic shift in Victoria's hospitality industry would have been sorely disappointed. When the Act came into force on 4 May 1988, there was no hurricane-like blast of the winds of change, no unrestrained displays of riotous drunken revelry in the vineyards, or mass rejoicing by exuberant crowds of newly liberated restaurateurs. Instead, Victoria lived up to its conservative, reined-in reputation and opted for a cautious wait-and-see approach. There is no doubt that change was in the works, but it would take some time before it made its presence felt. In the meantime, no-one seemed quite sure just how this new freedom was going to taste.

It seems fairly obvious that this hesitant approach on the part of the industry was just what the government wanted. That it took a year for the laws to come into effect was only part of the go-slow approach. The campaign by those opposed to the changes had successfully spread unease about the potential ramifications of more widely available alcohol, and so moving slowly was seen as the best option for keeping a potentially skittish population calm. Changing the name of the new licensing body from the Liquor Control Commission (LCC) to the Liquor Licensing Commission reflected this cautious approach by making any implementation of the new laws – even a name change – appear yawningly incremental. This tactic was reinforced by soothingly bland statements from the new liquor licensing commissioner, Tony Ryan, who was quoted in the *Age* as saying: 'If – IF – consumers want more of the kind of diverse licensing facilities allowed for in the Act, then the Act is there to make it easier for that to occur.'[1]

John Nieuwenhuysen's quite radical suggestion of only one general licence for all businesses wishing to serve or sell liquor had not been taken up by the government. Admittedly, the unwieldy twenty-nine licences under the old Act had been replaced by a more streamlined seven – General, Residential, Club, Producer's, On-Premises, Packaged Liquor and Limited Licence – but the idea of the slippery beast being constrained by a single legislative fence is not one anybody was willing to run with, either then or now.

> There was 'a feeling of jubilation, like a muzzle had been taken off'

There were other brakes applied to the Nieuwenhuysen Review's preference for unfettered deregulation, particularly in relation to restaurants. Perhaps responding to the results in the report's public opinion survey, which found 64 per cent of people against the idea of drinking in a restaurant without eating, the new Act introduced a couple of provisos that had not appeared among Nieuwenhuysen's recommendations. The first was an $800 levy on any restaurant applying for the On-Premises Licence, which would allow it to serve alcohol in association with its 'primary purpose'. No other type of business or organisation covered by this licence (caterers, entertainment and conference facilities, sporting and cultural activities and so on) was subject to this fee and it was seen by restaurateurs as a protectionist, competition-limiting move.

The other proviso, one that was to trip up a few businesses in the following years, was the so-called '25 per cent rule'. Again singling out restaurants applying for an On-Premises Licence, the 25 per cent rule allowed liquor to be served without meals only in an area set aside for that purpose, comprising one-quarter or less of the total licensed area. In other words, if you had a 100-seat restaurant, only twenty-five of your customers could drink without eating, so long as they were safely cordoned off from regular diners. Even when it first appeared in a time of stepping lightly and proceeding with caution, this rule was seen as silly, arbitrary and difficult to enforce. It compromised the supposed new freedoms for the industry and was, according to Nieuwenhuysen, evidence of the government giving ground in response to the intensive lobbying of various interest groups.

But despite these clumsy, timid moments, the new laws were mostly greeted favourably by the restaurant industry. Richard Frank says there was 'a feeling of jubilation, like a muzzle had been taken off ... you could plan and you could provide a service that you couldn't ... before'.[2] The *Age*'s Claude Forell also says that the industry 'certainly welcomed the report, particularly the cafes who saw the opportunity to expand their businesses', although some restaurants were 'apprehensive about the increased competition and worried about the expense of establishing or expanding their wine cellars'.[3]

In the unforgiving light of hindsight it may seem amusing that the response of some restaurant owners to their newfound liberation was to fixate on details like wine cellars (or lack thereof), but this is not so difficult to understand. When they had known nothing but the restrictive former laws and the insecurity that came from trying to satisfy the apparently arbitrary but binding whims and preferences of the LCC, it was not easy for restaurateurs to drop that mindset overnight. Those with a Restaurant Licence had jumped through any number of carpeted, wallpapered hoops to satisfy a list of exacting and very particular standards and were well aware of the potential fate that awaited restaurants and hotels that allowed those standards to slip. As Mietta O'Donnell wrote in the mid-1980s, 'most licensees would have received as a matter of course one or two convictions during their business lives'.[4] This well-documented fear of the LCC was never going to be erased at the mere stroke of a politician's pen. The industry needed some time to adjust – and learn to trust – to its new freedom.

Victorian restaurateurs had only ever done business in a system that allowed them to operate solely as a restaurant (food, wine, formal surroundings, no alcohol without a bona-fide meal), so it was going to take some time before the hospitality industry got its head around what it could and could not do under the new laws. In the early days, vague notions of 'European-style cafes' were about as far as the imagination travelled.

According to Erik Hopkinson, CEO of the new Liquor Licensing Commission at the time, there was 'relief and rush' when the new laws came in. But 'rush', it seems, is a relative term. In the Act's first two months, only twenty restaurants were granted licences that enabled them to serve alcohol without food. A further 200 other licence-related items were before the commission by the end of July. It was probably lucky for the Liquor Licensing Commission that the expected avalanche of applications had not materialised, as there were teething problems in implementing a whole new system of licensing, albeit a system that was supposedly more streamlined and efficient. Some commission employees talked to the *Herald* in July 1988 about 'lack of direction and low morale', saying that they had 'all the chiefs in the bloody world, but not enough Indians', and that the commission was 'running blind'. Hopkinson agrees things were difficult to start with, but for very good reason:

> Positions had ceased to exist; new positions took their place and people who had worked under the old system had to be allocated positions within the new organisation. It was challenging to most of us because it was a whole new approach to liquor licensing ... [The old system] worked on the basis that if we are going to give you a licence to sell liquor then the context in which that business is transacted is to be to our satisfaction ... whereas [the new system] talked about facilitating change and responding to the needs of the marketplace.[5]

The challenge was not just confined to those implementing the laws but extended to those who were trying to operate under them. In 1989, the limits of the new laws were put to the test in St Kilda, as a couple of businesses, Greasy Joe's and the Lager Bar, tested how far the boundaries and definitions could be stretched and just how much freedom the authorities were really willing to let them have.

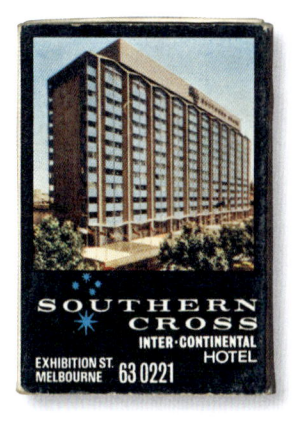

A Stellar Performer

Mietta O'Donnell's life ended tragically on a Tasmanian rural road in January 2001. She was one of the most illustrious and influential stars of Melbourne's constellation of restaurants for more than twenty-five years. Petite, demure and always impeccably groomed, she enhanced the city's reputation for fine dining and enriched its cultural life through her interests in music and the arts.

Mietta O'Donnell

She came from a distinguished family of Italian restaurateurs. Her grandparents, Mario and Teresa Vigano, were refugees from Mussolini's fascist regime in the 1920s. Their city restaurant, Mario's, was one of Melbourne's best in the 1940s and 1950s, and Mietta emulated and exceeded their success. The original Mietta's (now Matteo's) opened in Brunswick Street, Fitzroy, in 1974. At first an unassuming eatery with a bohemian air and adventurous cooking, it evolved into a superb formal restaurant in the European tradition.

By the mid-eighties, Mietta's moved to the former city home of the Naval and Military Club. Upstairs was a spacious dining room furnished in luxurious late-Victorian style, offering exquisite modern French cuisine by master chefs such as Jacques Reymond, whose excellence was matched by a list of fine Burgundian (and other) wines. The 'clubbish' yet raffish downstairs lounge doubled as a cultural salon, where Mietta hosted musical recitals, poetry readings, intellectual debates and the like. Mietta's was a haven for civilised dining and refined taste, and a magnet for a lively supper crowd. Besides this, she and her partner, Tony Knox, and sister Patricia bought and restored the Queenscliff Hotel, one of the grandiose, towered hotels built in this seaside resort in the 1880s.

In an industry dominated by men, Mietta O'Donnell stood out, along with Gloria Staley and Stephanie Alexander, as one of the three women who did most to extend the horizons and raise the standards of fine dining in Melbourne through the 1980s into the 1990s. After her restaurant closed in 1995, Mietta published a delightful book of Italian family recipes, with stories of her own heritage and that of Melbourne's other notable Italian restaurant families.

Behind a reserved, unfailingly courteous and seemingly unflappable demeanour, Mietta O'Donnell was intensely passionate about all she did. She personified dedication, professionalism and perfectionism, and, like her more ebullient partner, she was not afraid to be outspoken and sometimes controversial. CLAUDE FORELL

> While the new laws provided new freedoms, the commission was certainly no pushover

Maria Bortolotto was one of the owners of Greasy Joe's, an American-style burger joint operating under a General Licence and able to serve alcohol without food to 25 per cent of its customers. She admits that they probably didn't understand all their obligations under the new laws and became a little carried away with the freedoms they offered:

> All of a sudden everybody thought, fantastic. People could come in and have a drink without eating and we thought you could just serve a bowl of chips to the others. People used to love Greasy Joe's – there was loud music, eating and drinking, it was relaxed and casual. It was more like a bar really, and we hadn't been able to do that before and that was exciting. People felt free. We let people dance, we [became] overcrowded, but we really didn't understand what we were and weren't allowed to do until the licensing people came in and told us. They didn't close us down but they took away the 25 per cent and said, OK, now everybody has to eat and you are only allowed this many people.[6]

The Lager Bar didn't fare as well, probably because it pushed the conditions of the licence even further. With live bands, seating for hundreds and a party atmosphere where food and the 25 per cent rule were often ignored, the Lager Bar was ostensibly being run as a nightclub on a licence to run a restaurant. Not surprisingly, its licence was revoked and the place was closed down, sending out the message that while the new laws provided new freedoms, the commission was certainly no pushover. During such early days in the life of the new Liquor Control Act, the forced closure of a venue was bound to make others in the industry, if not exactly jumpy, certainly more cautious.

But it could be that the fairly muted response to the new laws was not just the result of caution on the part of the industry, or a fear of being caught in an administrative bottleneck at the fledgling commission. It was also a matter of timing, as the introduction of the new liquor laws coincided with a generational change on the Melbourne dining scene. At the end of the 1980s, many of the restaurants seen as Melbourne's best, at least according to *The Age Good Food Guide*, had been around for many years. Fanny's, Maxim's, Two Faces, Maria and Walter's and Rogalsky's had all been operating for a decade or more and, though still at the top of their game, were rightly seen as something of the old guard. These places had fought their battles and shaped their businesses under the old system. They had established themselves as standard setters, so probably saw few personal advantages or opportunities in the new laws, other than being able to run a bar for a quarter of their customers and shaking off the opinionated yoke of the LCC.

From his position in the Liquor Licensing Commission and then, after 1991, as a private consultant to the liquor and hospitality industry, Erik Hopkinson was in a good position to see how the laws began to reshape the industry. He believes that the real change began not with the old restaurants, which had been calling for the laws to be overhauled so that their operations would become more flexible (and lucrative), but with a new guard of people, who really understood the possibilities under the new regime:

> The restaurants have always been portrayed as being the innovative new group within the industry. And while there were some who sought to take advantage of the new opportunities in the legislation, by far the more significant changes were brought by the entry into the market of those who had a different background from the people who had traditionally been in the restaurant industry. In the 1980s and 1990s, there were people coming into the restaurant, bar and cafe industry who didn't necessarily have that kind of formal background. They were more lifestyle-savvy entrepreneurs, with business skills and a knowledge and appreciation of food and wine and good living. They were frequent overseas travellers. These are the people who started leading in the field. They carved a niche by tapping into the preferences and expectations of the market ... The '87 legislation gave those people the opportunity to come into the industry, take it by the throat and introduce the type of bar and cafe and restaurant that we see today.[7]

> **The real change began with a new guard of people, who really understood the possibilities under the new regime**

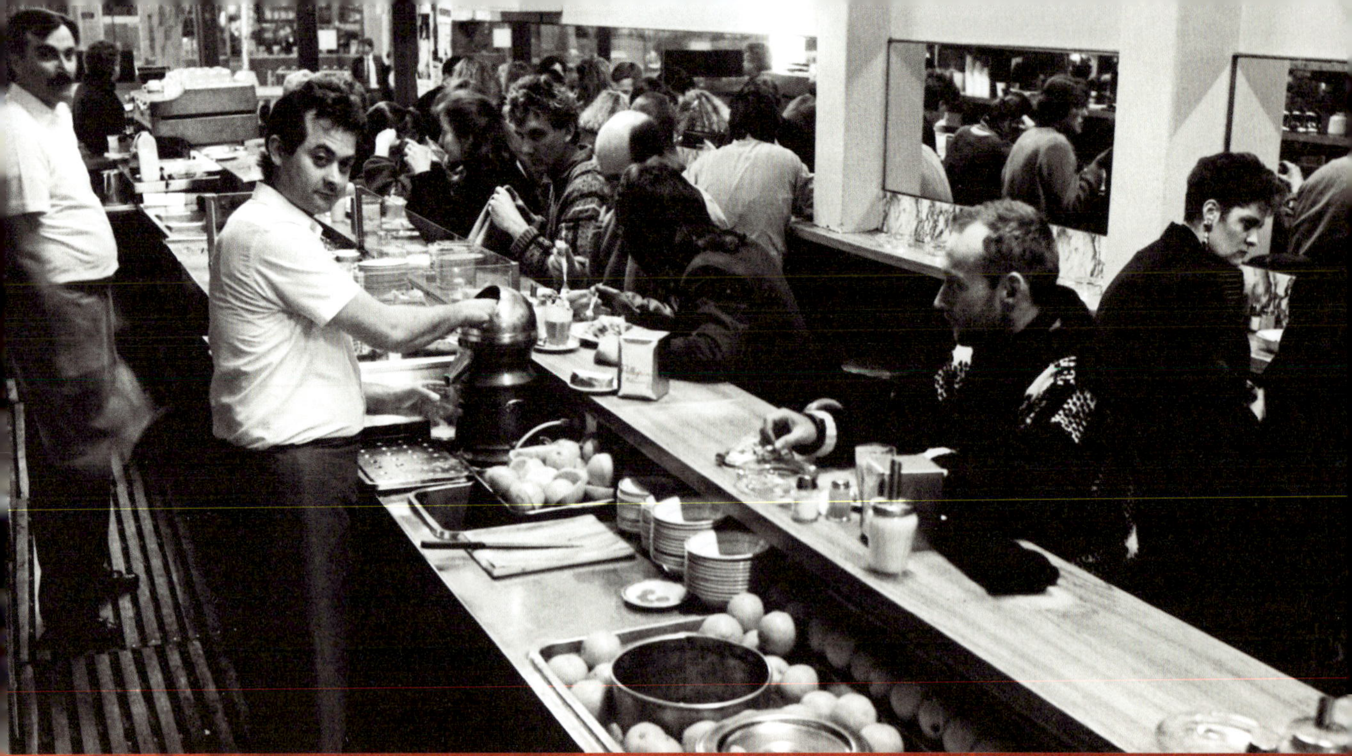

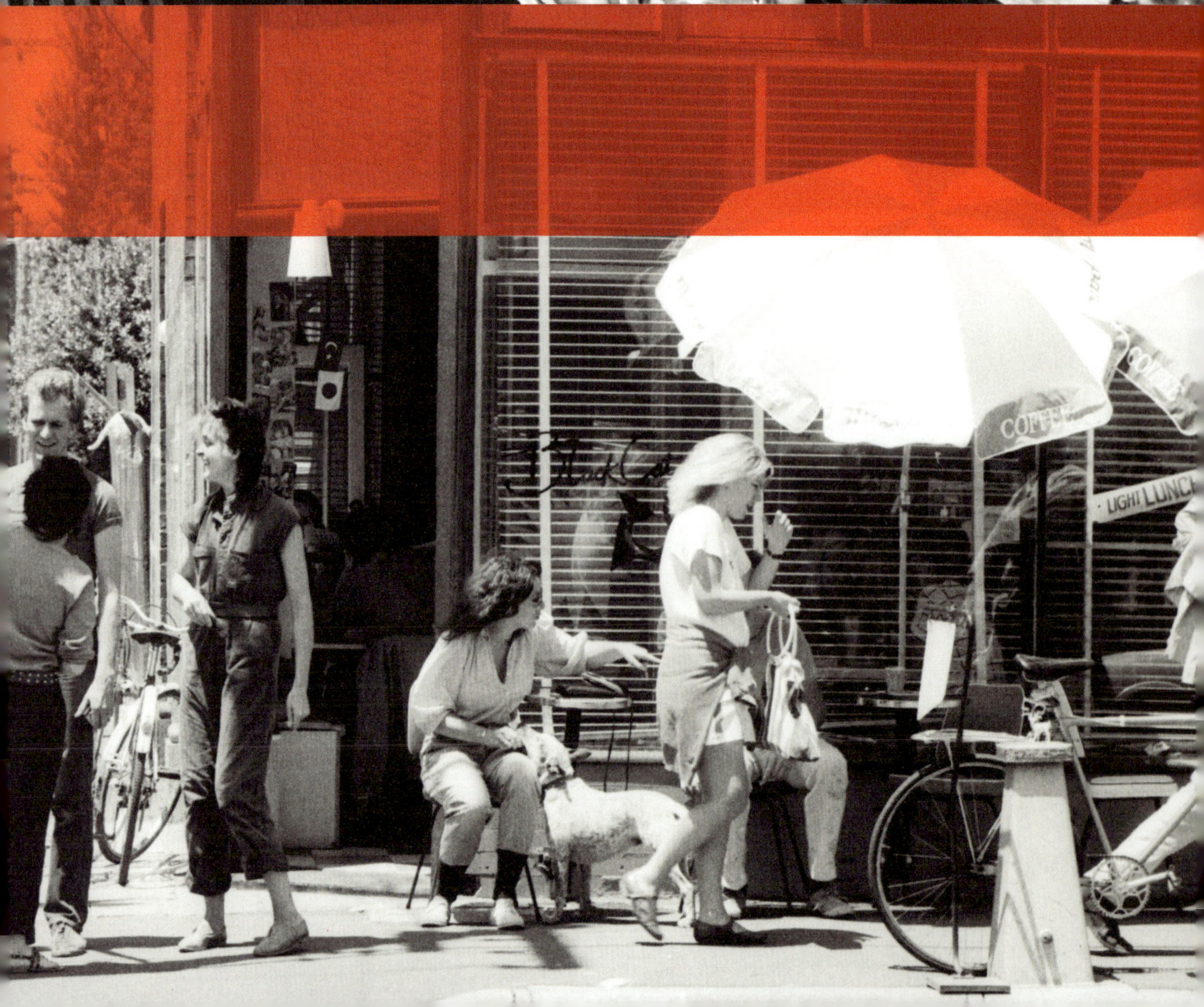

The first signs of the kind of operator Hopkinson refers to had already appeared in Melbourne at the beginning of the 1980s, when a new and distinctly Melbourne cafe culture began to take root, particularly in the artsy student hubs of Fitzroy and St Kilda. These new places were quite happy to pilfer the best and most colourful bits from Melbourne's culinary history – from the old espresso bars like Pellegrini's to Greek men's clubs and Italian bistros like Campari, Café Sport and Tiamo, to the family-run corner pub and the wine bars like the Weathercock in Carlton, which proliferated in the 1970s. These new places reassembled the old with an arty, bohemian, unlicensed but distinctly European spin. An increasingly well-travelled population that had experienced the various cafe cultures of Europe meant that these new cafe owners had little explaining to do to their potential clientele.

In 1982, Henry Maas and Toni Edwards opened the Black Cat cafe in Brunswick Street, Fitzroy. It was the first place to introduce this particular Melbourne-style aesthetic, which combined relaxed casual eating (Blue Heaven spiders, nutty chilli burgers, hot chocolate) with a 1950s formica and venetian blind touch and a soundtrack that was all about jazz and bossa nova. It quickly became a cultural flashpoint and a flurry of similar places with slight variations on the theme followed in the Black Cat's wake – places such as Rhumbarella and The Galleon, which also tapped into this desire that people had to eat and socialise in places that combined the familiar and the new. There was an endearing DIY sensibility to these places that was underlined by employees with wildly varying levels of skill and attitude but a similar non-uniform bohemian look. It was certainly amateur hour, but, in the beginning at least, that was part of the cafe culture's charm.

{*Opposite, above*} Pellegrini's Espresso Bar; {*below*} the Black Cat cafe

{*Below, left*} Henry Maas and Toni Edwards

TIAMO

DEALER
Rawleigh's
GOOD HEALTH
PRODUCTS
and SERVICE
SPECIALS
TIAMO

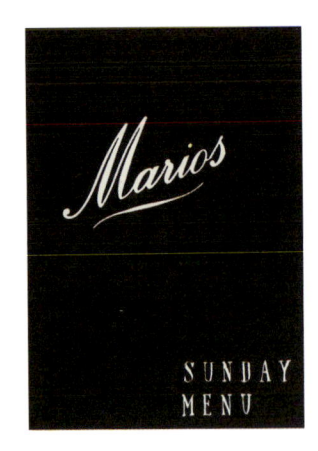

It was not long before some in the industry saw potential in pushing the Melbourne-style cafe idea in new and more sophisticated directions. This push was driven in part by a booming Melbourne restaurant scene. People working as waiters in the city's more upmarket restaurants were becoming frustrated by the lack of places for them to go after finishing their shifts. It was not just the night waiters who found a dearth of venues to go to for a quick bowl of pasta after they finished work. Those who worked lunches also discovered there were few places in Melbourne where you could get something to eat at 4 pm. As if to increase the sense of frustration, the joints that did serve food at odd hours were mostly of the fried food and toasted sandwich variety, which did not always sit well with people who had been silver-serving meticulously prepared food all day long. So some of these waiters decided to open their own places.

In April 1986, Mario De Pasquale, a former waiter at the city's Tsindos Bistro, and Mario Maccarone, who had been working at Mietta's, opened a cafe in Brunswick Street, Fitzroy, that revolutionised the way the Melbourne-style cafe was run. Marios opened late every day, embodying a philosophy that people should never have to think 'Are they open?' It served breakfast all day every day, kept prices down but quality up and, perhaps most importantly, concentrated on excellent service, courtesy of a fleet of smartly dressed, smart-mouthed waiters. It was exactly the sort of venue the two Marios had pined for when they were working for others. It was not formal or starchy, but neither was it annoyingly amateurish. The food was simple but well cooked and the coffee was good. It was this flexible blend of casual and quality that created a blueprint for how things could be done. It provided a departure that had even more resonance after the licensing laws were relaxed.

{*Opposite, below*} The two Marios: De Pasquale and Maccarone

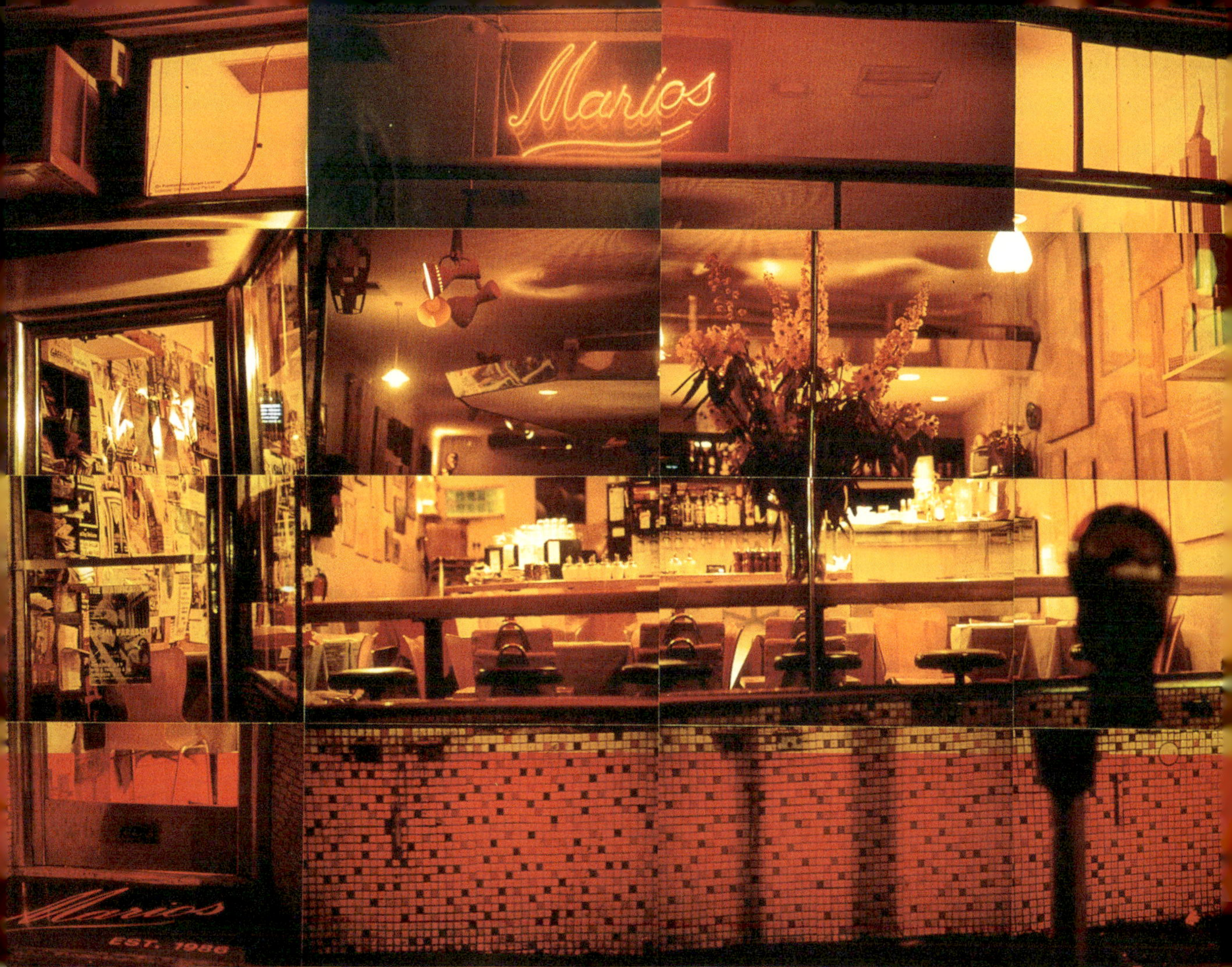
Marios
Marios
EST. 1986

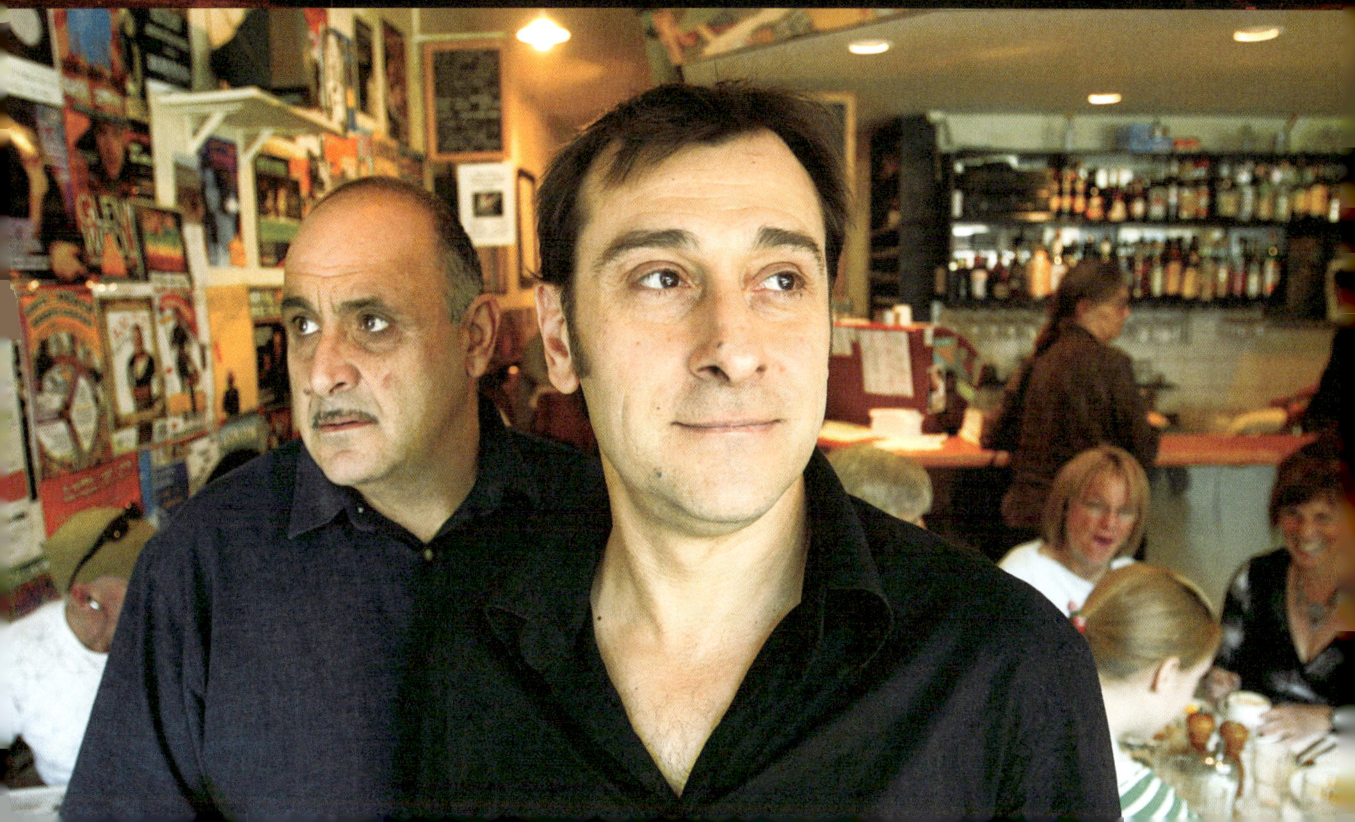

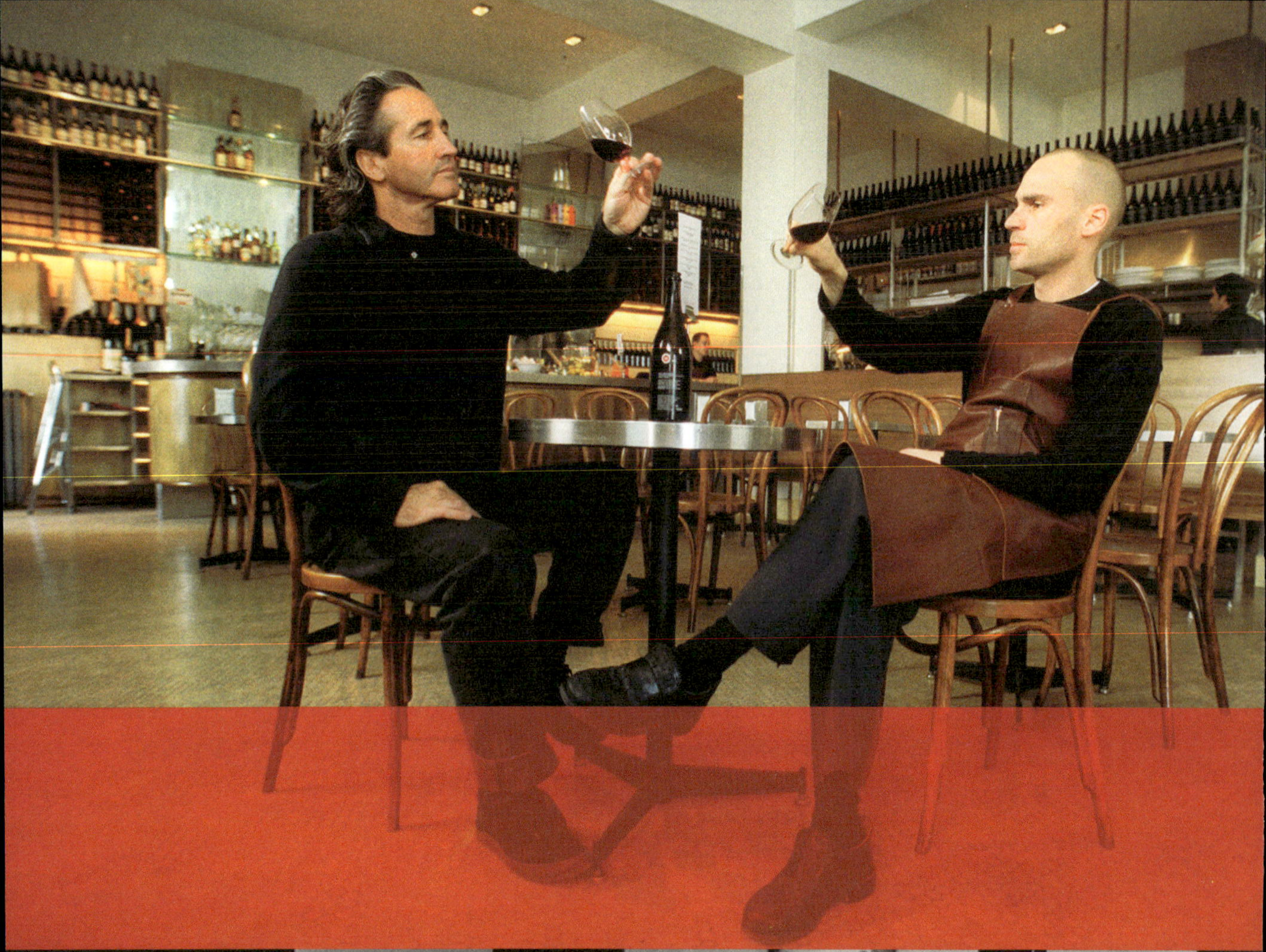

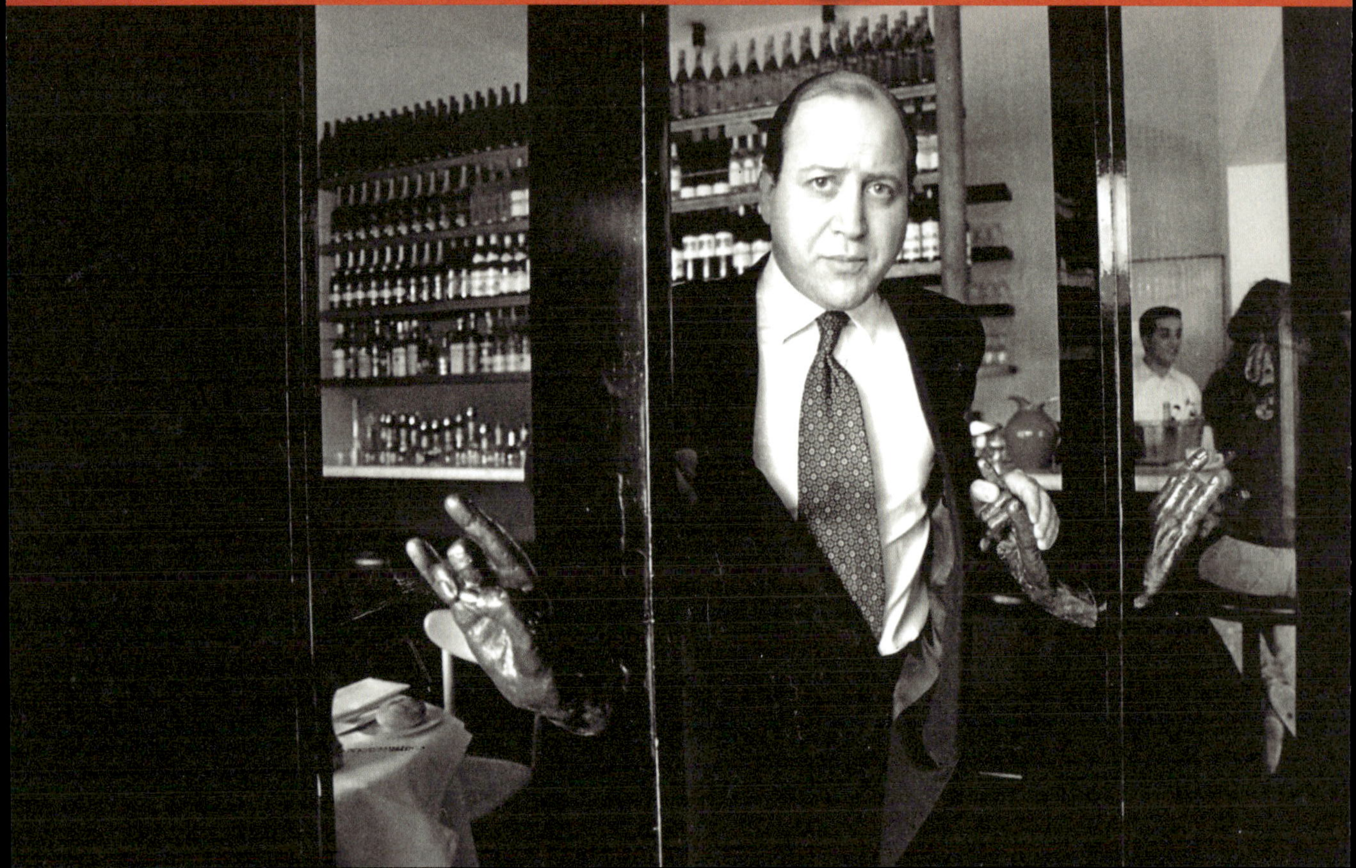

Another style-setting former waiter was Ronnie Di Stasio. Some of Ronnie's earliest memories are of accompanying his father to an Italian espresso bar in Thornbury where, on Sundays, the men would get dressed up in the sharp suits and ties they had brought with them from Italy and gather at the formica, stainless steel and terrazzo-clad espresso bar to drink coffee and chat. It was the sense of style that the men, many of whom were factory workers during the week, brought to these gatherings that the future restaurateur remembered. He came to believe that such style should be an integral part of eating and drinking in public. He began working in pubs as a teenager and added the homey conviviality he experienced there to his portrait of what an ideal restaurant should be. When he graduated from pubs to restaurants, Ronnie Di Stasio saw in Melbourne's dining scene a style that belonged to another era and one that included few of the elements he believed to be essential:

> I started working as a waiter in the early 1980s. And what did I see? I saw silver, I saw damask, I saw people going out to dinner in a very stiff and formal way. And I thought, 'How long has this been going on?' Not long after that I went to Paris for six months, which is what I consider to be my PhD in hospitality. It opened my eyes to what could be done, and so after I returned to Australia I opened Rosati.[8]

Rosati – opened in partnership with Piero Gesualdi at the end of 1986 in a massive former clothing warehouse in Flinders Lane – was nothing like Melbourne had seen before and was very much a product of the exuberant late 1980s. It seated 500 people, had a massive central glass and wood bar, mosaic floors, funky furniture and murals. It also had an attitude and style far closer to Rome than Melbourne. Although people were still required to eat a meal if they wished to drink wine at the bar, the fact that the bar was the central feature of the restaurant and was surrounded with comfortable stools taught the hordes of locals that eating out did not have to be just about sitting at a table in a carpeted room. It also provided one of the first inklings that the city's smaller streets and unused former industrial buildings could, with a bit of imagination, make brilliantly atmospheric places to set up shop.

There was another opening around this time that was equally influential in developing Melbourne's unique wine and food style. In late 1986, Donlevy Fitzpatrick bought two residential buildings – Colombo Court and Harley Court – at the sleepy, tucked-away end of Acland Street in St Kilda. His original vision was never fully realised: to create a European-style bar below an Italian-style pensione that would have a rooftop terrace complete with wood-fired pizza oven. But in 1989, part of the plan did come to fruition and the Dogs Bar, a place that arguably did

{*Opposite, above*} Donlevy Fitzpatrick and Maurice Terzini at the Melbourne Wine Room; {*below*} Ronnie Di Stasio at Cafe Di Stasio

Gastronomic Revolution

Thirty or so years ago, the food tastes of the average diner tended to be as limited as the liquor licensing laws were restrictive. Most of Melbourne's top restaurants offered a French-influenced cuisine, or called their slightly broader style 'international'. Beef Wellington was a winning dish, along with pepper steak, chicken Kiev, duck à l'orange and whiting Caprice – preceded, perhaps, by prawn cocktail and followed by chocolate mousse.

Of course, trendsetters such as Fanny's, Glo Glo's and Two Faces were more daring in their menus. Some even toyed, for a while, with 'nouvelle cuisine', which cynics described as small helpings on large plates at high prices, or the triumph of artistry over substance.

What has emerged from this clash of culinary cultures is a swing away from old-fashioned cooking and kilojoule-laden, high-cholesterol, cream- and butter-based sauces towards lighter dishes based on natural flavours. Chefs were encouraged to be more creative and diners to be more adventurous in their choices. Most of the top-rated restaurants today describe their culinary style as 'modern Australian' or, drawing on the long-established Italian and Greek heritage, 'modern Mediterranean'. Classic French cuisine has been replaced by broader European, Middle Eastern and Asian influences, also made possible by a greater diversity and higher quality of locally grown and specially imported ingredients. Burgundy-born Jacques Reymond, for example, has integrated some Asian flavours into his *cuisine du temps*, truly a sign of changing times.

What else has changed? Coffee has superseded tea as the hot beverage of choice, popularised by the ubiquitous Italian espresso machine. Cafes are no longer purveyors of greasy steak and eggs with chips, but chic rendezvous where you may enjoy a glass of wine with a range of snacks. Pubs have had to lift their game in an increasingly competitive environment, some now offering meals of top-restaurant quality. Gastronomically, we are indeed a lucky country – no irony intended. CLAUDE FORELL

Gastronomy

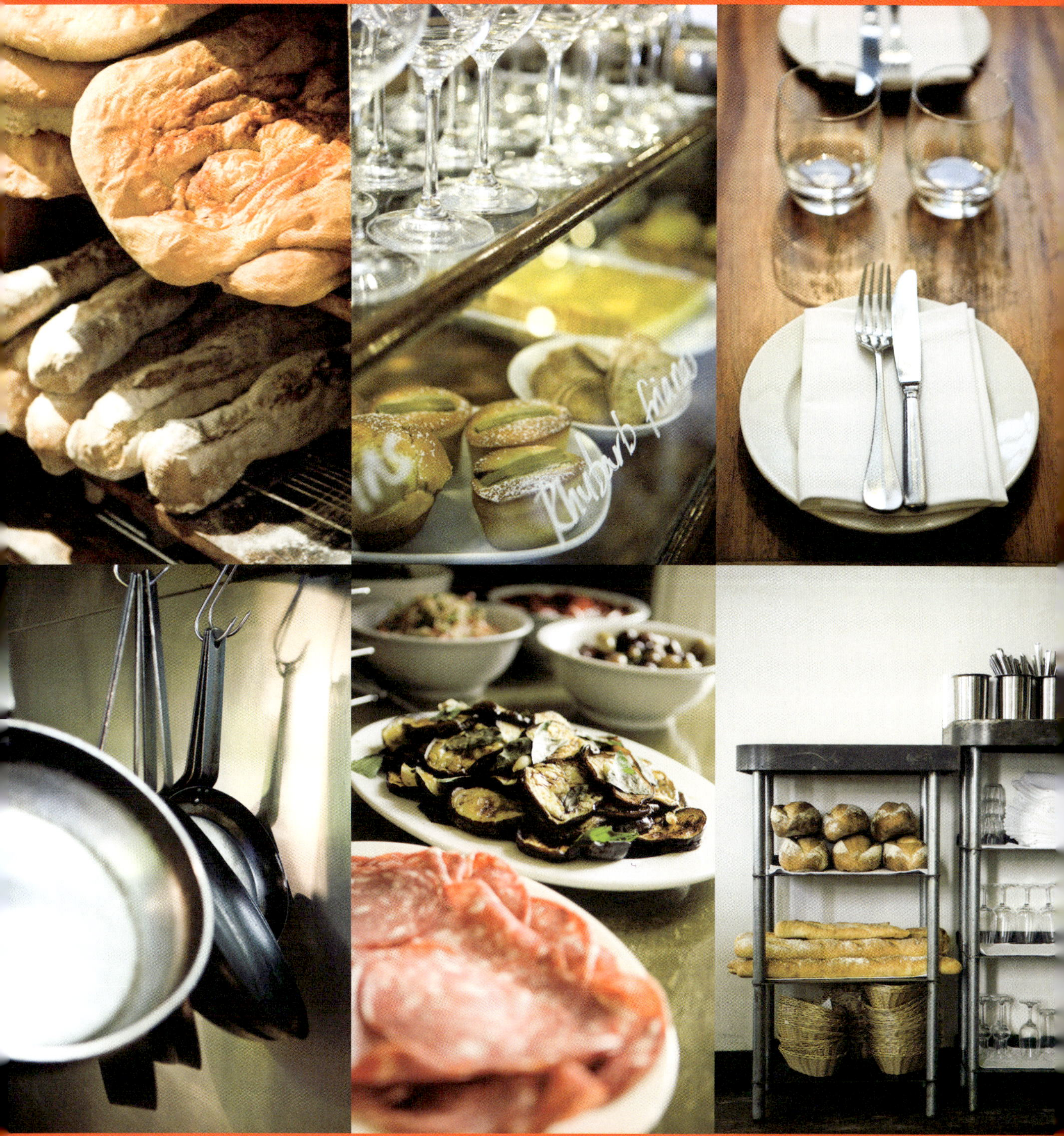
Rhubarb

more than any other business at the time to educate people about the infinite possibilities of eating and drinking in a relaxed, non-regulated environment, opened its double glass doors.

Fitzpatrick had been loosening up what he saw as the starched seriousness of Melbourne's dining scene for many years, particularly at places like the Smith Street Bar & Bistro in Collingwood and his Italian-style trattoria Vic Ave, in Albert Park. As friends tell it, the restrictive licensing laws at the time infuriated Fitzpatrick, who was a regular visitor to Europe and a staunch proponent of the relaxed, mature, continental approach to eating and drinking he found there. Even working under the old liquor laws, Fitzpatrick was all about breaking down the stuffiness and intimidation he believed characterised many of Australia's top-end restaurants. One of the ways he did this at Vic Ave was to serve wine in tumblers rather than stemmed wineglasses. It was a move that appalled some wine buffs – 'I'm not drinking my wine out of a Vegemite jar!' – but appealed to other drinkers. It made wine just another part of the experience of eating out, rather than an intimidating rarity only to be enjoyed by those with encyclopedic wine knowledge and a finely tuned palate. It was an attitude that was, in many ways, in direct conflict with the standards the LCC was supposed to be upholding. But the popularity of Fitzpatrick's ventures showed that it was not he who was out of step with the laws, but the laws that were out of touch with the community.

The Dogs Bar introduced Melburnians to the type of casual and flexible eating space that would become increasingly common over the coming years. In many ways, it was the poster child for the new Liquor Control Act, perfectly realising the 'civilised imbibing' that John Nieuwenhuysen held up as the ideal in his report. People dropped in to read the papers over a coffee in the sun outside, or met friends for a snack and a drink in front of open fires in the winter. Wine was an integral part of the bar. Its mock antique style, complete with wrought-iron gates, combined with down-to-earth touches such as drinking bowls for local dogs, struck a chord with locals, who began to see it as an extension of their own living rooms. The queues of people waiting for tables were not exactly in keeping with Fitzpatrick's relaxed vision, but, if nothing else, they clearly showed other entrepreneurs that the market had plenty of room for places like his.

The immediate success of these new-style businesses showed that Melburnians were amenable to a style of eating out that had nothing to do with damask and silver. The fact that the 1990s saw many of Melbourne's fine dining institutions close their doors may have had something to do with the increased competition, but it also reflected a change in approach to the way people wanted to eat out. Just as the Nieuwenhuysen Review had pointed out, the rigid definition of what a restaurant

{*Above and opposite*} Fitzpatrick's Dogs Bar was a fine example of the new breed of civilised drinking establishments

PECIALS

, SWEET PEPPERS

Stephanie's

A salad bowl... of carefully selected salad leaves, tossed with olive oil and Hill Smith wine vinegar

Buttery, baked vanilla pears, with a caramel sauce

Wicked chocolate pudding with a ginger cream sauce
...served cold with a chocolate sorbet and a crisp wafer

Old fashioned rhubarb and apple crumble with a rhubarb ice and King Island farm cream

should be was no longer applicable and people seemed to relish the casual, flexible nature of what came in its wake.

But while the new businesses were pioneering the biggest changes, there were restaurants at the top end that were also taking note of changing attitudes and responding to them in ways that influenced the Melbourne style of dining.

Stephanie Alexander was one restaurateur who understood both the changes in attitudes occurring in the 1980s and the possibilities that opened up after the Nieuwenhuysen recommendations were made into law. Alexander had always had a good eye for the dining scene in Melbourne. In 1969, she opened her first restaurant, Jamaica House, in Lygon Street, Carlton, just as the street was beginning to attract attention as a cosmopolitan and bohemian destination. In 1976, she opened Stephanie's restaurant in Brunswick Street, Fitzroy, and in 1980, just as Fitzroy was moving towards 'cafeville' and the industry and the economy were ripe for some opulence, she moved the restaurant to a mansion in Hawthorn. It was during this time, she wrote in 1997, that she and others like Mietta O'Donnell, 'set new standards, provoked discussion, changed menus with dizzying speed, honed techniques, sought out special produce, and turned eating-out into a favourite pastime'.[9]

Stephanie's also helped change the way the front of house was run, courtesy of one-time head waitress and then business partner Dur-e Dara. Dara pioneered a style of service that perfectly matched the changing times, with an approach that made the customer feel comfortable and welcome, as if they were in somebody's home rather than being attended to by haughty, robotic waiters in a tradition-bound fine dining establishment. Standards of service were still exacting but they were accompanied by a friendly, down-to-earth and often humorous style. Perhaps the best example of Dara's approach was the way the bread was served. Rather than having bread silver-served onto a side plate, the waiters at Stephanie's would present the customers with a basket of assorted types of bread and get the customer to take what they wanted with their own hands. A small thing perhaps, but revolutionary in helping to break down ingrained preconceptions about what should and should not happen in a restaurant.

It is interesting to note that when Stephanie's closed in 1998, both Alexander and Dara went on to businesses that were very much in tune with the post-Nieuwenhuysen times. Alexander became partner in the cafe/bistro Richmond Hill Cafe & Larder, with its attached produce store and cheese room, while Dara, with a group of partners, opened Nudel Bar, a canteen-style place in the city specialising in noodle dishes from across the globe, accompanied by an ever-changing list of Australian wine.

It would seem that this upswing in interest and innovation during the 1980s would naturally have created the perfect conditions for galvanising the people to

{*Opposite*} Dur-e Dara {*left*} and Stephanie Alexander outside their Hawthorn establishment, Stephanie's

> It is often difficult to remember how groundbreaking some of the businesses of the late 1980s and early 1990s were

rise up and force a change in the restrictive licensing laws. But the muted – albeit mostly positive – attitude towards loosening up the availability of alcohol showed that many people were reasonably content with the way things were. In fact, even the Australian Hotels Association pointed to the restaurant and cafe boom of the 1980s as evidence that the existing laws were fine and, at best, probably just needed a little tweak here and there. It was true that Melbourne's restaurateurs, cafe owners and hoteliers were doing quite well with what they had to work with. But when, in the early 1990s, the young bloods in the industry began to truly understand the potential of the new laws, it became apparent just how much the boom of the 1980s had been muffled by the old regime.

Even though it is less than two decades since Melbourne's dining scene underwent a seismic shift, it is often difficult to remember how groundbreaking some of the businesses of the late 1980s and early 1990s were. Perhaps it was because the places that opened at this time so accurately reflected the culture of Melbourne that they were able to become such an accepted part of the city's fabric so quickly. The recession that Victoria slid into so emphatically in the early 1990s may also have had something to do with the perception that these more casual places were responding to economic times, making do rather than making history. But much of what was happening in the industry was not about responding to change, but driving it.

In Chapel Street, South Yarra, Maurice Terzini opened Caffè e Cucina, a place that, according to the restaurateur and developer Chris Lucas, 'turbo-boosted the Italian culture from a shoebox'. The tiny space pulled together many elements that would come to define a Melbourne-style Italian bistro. Cloth-covered tables were packed closely together against a background of dark wood panelling. There were table lamps, wooden venetian blinds in the gold-lettered front windows, and shelves lined with bottles of wine, Campari, mineral water and olive oil. Smartly kitted-out waiters flirted with customers and called to each other in Italian, creating what came to be known as the 'Ciao, bella!' style of service. The food was straightforward, rustic, well-cooked Italian that emphasised good ingredients and shunned tricked-up presentation. It felt like Italy, but it buzzed with a distinctly Melbourne style and was constantly packed with a crowd always liberally sprinkled with celebrities of every creed. Terzini went on to refine and redefine this style at other places around town – Il Bacaro and the Melbourne Wine Room among them – but there were others who were also tapping into this new energy.

Ronnie Di Stasio left the cavernous Rosati in the city and headed for the atmospherically grungy Fitzroy Street in St Kilda, where he opened Cafe Di Stasio, a place that seamlessly teamed all the stylish, theatrical ingredients Di Stasio had yearned for since his first experience with the espresso bar in Thornbury.

{*Opposite, above*} Il Bacaro;
{*below*} Caffé e Cucina

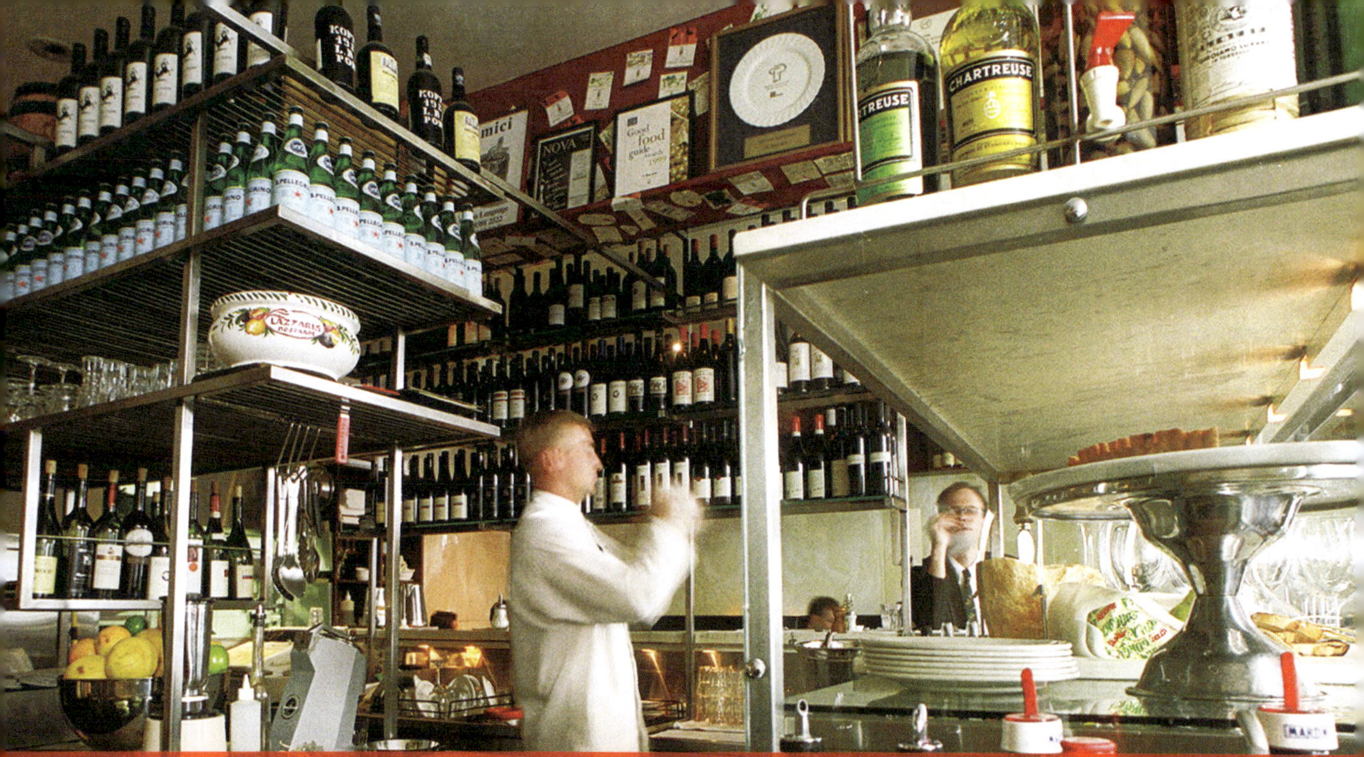
CHARTREUSE

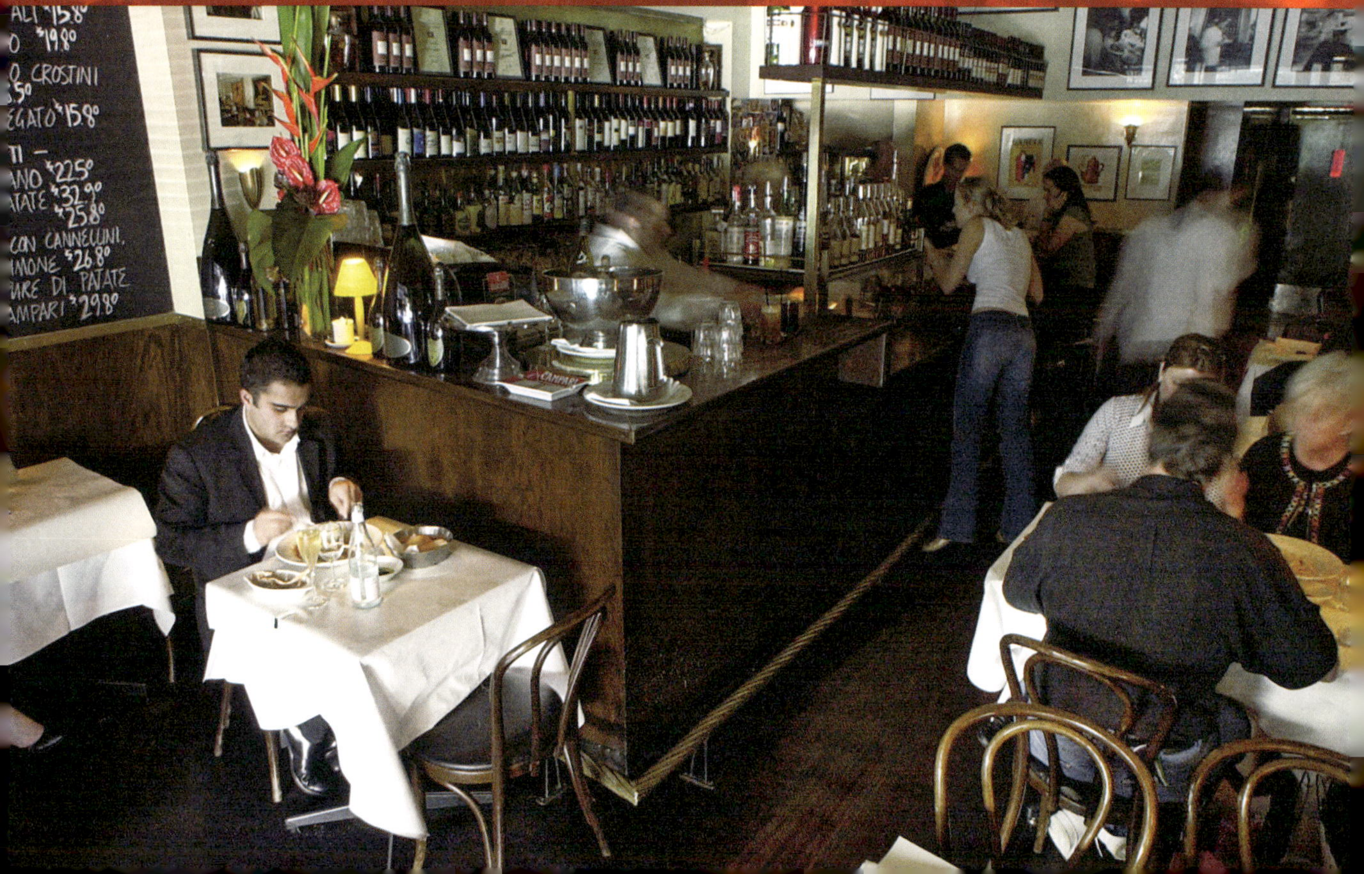
CROSTINI
CON CANNELLINI

More Than a Cook

Given her pre-eminence as a passionate and influential exponent of good food, it's surprising that Stephanie Alexander was not professionally trained as a chef. She did not set out to make cooking and writing about it her career, nor was she an immediate success as a restaurateur.

Stephanie Alexander qualified as a librarian, but a visit to France as a postgraduate kindled her love of French provincial cooking. She met a gentle Jamaican, Monty, with whom she returned to Melbourne and opened a Caribbean-style restaurant, Jamaica House, in Carlton. The partnership did not survive, but in 1976 she opened the original Stephanie's restaurant behind a simple shopfront in Fitzroy.

Her interpretation of French provincial cuisine won such critical acclaim that after four years she moved her eponymous restaurant to a grand old mansion in Hawthorn East. There she developed a distinctive personal style based on the best seasonal ingredients, championing small, specialty food producers and a creative approach to classic techniques. Stephanie's was soon recognised as one of Australia's best fine-dining restaurants. She also found time to start writing evocative books on food, cooking and her travels abroad. Most notable of these is the encyclopedic *Cook's Companion,* intended to inspire young people to understand the joys of cooking and good eating.

Since closing Stephanie's in 1997 and becoming a partner in the more casual Richmond Hill Cafe & Larder, she has turned her formidable talents to encouraging children and their parents to appreciate fresh food. Her kitchen garden at Collingwood has set an example that many primary schools – aided by a foundation she sponsored – have followed.

Although Stephanie Alexander has been credited with being at the forefront of developing a contemporary 'Australian cuisine', she disputes that there is, or will be, such a new phenomenon. 'We should not be preoccupied with whether what we are doing is unique, but rather whether it is good,' she once told me in an interview. 'What is important is that we use the very best of all the fine produce now available to us, and I believe we will continue to reflect all the influences to which we are exposed in a multicultural society.' CLAUDE FORELL

ander

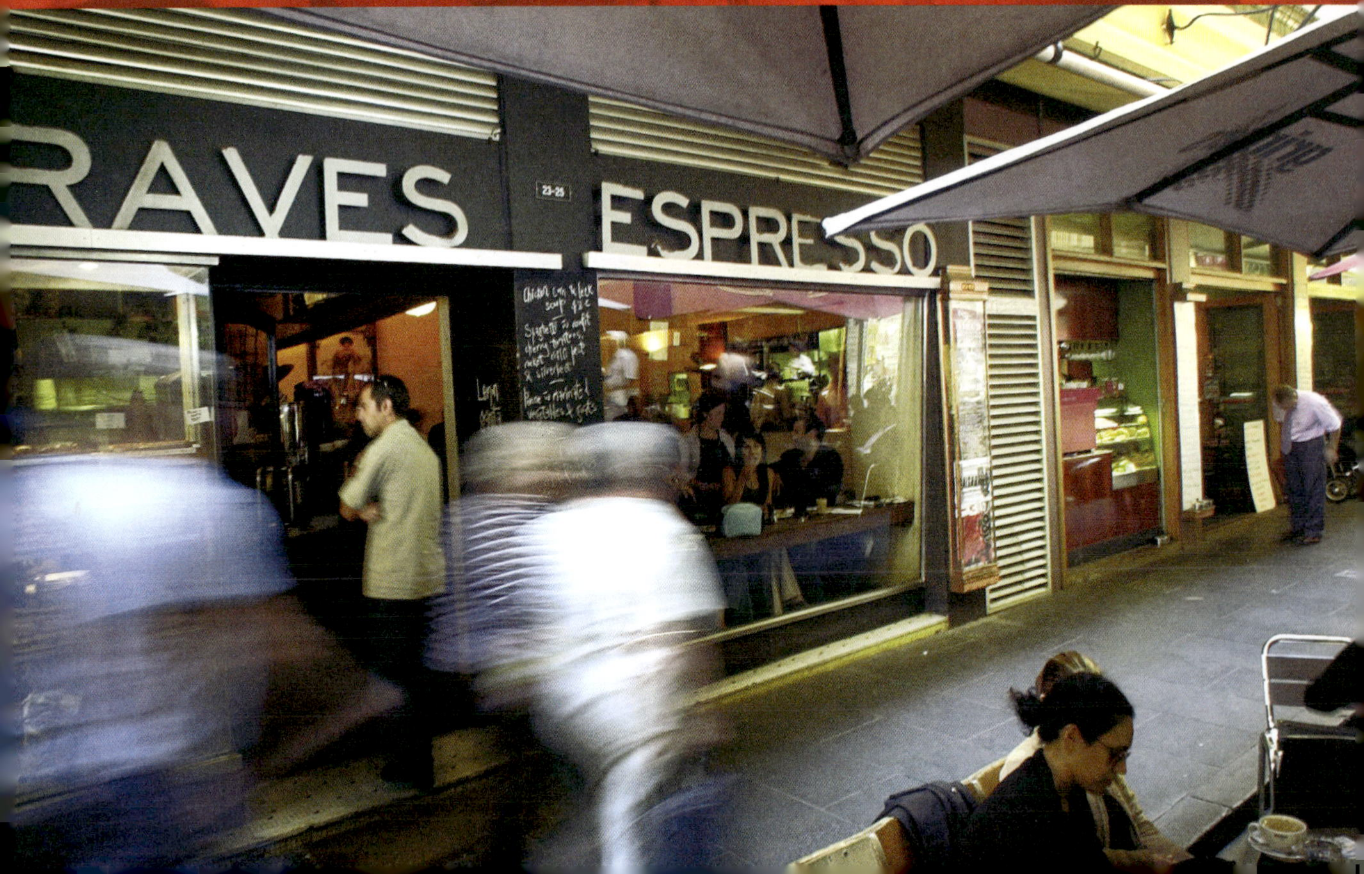
RAVES
23-25
ESPRESSO

Donlevy Fitzpatrick took over the grand but dilapidated George Hotel in St Kilda, transforming the public bar into one of the most stylish watering holes in the city and teamed up with Terzini to create the gloomily glamorous Melbourne Wine Room.

Brothers John and Frank van Haandel were awarded the lease on a 1920s-era boathouse on the St Kilda foreshore and turned it into one of Australia's iconic restaurants, Stokehouse. The upstairs restaurant, with its modern Australian menu and brilliant views over the bay, and the downstairs cafe with its wood-fired pizza oven and boardwalk-level outside area brilliantly captured the essence and spirit of the licensing law reforms. A few years later the van Haandels revitalised another grungy St Kilda pub, the Prince of Wales, maintaining its egalitarian public bar and legendary band room while adding a much-lauded restaurant (Circa), a boutique hotel and, later, a day spa.

In the city, Con Christopoulos was helping lead the charge into the CBD's neglected laneways. Starting off with Cafe Segovia, in Block Place — one of the first places in the city to begin serving wine by the glass — he then opened Degraves Espresso, in Degraves Street, and Syracuse, in Bank Place. It was in these places with their faux-aged interiors and darkly romantic aesthetic that Christopoulos and his various partners helped define the Melbourne palette — dark wood, red wine and espresso coffee. As he says:

> It wasn't all about getting in and making money; it was about expressing yourself and having fun creating a life for yourself. There was an excitement about colonising the empty spaces — laneways, basements, first floors. It was like a blank canvas and that's what I loved about it. It wasn't just about taking advantage of these new laws that were like a pot of gold — you actually had to find out what worked, you had to earn it. But the new laws certainly gave you more colours for you to paint your masterpiece.[10]

The rush occurring in St Kilda and the city was happening in Fitzroy too. Marios, the style-setter, was granted a licence and was joined by places such as the Gypsy Bar and Paul Mathis' enormous diner, Joe's Garage. Brunswick Street's Provincial Hotel was taken over by Max Fink and, with a renovation that simultaneously aged and renewed the large building, he turned the former bloodhouse into a hugely popular combination of bar, bistro and burger joint.

Boom and bust in the restaurant scene is a phenomenon that will always be with us. But the boom that followed the revolution in Victoria's licensing laws was remarkable in that it saw the introduction of many new styles of eating and drinking that Melburnians — and arguably Australians — had never experienced before.

{*Opposite, above*} Syracuse; {*below*} Degraves Espresso

{*Above*} Frank van Haandel with his son at Mr Tulk

One of the key differences with this boom was that wine was front and centre. This is not surprising when Australian consumption of wine had risen from five litres annually per capita in the 1960s to twenty-two litres in the 1980s. Though changes to Victoria's licensing laws meant that the number of places able to sell alcohol began to boom in the 1990s, the consumption of wine and all other forms of alcohol actually decreased, which could show a switch in drinking habits to an emphasis on quality from quantity. Certainly many of the newly licensed businesses began to make wine a selling point. The ubiquitous 'house wine' gave way to lists of wines by the glass, as people became more knowledgeable about what they were drinking and where it came from. It suddenly became apparent that Victoria had a wine industry that was worth taking seriously.

The Nieuwenhuysen Review and the subsequent Liquor Control Act were integral in creating this awareness of and interest in local wine. The report was not just about unshackling the hospitality industry from restrictive and uncompetitive laws, but it aimed at applying deregulation across all industries that involved alcohol. This included the wine industry, which had also been hobbled by the 1968 Liquor Control Act and its predecessors.

Under the old laws, the only way to be granted a Vigneron's Licence (that is, a licence to make and sell wine) was to have both a vineyard under cultivation and a fully equipped winery to process the grapes. It was illegal for those who grew grapes and then had them made into wine at someone else's winery to sell that wine from their own premises, either to passersby or into the retail market. They would have to rely on the winery that made the wine to sell it for them.

Just like the low-level law breaking that previous legislation seemed to encourage — from the old wine-in-the-coffee-cup trick to the pretence that late-night drinkers in restaurants were actually waiting for a bona-fide meal — many vineyards were also fudging the legal requirements in order to get a licence. Some would set up the bare minimum of wine production facilities, with no intention of ever using them, just so they could get a licence to sell their own wine. It was again a case of everybody knowing it was going on but there being little will to police laws that had drifted so far from reality.

John Ellis, a winemaker and owner of Hanging Rock Winery, became the first CEO of the newly formed Victorian Wine Industry Association in 1985. He says that the issues surrounding licensing were a topic of much debate among winemakers at the time:

> There were all sorts of constraints that said you don't get a cellar door unless you're a fully operational winery and your facilities comply with our

ard cooked

MIGIANO REGGIANO
 Romagna. Italy
rzio controlled
milk - 5 provinces

resh grass

morning\eve milk
d in cauldrons

MELBOURNE WINE ROOM

MELBOURNE WINE

inspectors' wishes. There was nothing you could do about it and there was a view in the industry that the existing laws amounted to a restraint of trade and that we should argue for them to be fixed. But others [in the industry] held the view that they didn't want a little vineyard in every corner with its own cellar door. These people believed that the laws should be tightened and that the strength of the industry lay in having a limited number of strong producers.[11]

The 1987 laws that followed the Nieuwenhuysen Review changed the Vigneron's Licence to a Producer's Licence, which became available to businesses whose primary purpose was the production or distribution of liquor. In other words, the new licence enabled vineyard owners who had their grapes made into wine elsewhere to open a cellar door and sell their wine directly to the licensed trade. As Ellis says, the growth in the number of licensed vineyards and wineries after the laws changed was 'logarithmic', with 'about 200 wineries at the time of the Nieuwenhuysen Report and nearly 700 now'.

This new freedom gave an obvious boost to the industry and allowed for an incredible expansion in wine tourism in regional Victoria. Many vineyards with winery facilities now invested in restaurants, cafes, landscaping, barbecue areas, even art galleries and reception centres, instead of pouring money into winemaking equipment they could never use. Areas like the Yarra Valley, the Mornington Peninsula, King Valley, Heathcote, Bendigo and the Macedon Ranges are now liberally dotted with small and large wineries, a boom that would not have been possible without the change in laws.

But perhaps more importantly for Victoria's wine industry was that the 1987 Act saw a massive increase in the number of outlets – restaurants, cafes, retail stores – in which the state's wine producers could sell their wine. Ellis says that with the sudden interest in wine on the part of cafes and restaurants, and subsequently the public, many of these places wanted to know more about the smaller, boutique wineries. The restaurateurs had an obvious interest in 'famous wines', he says, 'but if your wine wasn't famous they wanted to know whether you were going to sell it to Dan Murphy's. If you weren't, they would be happy to take it on'. It was an ideal situation for many of the small growers with the new Producer's Licences. It meant that making money or even a living from their grapes was a possibility, at least for some in the industry.

Ellis believes that though there was already a notable growth in interest and consumption of Victorian wine prior to the Nieuwenhuysen Review, the overall effect the report had – from nurturing a European-style wine-drinking culture in

{*Above*} John Ellis

{*Following page*} Melbourne's laneway culture in action

COOPERS BREWERY
ORIGINAL PALE ALE
BLU
Vicolino
FOKUS
kinki ger
AIX

the city to allowing small vineyards to sell their own wine – helped create the diversity and strength the Victorian wine industry enjoys today.

The wide-reaching consequences of the 1987 Act and its timeliness were felt in other corners of the industry. Under the new laws, the catering industry was able to apply for a General Licence, which was mobile. The first of these new licences was granted to hotelier-turned-caterer Peter Rowland. He says:

> The new General Licence meant that wherever we went, the licence went with us. Before that we had to apply for a licence for every event where we wanted to serve alcohol. It could take up to 28 days to get a licence and so if someone wanted you to do a function the next week, you were snookered or you sly-grogged. As long as we looked after the conditions of the licence it could now move with us and made the whole catering industry much more flexible.[12]

It was this flexibility that provided the engine for the innovation and energy that characterised the hospitality industry in Victoria during the 1990s. Nieuwenhuysen's recommendations arrived at a time when the population and the industry were looking for a new way of doing things and, by knocking down many of the antiquated restrictions that hemmed people in, allowed the industry to flourish and to find a style that was uniquely Victorian.

Amendments to the Act in 1994 and 1998 took up most of Nieuwenhuysen's recommendations that had failed to make the original cut, though the 25 per cent rule remained – relegated to a dusty and mostly ignored corner. Hotels, restaurants, cafes, cellar doors, catering companies, wineries and retailers all responded to the new flexibility, and the much-talked-about European-style eating culture quickly became part of everyday life. But the innovation did not stop there. A brand-new phenomenon was also unleashed by the revamped liquor laws, one that was to become as integral to the city's lifestyle as the new wave of cafes and restaurants.

> It was this flexibility that provided the engine for the innovation and energy that characterised the hospitality industry during the 1990s

Melbourne's bar culture, which has arisen from reforms to liquor licensing last century, leaves Sydney for dead.

CLOVER MOORE, MP NSW PARLIAMENT, 2007

Raising the Bar

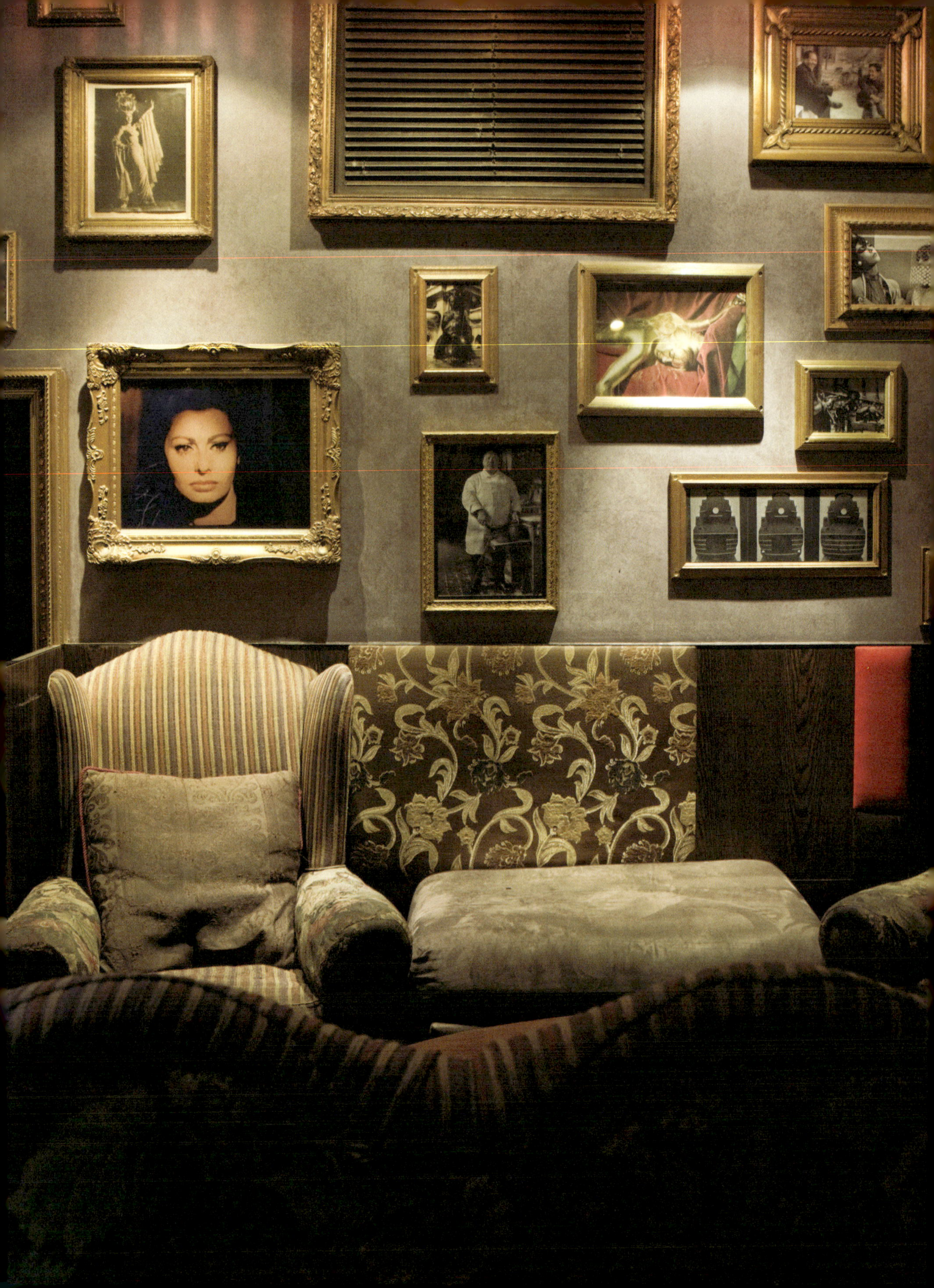

*I*f you were after an example of how ingenuity can outpace the law, Melbourne's small bars would be a good place to start. Melbourne's CBD has been so successfully colonised by idiosyncratic bars that it is almost impossible to imagine the city's laneways, rooftops, storage spaces, car parks and basements without them. Now spreading from the city into the suburbs, the bars have become such an established part of Melbourne's fabric that it is as if they have always been with us. But despite this impression of their longevity, these bars have been around for mere years rather than decades, and they have taken on a form and style that was never imagined by the architect of Victoria's revamped liquor laws. John Nieuwenhuysen marvels when contemplating the city's bar scene: 'I kept saying that the people of Melbourne were quite mature enough to accept these changes, but what I didn't realise was how entrepreneurial the licensees were going to be and how quickly the public was going to take to the new system.'[1]

There is little doubt that the liberalised licensing laws paved the way for Melbourne's bar wave, but the change in law coincided with a number of other factors – economic, social, political, geographical – that created the unique conditions that gave birth to a genre of drinking venue that had never before been seen in Australia.

'Melbourne-style bar' has become the nationally recognised shorthand for a small, quirky, creative watering hole that is the antithesis of the large, generic, binging and blipping pokie joints that proliferate everywhere across the land. When states other than Victoria begin to make noises about liberalising their licensing laws, with a view to allowing smaller, more intimate drinking venues to become established, it is always the Melbourne model that is flagged as the way to go. For those opposed to such changes, they also drag Melbourne's bars into the spotlight – this time to deride as symbols of elitist, un-Australian wankerism. As recently as 2007, John Thorpe, president of the New South Wales branch of the Australian Hotels Association (AHA), argued against laws that would open the way for small bars in that state, saying, 'We aren't barbarians, but we don't want to sit in a hole and drink chardonnay and read a book.'[2] Even without his mentioning 'Melbourne-

{*Opposite*} The genre-defining Gin Palace

> The Melbourne-style bar was also a product of good timing

style bar', most people who heard (and responded to) Thorpe's comments knew what he meant.

But while the success of the Melbourne bar scene has become the envy (or the nemesis) of other parts of the country, and is certainly worth studying as some kind of civilised boozing blueprint, it can be argued that the circumstances that brought it into being would be difficult to duplicate elsewhere. Regular murmurings of disquiet within Victoria from sections of the press and the government about there being too many bars seem to show that the Melbourne-style bar was also a product of good timing, arriving as it did during a patch of open-mindedness that was probably much rarer than it appeared at the time.

Certainly there had been few precedents of it before most of Nieuwenhuysen's recommendations were implemented. Prior to the changes, the most obvious place to get a drink without a meal was in hotel bars and, until the 1960s, those had been forced to close by 6 pm. Despite the pub-centred notoriety of the six o'clock swill, there were hotel bars where you could drink alcohol without running the gamut of hordes of desperate men chugging down one pot after another in a raucous, tile-lined public bar as the clock ticked towards six. The city's smarter hotels, such as the Windsor and the Menzies, all had bars (or smoking rooms and lounges, as they were euphemistically called), where you could enjoy the swill in more genteel style. Hotels that were built a bit later, such as the Southern Cross, which opened in 1962, tapped into the public's desire to drink in venues other than pubs by creating space for cocktail bars, like the ultra-chic, Hollywood-glamour-style Wilawa Cocktail Bar. But these types of hotel bars were mainly for the well heeled and suitably dressed and so the options for those who couldn't afford the upmarket and didn't want to brave the rowdy, overwhelmingly masculine corner pub were fairly limited. In an early example of ingenuity outpacing the law – or, at least, proof that where there's a will there's a way – Melbourne did have some places that were able to sidestep the upmarket–downmarket divide.

One place that could be considered the direct ancestor of the modern-day Melbourne bar is Jimmy Watson's Wine Bar in Lygon Street, Carlton. In 1935, Jimmy Watson bought an existing wine saloon that was operating under an Australian Wine Licence (AWL). This meant that it was able to sell Australian wine only (no beer, no spirits and nothing imported) to drink on the premises or to take away. Most places operating under these licences at the time were half-derelict hell holes filled with drunks who would stagger out onto the street at six o'clock, after drinking 'penny dreadfuls' all day; they would then collapse onto the footpath before being dragged off by the police. Wine was not widely loved in these years and being called a 'wino' meant that you were probably clinging to the bottom rungs of society's ladder.

{*Opposite*} The reliable Melbourne bar, Jimmy Watson's Wine Bar

J.C.WATSON LICENSEE

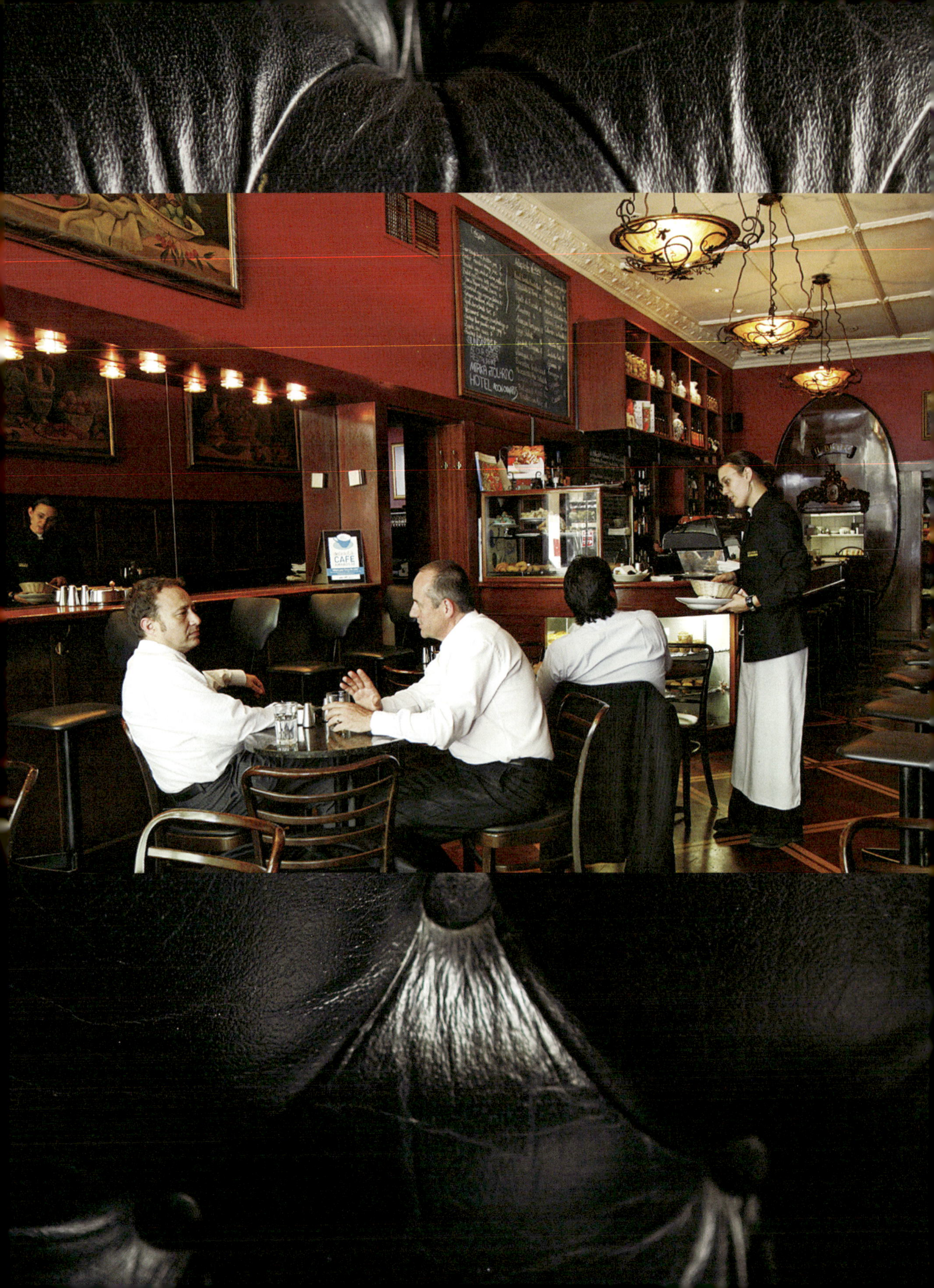

Watson's mother was an Italian who came from a family of wine bar owners. Watson himself was a professional musician who used to play in orchestras at cinemas during the silent-movie era. With the advent of talkies, work began to drop off and so as a fallback he decided to follow his family into the wine bar trade.

Jimmy was not interested in serving rotgut to chronic alcoholics and he had a passionate belief in the quality of Australian wine – a good thing, seeing that it was all he was allowed to sell. From the day he took over the wine saloon he began to rid it of aggressive drinkers and limit the intake of the more harmless ones. He enforced strict rules of behaviour, began to sell better quality wine, hold wine-tastings, organise trips to wineries throughout Victoria – particularly to Rutherglen, home to some of the world's great fortified wines – and generally tried to raise the tone and change perceptions of what a wine bar could be.

It worked a treat. Watson's musician contacts meant that Melbourne's bohemian crowd discovered the place, as did the academics from the nearby University of Melbourne. The Jewish and Italian populations that had settled in Carlton frequented Jimmy Watson's because it provided them with a more familiar atmosphere than the public bars of the local hotels. It was also a popular drinking hole for some members of the armed forces and the business community. Women were made to feel welcome (and secure) at Jimmy Watson's, something that could not be said for the majority of hotel public bars. It became a place that people relished because of its perceived European-flavoured sophistication and the fact that it provided one of the few viable drinking venues in town.

Places like Jimmy Watson's and Il Bistro (now the Cellar Bar) at Cafe Florentino flew under the radar of the Licensing Court until the late 1950s, when more people began to discover these places and so drew the attention of the authorities. Il Bistro, located just a block from Victoria's Parliament, had become so popular after a renovation in the mid-1950s that people often spilled out onto the street with their glasses of wine. Drinking wine on the street was strictly illegal. Drinking wine on the street right under the noses of parliamentarians was asking for trouble. When the liquor laws were reviewed in 1960 it was decided that the terms of the AWL needed to be changed, perhaps to stop this outbreak of civilised, European-style wine drinking. Il Bistro was mentioned by name in Parliament when the laws were changed.

The new AWL prohibited wine being consumed on the premises, ostensibly turning the saloons into bottle shops. Those that wanted to continue serving wine were invited to apply for the new Restaurant Licence, which allowed them to sell wine only to customers partaking in a bona-fide meal. (Jimmy Watson's was able to keep selling wine to take away because the business consisted of several

{*Opposite*} City stalwart Florentino's Cellar Bar

A State Treasure

In his signature leather brewery apron, Jimmy Watson was the very model of a jovial, rotund host. He took over a lowly Lygon Street wine saloon in 1935 and founded a family dynasty that still runs Melbourne's most revered wine bar and wine lovers' rendezvous for long lunches. A champion of the robust red wines of Victoria's north-east, Jimmy bought them and others by the hogshead to bottle under his own label.

Generations of Melbourne University students like myself can recall learning to appreciate good wine under Jimmy's generous tutelage. When he died in 1962, his son Allan – later a Lord Mayor of Melbourne – took over. He commissioned the renowned Melbourne architect Robin Boyd to redesign the historic two-storey corner building, with its clubby bar and leafy courtyard. The new design encompassed a smart new bistro downstairs and preserved the historic, memento-filled private rooms upstairs, haunts of regular luncheon clubs. Jimmy's grandsons Nigel and Simon now have joined the business.

The name of Jimmy Watson is commemorated by the Royal Melbourne Show's valued trophy for the best young red wine. Among the many stories about the quick-witted bon vivant and raconteur is one recounted by Grania Poliness, author of *Jimmy Watson's Wine Bar*. A pompous overseas visitor was sounding off that Melbourne was the 'arse end of the world'. 'Oh,' said Jimmy, 'just passing through, are you?' CLAUDE FORELL

Jimmy Watson

separate shopfronts.) The legal loophole that had allowed places other than hotels to operate as de facto bars in Melbourne had been firmly closed.

For the next couple of decades, Melbourne was a small-bar desert; it was an accepted part of life that hotels were the only place you could get a drink without a meal. Other than a few restaurants with room enough to provide a band and a dance floor, and a handful of nightclubs, pubs were also one of the few places where you could have a drink while watching live music. Some restaurants, such as Top of the Town, in the city and Ferdi's Bistro, in Carlton, managed to sidestep the no-bar rule with the aid of tricky wording and expensive lawyers, but until the 1987 changes to the Liquor Control Act mostly it was the pubs that dominated bar culture, with little room in the Act for any other type of business to gain a foothold.

Admittedly, many pubs did respond to the changing desires of the drinking public. Years before the Melbourne-style bar had even been contemplated, the radical idea that men and women might like to enjoy a drink together in the same room began to take hold. At the same time, hotel owners began to countenance the idea that serving beer to people like they were pigs at a trough was perhaps not the only business model that would work. In his book *The Australian Pub*, J.M. Freeland describes how many pubs changed their tune to appeal to a wider demographic and possibly to reverse the drift to the clubs, which were seen by many to offer a more genteel atmosphere:

> Open air beer gardens with tables and chairs set amidst rock-gardens, stone paths, shrubs and gay sun umbrellas were added to encourage wives to share their husbands' conviviality and bring restraint and respectability to leisured family drinking … Carpeted lounge bars, with ample sit-down drinking facilities and waiter service were incorporated or extended … [and] entertainers were engaged to perform in the lounge bars where people could dance or sing, or just listen and drink without being obliged to take part. A variety of entertainers designed to add variety to the previous one-note drinking-theme were enticed to bring their wares to amuse the customers … Warm colours returned [and the] pubs broke out in a rash of lime and coffee-coloured paint, striated plywood, chrome tube furniture, bright-coloured laminated plastic, satin finish tiles and fluorescent lighting. It was a jazzy combination, but its bright cheerfulness captured the reformed image the pubs were trying to establish.[3]

Cheerful perhaps, but it was a sort of rigidly grinning cheerfulness, as these pubs tried, with an air of slightly befuddled desperation, to alter the way they did things. It was not an easy balancing act. Not only were pubs trying to satisfy a clientele that was increasingly looking for more sophisticated drinking venues, but they

> The radical idea that men and women might like to enjoy a drink together in the same room began to take hold

had to do so within the strictly proscribed guidelines of the Liquor Control Act and under the watchful eye of both the Liquor Control Commission and the AHA. Nieuwenhuysen's comments about the laws being like a procrustean bed seem particularly accurate in the context of Victoria's hotel bars at the time. During the 1980s, another example of the ingenuity of the Melbourne hospitality community showed itself, as a new generation began to experiment with old pub formula.

Places such as Mietta's Melbourne Hotel, in the grandly ornate former Naval and Military Club in the city; the Smith Street Bar and Bistro, a pub in Collingwood run by Donlevy Fitzpatrick, who spruced it up with plenty of wood and glass; and the ad-crowd magnet the Red Eagle, in Albert Park, were very much about providing good food in their restaurants. But they also provided dedicated drinking areas that were completely different beasts to the typical hotel bar. Wine had just as important a place on the drinks list as beer. Fit-outs – all sleek, polished surfaces or ornate, slightly ironic retro-kitsch – were the antithesis of the old tiled, fluoro-lit public bar. Hours were extended, women and men frequented these places in equal numbers and it all seemed very modern and civilised.

Though they were still attached to restaurants, and food continued to be a main focus for these hotels, the bars were attracting a crowd of younger drinkers who came with no intention of eating. For many in this crowd, the traditional pub was a place where you would go to see a band, not necessarily to hang out with friends. The bars in places like Mietta's and the Smith Street Bar and Bistro provided a different atmosphere, and arguably they played an integral part in planting the seed for the small-bar wave that would hit Melbourne a few years down the track. But there was no chance of anything like that happening under existing laws.

There were few immediate signs of a potentially flourishing small-bar culture after the Nieuwenhuysen recommendations were made into law. There was confusion about what could and could not be done, typified by the baffling '25 per cent rule'. With some places losing their licences for allowing too many patrons to drink without eating, there was a feeling of caution about how far the laws could be pushed. The gist of the laws – endlessly spruiked by Nieuwenhuysen, sections of the press and the government – was that the new regime would encourage small European-style cafes where patrons could drink a glass of wine with a piece of cake in the morning and have a focaccia and a couple of beers in the evening.

Certainly, many cafes took advantage of being able to serve alcohol and the Euro-style cafe boom in Melbourne was noticeably gathering a head of steam. But few operators saw the potential of running a bar with the main focus being on alcohol, with a little bit of food on the side. Then, in 1989, Le Monde opened at the top end of Bourke Street in the city.

[*Opposite*] The European encapsulates Melbourne style

- Crumbed King George
  Whiting fillets w̄ a fennel +
  blood orange salad
  $32

- Whole oven-roasted Barramundi
  w̄ zucchini beignet $36

- Veal Holstein w̄ celeriac
  remoulade, rocket, fried eggs +
  white anchovies $32.50

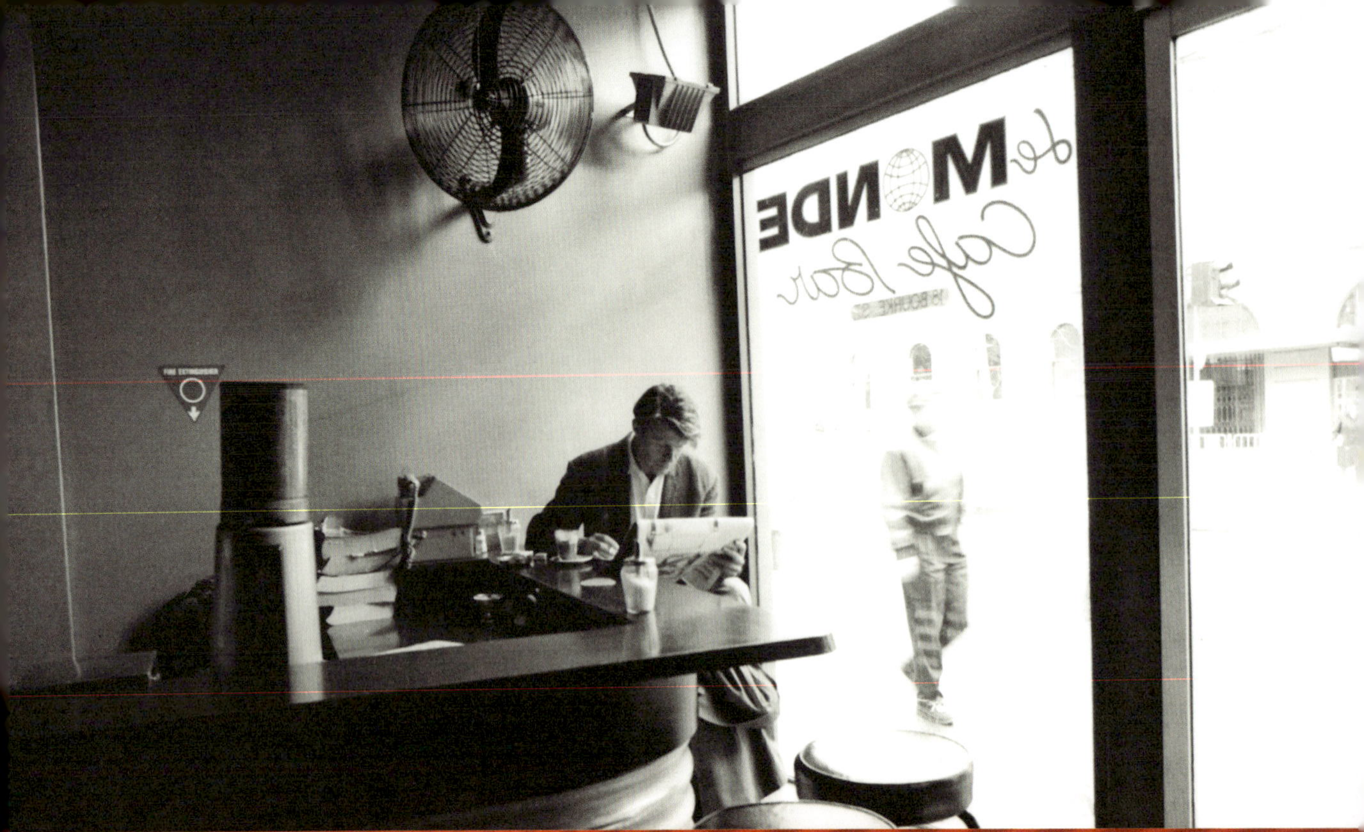
le MONDE
Cafe Bar

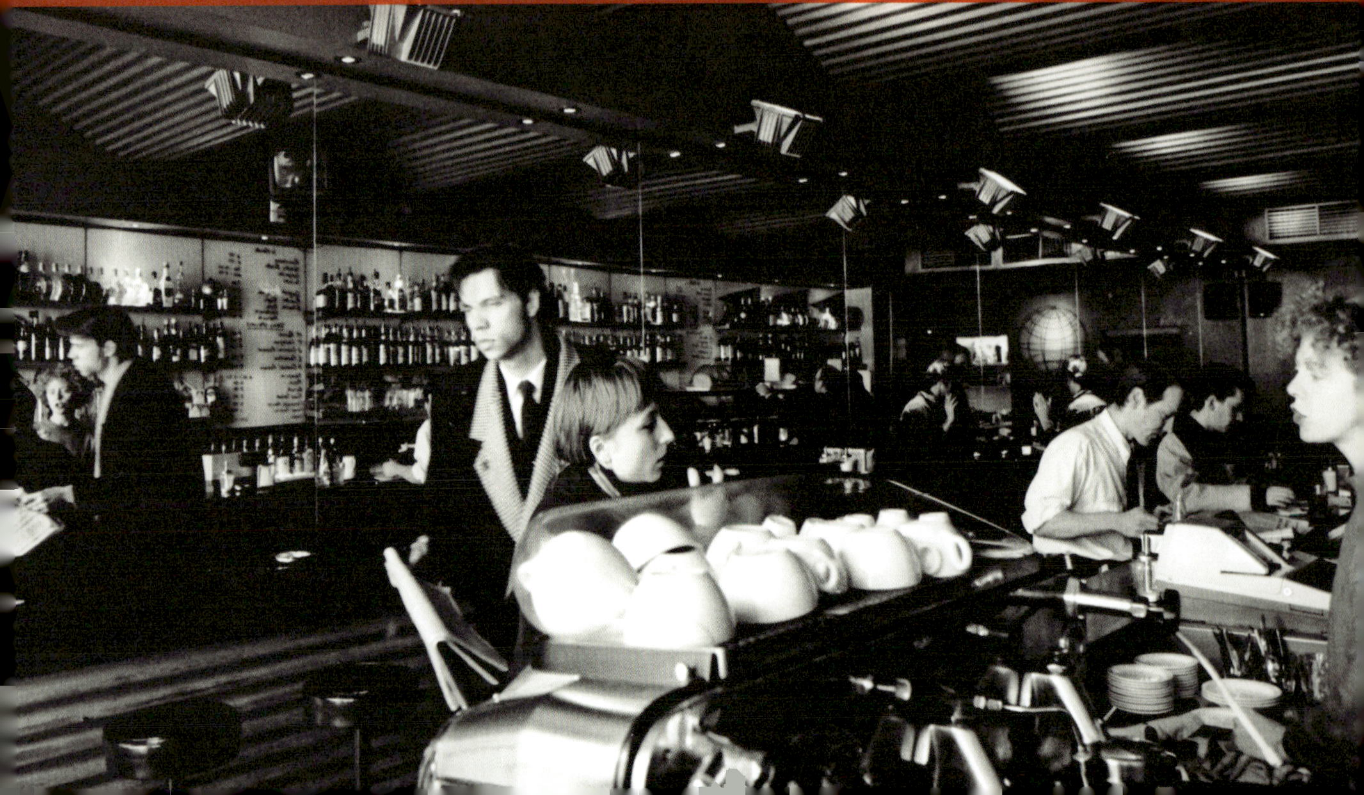

Le Monde was a bar that looked like a bar and acted like a bar. It was small, it opened late (it had a 24-hour licence), it served pretty good quality alcohol and mainly antipasto-type snacks, it made decent coffee and it played good music, which became louder as the night progressed. The main seating was on stools at a bar that ran the length of the long, narrow space. There were stylish touches such as cast-metal handles in the shape of the world on the glass front doors and a mosaic-tiled doorstep that echoed, in miniature, the exuberant style of Rosati around the corner. It channelled Pellegrini's, deliberately tapped into the small-bar culture of places like Manhattan and Paris and it started light bulbs flashing in the heads of some of the city's future style-makers. As Con Christopoulos, originator of several pace-setting city bars and cafes, says, 'My first experience of the new freedom of the laws was as a customer at Le Monde.'[4]

One of the main factors that helped bring Melbourne's small-bar culture into being was that the liberalising of the licensing laws coincided with the appearance of a fairly sizeable – that is, economically viable – group of people who were deliberately and actively seeking an alternative to the mainstream drinking culture. It was a collection of people that included bohemian artistic types, who liked to keep night-owl hours, and legions of hospitality workers, who were searching for a place to wind down after their night's work. Among the first people to provide a viable and permanent home in the city for this group was Carlo Colosimo, the man who opened Lounge, in Swanston Street in 1989, six months after Le Monde had opened its doors.

Colosimo had been working in clubs and organising events since he was a teenager. After running the Bridge Road Club in Richmond, in the mid-1980s he went overseas, and when he returned to Melbourne he noticed a series of clubs being run in existing nightclubs or licensed venues on certain nights of the week – places with names like Razor, Hard Times, Swelter and Hardware, which were identifying an alternative crowd, artists and the like.

Thinking 'there might be enough room to make it every night of the week',[5] he began looking around the city for a venue with an existing licence, knowing from previous experience that getting a new licence for what he had in mind would be time consuming and potentially costly. He discovered a two-storey business on Swanston Street that had both a restaurant and cabaret licence, and which had been running for nearly thirty years in one form or another – cabaret, gambling den, strip club and reggae club among its various incarnations. The two licences meant that he was able to open twenty-four hours a day and, under the new Liquor Control Act, he was able to keep those hours under a General Licence. In late 1989, he opened the first floor as a bar, though food was also available. There were pool tables, DJs,

[*Opposite*] Le Monde led the way in Bourke Street

[*Above*] Carlo Colosimo from Lounge

> Much of the cheapest vacant space was in the CBD's laneways, in the basements and the upper floors of buildings

the occasional band, a lot of dancing and imbibing, and from Thursday night until Monday morning it didn't close:

> We realised there was a lot of these people out there that weren't about the mainstream or the 'too tight and too bright' crowd or the yobbos, but were a bit left of centre, reasonably well dressed, some of them well heeled, some not. They were, theoretically, the thinkers of our community and they hadn't been catered to before.

Lounge was definitely something of a template for the bars that followed, if not so much in looks – though the second-hand furniture aesthetic was certainly repeated ad nauseam in the following years – but in attitude and approach. There was a certain free-spirited, smell-of-an-oily-rag, DIY sensibility to Lounge that not only appealed to the punters who packed the place, but to the people who began to see, by checking out Lounge, that it was possible for them to start their own businesses without having to outlay a million bucks. Colosimo says:

> What we tried to achieve was to create a Melbourne bar as distinct from a European bar. I'm not saying that the European feel is bad – I think it is fantastic and it is part of my background – but Lounge was about bringing the Melbourne culture in, the elements that make Melbourne Melbourne. It was a way of acknowledging the people that contributed to that – the people who were the thinkers, the designers, the artists.

If Lounge and Le Monde provided a kind of blueprint for the Melbourne-style bar, there were other important factors that came together to create the bar boom. The recession of the early 1990s hit Victoria with particular force. Unemployment rose by 8 per cent and the city saw an increasing number of vacant shops and businesses and a corresponding drop in rents. Much of the cheapest vacant space was in the CBD's laneways, in the basements and the upper floors of buildings – locations perfectly suited to bars that don't rely on passing daytime traffic. Bars, by their nature, are one of the few businesses where being hidden away and hard to find actually constitutes a plus.

At the same time retail space was becoming available, the Melbourne City Council was working on strategies to bring life back into the city centre. Traffic flows were reduced on certain streets, strong building-design policies were put in place to help preserve older buildings, and plans were afoot to upgrade the streetscapes. Probably most important for Melbourne's bars, however, was the policy the council had towards attracting new businesses. While it actively encouraged certain types of businesses, particularly those run by the young, the council also had something

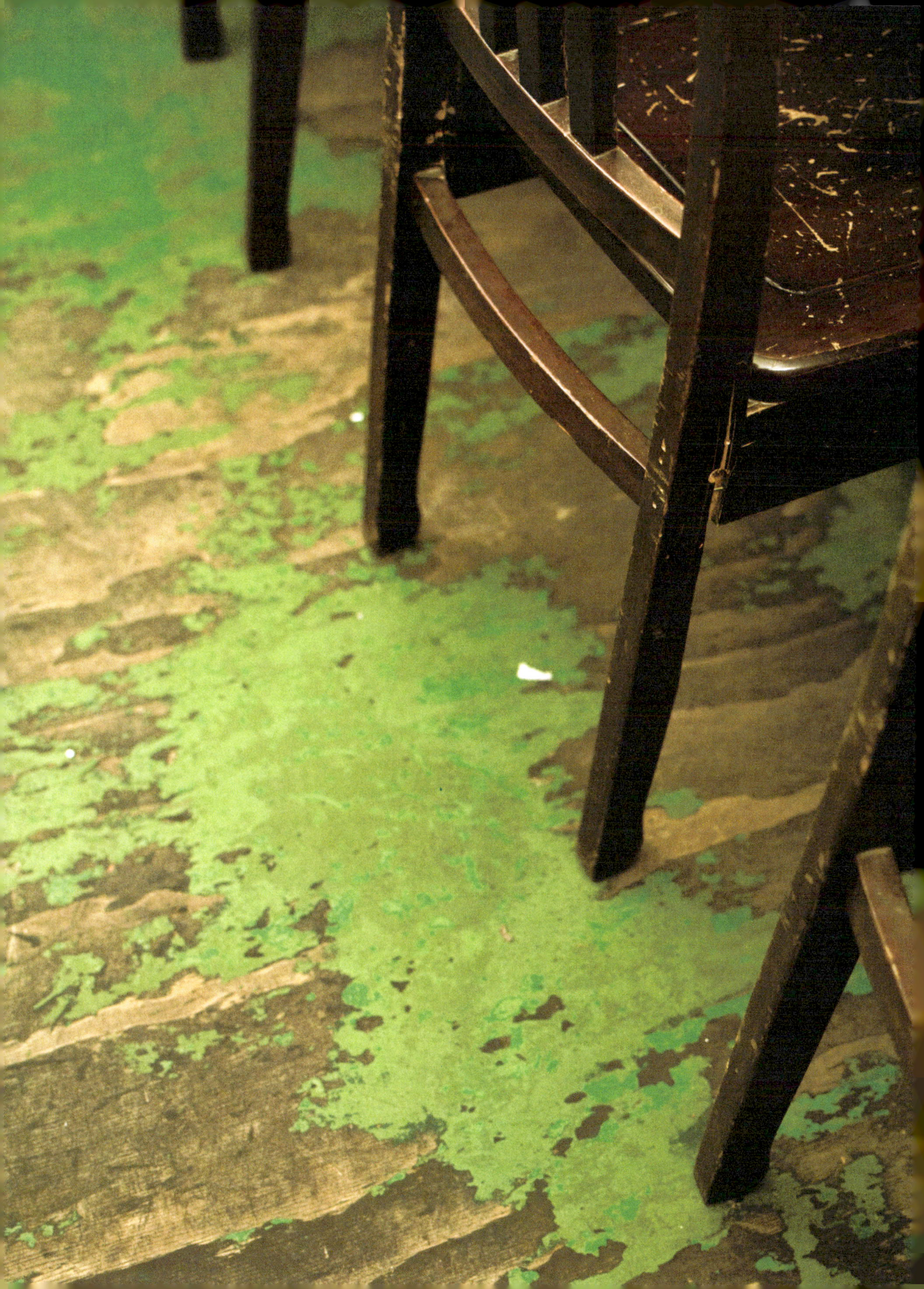

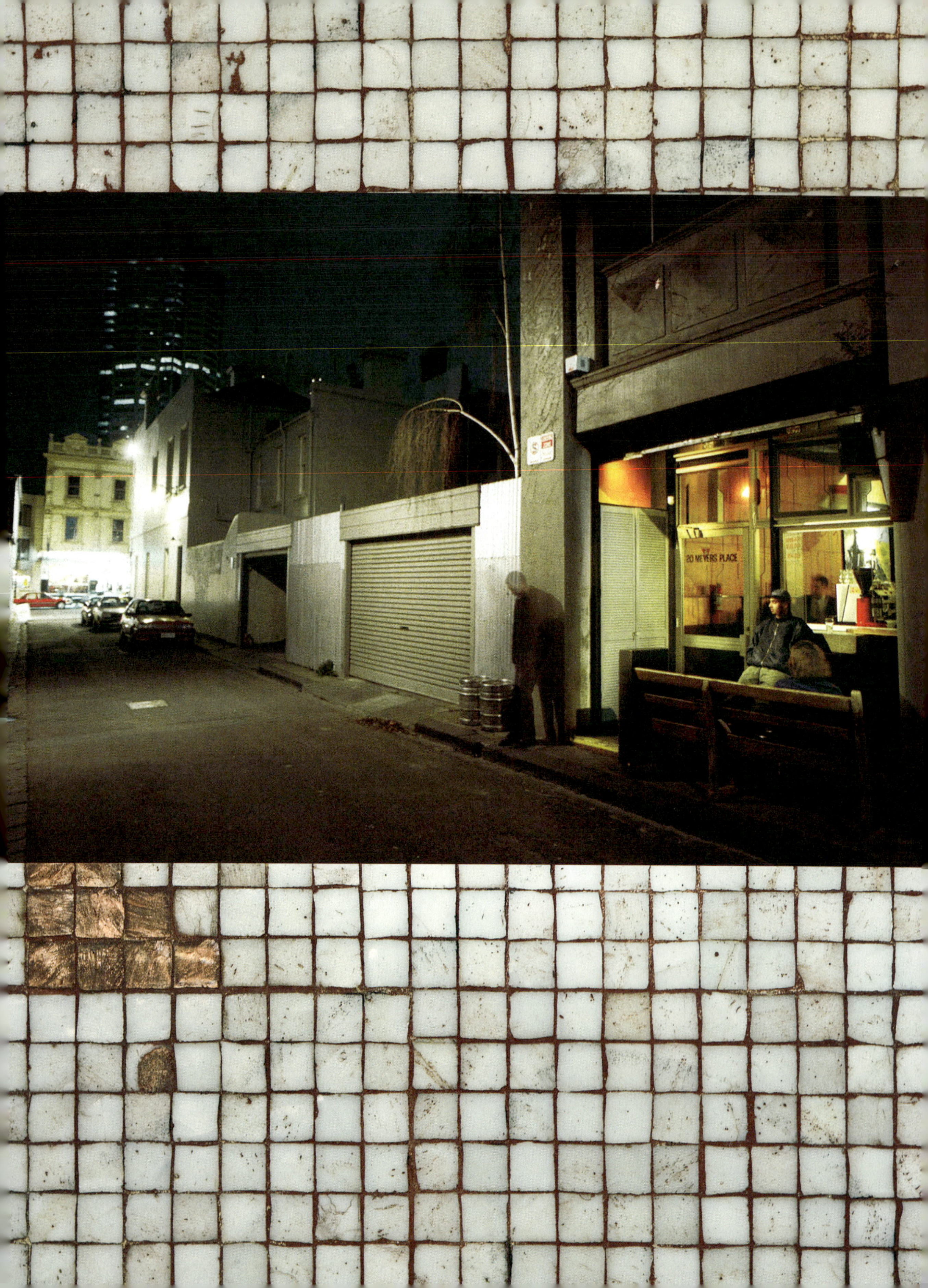
20 MEYERS PLACE

of a hands-off policy, which allowed the city centre to develop its own character without the help of some marketing genius directing all the moves.

But none of this would have helped establish the Melbourne bar scene if it weren't for the newly relaxed licensing laws. The European-style cafes and restaurants envisioned by the architect of the reforms in the late 1980s had certainly started to take hold in the city centre, but it wasn't until 1994, when the Kennett Liberal government revisited the laws, that Melbourne's bar culture was given the green light.

The main reason for revisiting liquor laws at this time was the arrival, in the city, of Crown Casino. To allow the casino's bars to sell alcohol without the requirement of the consumption of food, the government created a new type of licence, the General Licence Class B. Though it may have created a dangerous precedent for regularly amending the Victorian laws to suit the way Crown Casino likes to trade, the arrival of General Licence Class B was a significant factor in the revitalisation of Melbourne's CBD. Not only were places now able to open up without the expense of installing kitchens and all the paraphernalia that accompanies them, they were able to obtain one of these licences for a very modest $2000.

It did not take long for those who had seen other possibilities in the way Colosimo's Lounge operated to take advantage of the 1994 amendment. The second of these new Class B licences was claimed by a fledgling group of architects that ran a practice called Six Degrees. These six architects, sick of noisy, expensive nightclubs and dowdy, uninteresting pubs, had decided to open a place that was all about gathering at a small, stylish place for a chat over a reasonably priced drink. They took out the lease on a former hairdressing salon in a little laneway off Bourke Street called Meyers Place.

It is hard to imagine that Melbourne's small bars, the Melbourne-style bar in fact, would have headed in the same direction if it hadn't been for the early intervention of these young architects, with their minuscule budget and unique aesthetic. With a budget of about $30,000, they renovated the small narrow shopfront, using mostly recycled materials. The walls were panelled with timber from the stage at the Melbourne Town Hall (traded with the builders, who were demolishing it, for a slab of beer), parts of the ceiling were lined with shag-pile carpet pulled from a house in Doncaster and a complete cool room and beer system was obtained from a closed-down pub and reassembled at the site. The dimensions of the concrete bar were modelled on those of nearby Pellegrini's, a favourite hangout. There was no official name, no signage, only cheese, kabana and crackers to eat, four types of spirits, one beer and, when it was closed, no sign that it even existed behind the blank metal roller door. There were no DJs, just a constant soundtrack of music played at

{*Opposite and above*} The original laneways bar, Meyers Place

A Coming of Age

There are twenty-eight wines served by the glass at Melbourne's Taxi Dining Room; twenty-two hail from overseas. It's an impressive, lip-smacking international smorgasbord. Your aperitif might be a fifteen-year-old Malmsey, a Tateyama umeshu plum wine from Japan, or perhaps a more traditional rosé champagne. You could spend your entire meal cherry-picking from the wines-by-the-glass list, but there are bottled wines to follow – thirty-nine pages of them – offering a challenging and eclectic mix of Australian and international wines. In 2008, this won Taxi Dining Room the Australian Wine List of the Year Award.

In the award's twelve-year history, Melbourne restaurants have won seven times. Not a bad record. A Melbourne wine list challenges, educates, stimulates, can be daring as well as conservative and, occasionally, defies convention. Who would have thought a wine list devoted exclusively to European wines would survive past its fad date, but The European is now firmly entrenched as a Melbourne favourite. And what do we make of a restaurant that delights in new-wave Greek wines (The Press Club) or a wine bar firmly focused on Spanish and Italian grape varieties (Bar Lourinha)? We go there, of course.

A strong wine selection is reason enough to go out these days, and edgy wine lists are attracting loyal followings. An interesting selection of imported wines is almost obligatory, with German, Austrian, Italian and Spanish becoming commonplace alongside more familiar French names. Less commonplace are the big, well-known brands of the past.

The wine list of today is all but unrecognisable to the wine list of twenty to thirty years ago. Back then, the imported wine section might offer the obligatory (and semi-sweet) Blue Nun Liebfraumilch, Italian lambrusco or Mateus rosé from Portugal. Australian big-company wines – Orlando Jacob's Creek claret, Kaiser Stuhl rosé, Seaview cabernet sauvignon, Houghton white burgundy – dominated.

Wine Lists

Wines by the glass? No way. That phenomenon arrived in Melbourne in the 1990s, following the deregulation of liquor laws and the dropping of the rule stating that wine could only be served when accompanied by a meal. And what about the 'wine flight'– a comparative tasting of three or four wines in tasting-size glasses (60 ml or 80 ml)? It has only been around since the mid to late 1990s.

In the 1980s the sommelier was your wine waiter, who was also your food waiter, who was probably a uni student or an aspiring actor. A sound wine knowledge didn't come with the job description. There are not many things from the 1980s we would recognise today. The wine list is no longer handed automatically to the male diner. Wine glasses are bigger, deeper, better organoleptic devices. We are no longer insecure and parochial in our wine tastes. Our sommeliers are professionals and the wines they buy are more often than not changed daily or weekly on their lists – not annually.

At Taxi, sommelier Lincoln Riley – 2008 Sommelier of the Year – moves fifty wines in and out of his list weekly. He's likened it to writing the great Australian novel. He's got forty pages of blank space in front of him and 1000 wines that have to be whipped into shape, brought to life upon the page. They have to attract the eye of the reader from the very start and keep that attention right through to the end. JENI PORT

AUSTRALIAN WINE LIST OF THE YEAR AWARD

MELBOURNE WINNERS

Taxi Dining Room – 2008

Asiana – 2004

Circa, The Prince – 2001

Melbourne Wine Room – 2000

Syracuse – 1999

France-Soir – 1997

Walter's Wine Bar – 1996

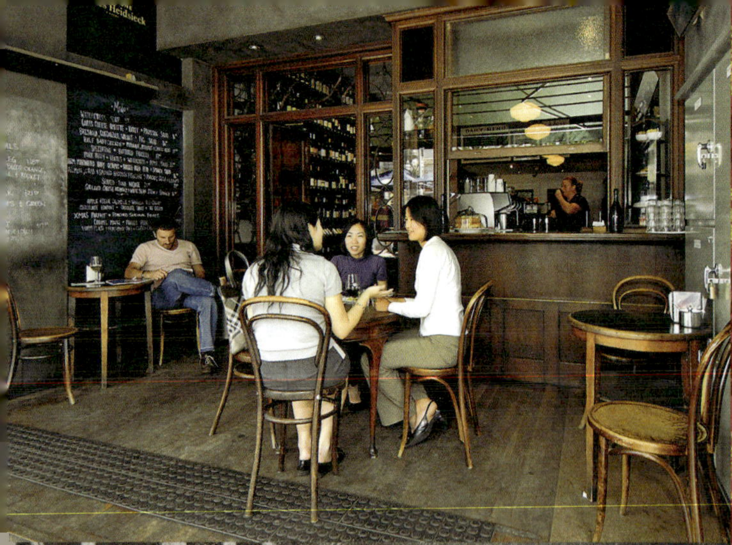

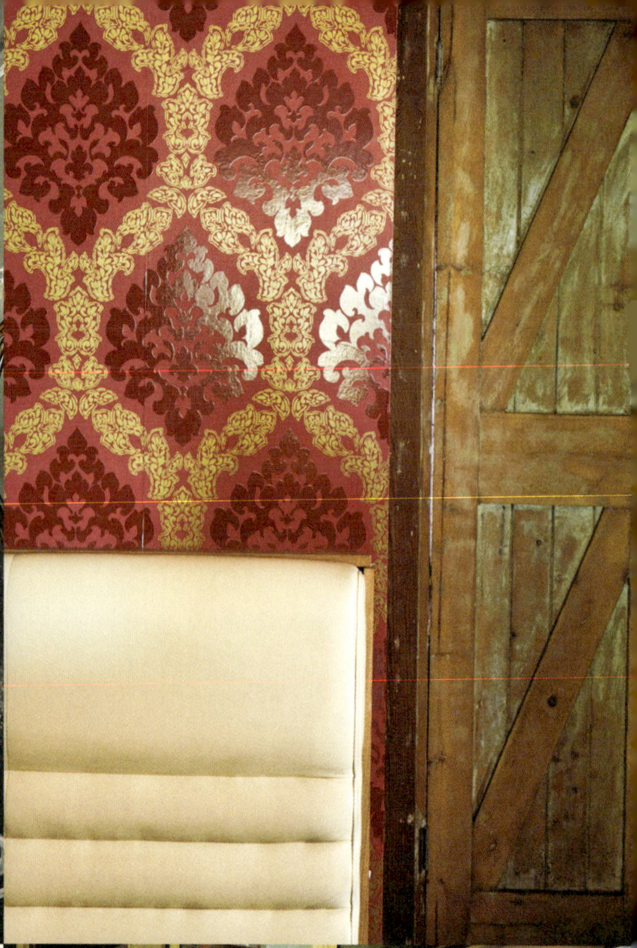

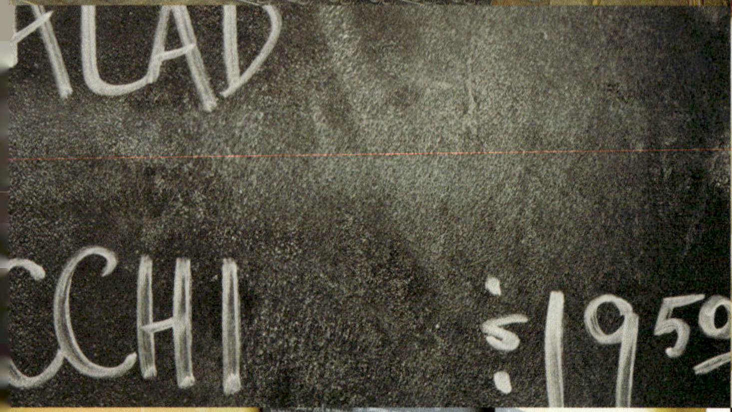

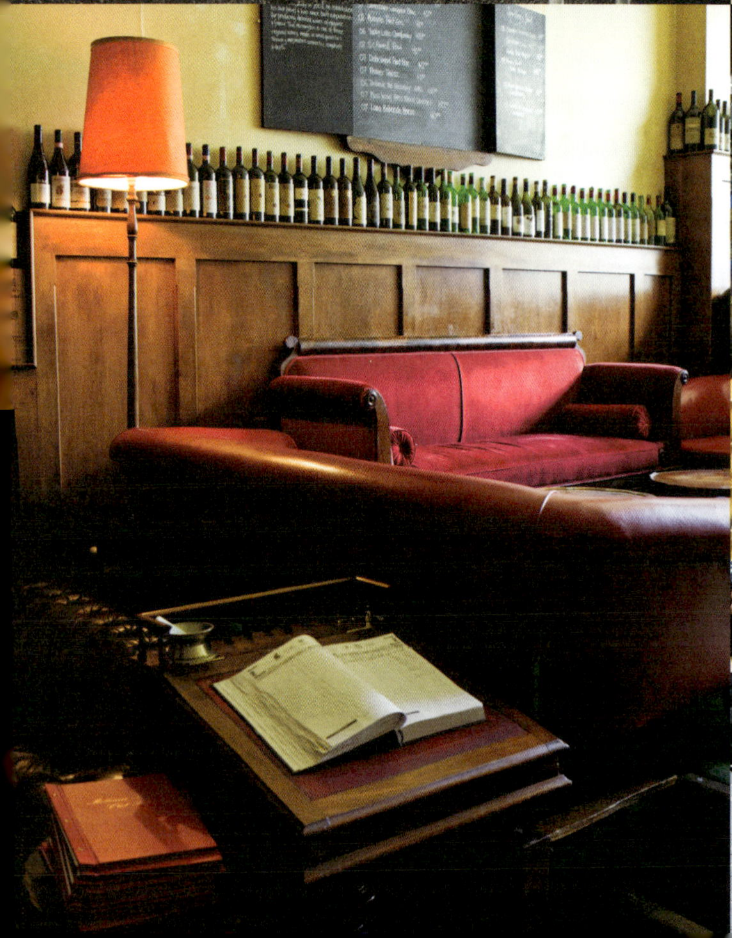

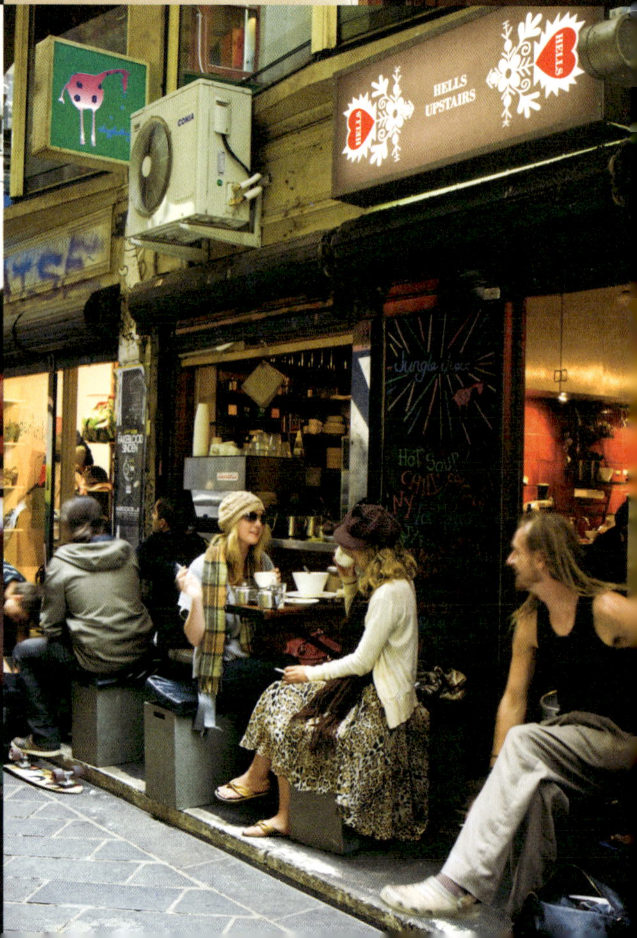
HELLS UPSTAIRS

City Wine Shop Tastings
So Where Does Flavour Come From?
San Pell
*Arancia

a volume that encouraged conversation. A particular aesthetic had been coined and it was nothing like anything Melbourne had seen before. People went mad for it immediately and the first rumble of the bar boom sounded.

Within months, more bars began to appear, down lanes and above shops. There was Sadie's, opened in a tiny two-storey former Japanese restaurant down the end of Coverlid Lane; Rue Bebelon, with its two turntables spinning eclectic vinyl behind the bar in Little Lonsdale Street; Up Top, with its 1950s cabaret aesthetic above a souvlaki shop on Russell Street; and The International making its 1960s airport-lounge moves upstairs in Market Lane. Though they were all discernibly different – some were about music and dancing, others provided food or began to concentrate on obscure alcohol and meticulously constructed cocktails – all of the CBD bars shared similar traits. They were small and intimate, tucked away, fitted out on a tight budget and all buzzed with an energy that can only come from pioneering something new.

In 1994, there were eight small-bar applications. In 1995, this number rose to forty and by 1997 the total had reached 152. By the turn of the century, dedicated bar guides began to appear, bar hopping had become a popular nightlife pastime and there was a rise in bar specialisation. Though places like the Meyers Place bar and others like the bar at laneway restaurant Becco successfully continued with the by-now old-school approach to the Melbourne-style bar, others began to hone the simple, general approach into something much more specific.

In 1997, Vernon Chalker opened Gin Palace in a former light-bulb factory in Russell Place, bringing in a new phase in Melbourne's bar development. Gin Palace

{*Below, left*} Madame Brussels; {*right*} Vernon Chalker

{*Opposite and following pages*} Gin Palace

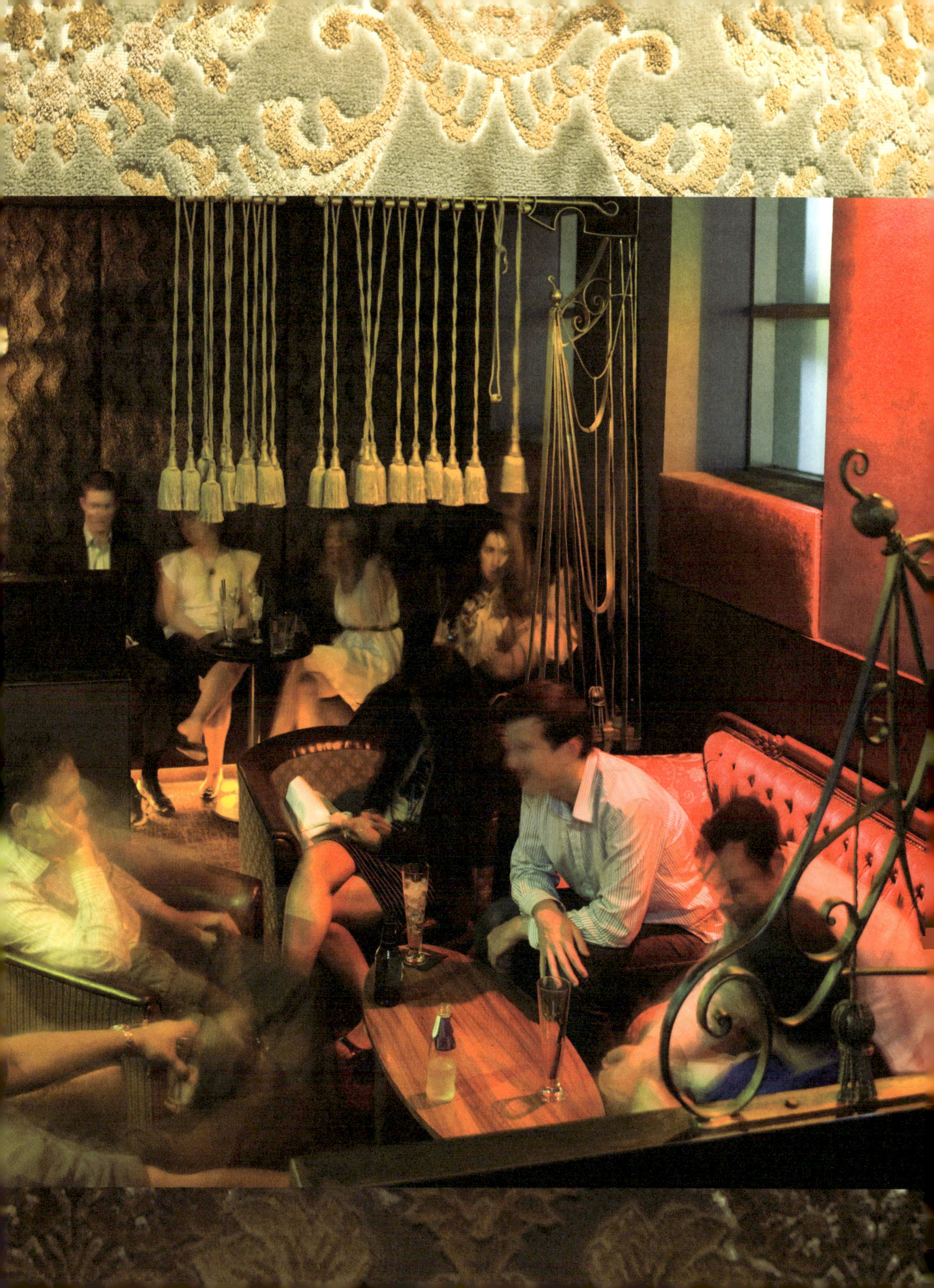

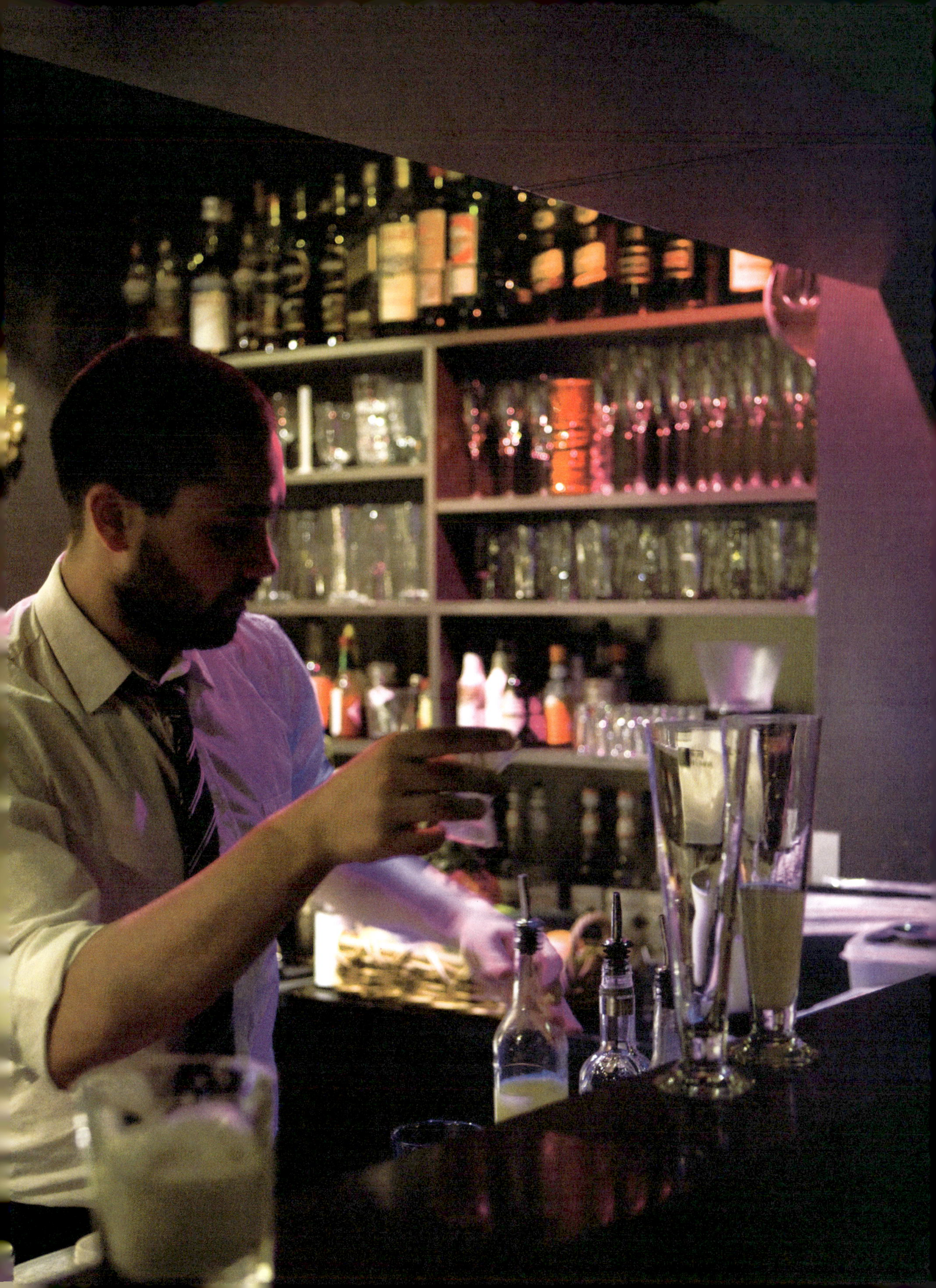

EXIT

was all about luxury and decadence, albeit in slightly ironic and witty form. The glamorously gloomy room was stuffed with hidden nooks, upholstered couches, low tables and voluminous deep-coloured curtains. The obscure entrance and glamorous fit-out gave it the feeling of a speakeasy. With a menu dedicated to martinis and another to champagne, table service from smartly-attired waiters and with a constantly ginned-up crowd, Gin Palace put another spin on the Melbourne-style bar.

Chalker has become one of the true style-makers of Melbourne's bars, with a stable of watering holes that includes Collins Quarter, the Order of Melbourne and Madame Brussels – named after a famous nineteenth-century brothel owner. The latter is an eccentric bar on the third level of a nondescript city building, featuring indoor Astroturf and garden furniture, a huge outdoor terrace and a propensity for pink drinks, dark rum and cucumber sandwiches.

Con Christopoulos has also stamped his particular and much-emulated mark on the city's bar scene. Probably better known for his cafes and restaurants, with their trademark dark-wood-panelled, European-channelling, well-lived-in interiors, Christopoulos has also made an indelible impression on the bar scene with the Melbourne Supper Club. Overlooking Parliament House and St Patrick's Cathedral, behind an unmarked door and up a flight of stairs, the Supper Club is all leather couches, upholstered furniture, low tables and, until the 2007 smoking ban, a rich patina-creating cloud of cigar smoke. It is like a private gentlemen's club let off the

{*Opposite, above*} The European; {*below*} City Wine Shop

{*Below, left*} Siglo; {*right*} Con Christopoulos

> There is a whole subset of bars that thumbs its nose at comfort and luxury

leash. With a voluminous wine list that favours Old World wine, a democratic list of bar snacks that runs the gamut from party pies to caviar, wine-savvy service and a 6 am closing time, the Melbourne Supper Club embodies the kind of civilised, market-driven place that was one of the lucky, unforeseen consequences of liberalised liquor laws. Smoking laws have seen the Supper Club sprout a rooftop terrace bar called Siglo and next door there is a bottle shop–cum–bar called City Wine Shop, but it is the original bar with its quality wine, dark wood, late hours and excellent coffee that, for many imbibers, defines what makes a Melbourne bar a Melbourne bar.

Camillo Ippoliti, who opened the Lounge-like Revolver in Chapel Street, Prahran, in the late 1990s, has also helped define and redefine imbibing in Melbourne, with a series of businesses in Swanston Street's Curtin House. Perhaps the best known of the city's 'vertical laneways', Curtin House is home to Cookie, a bar, cocktail bar, beer hall and Thai restaurant that occupies one vast floor of the 1920s building. One floor up is The Toff In Town, a two-part bar that features a live music venue on one side and a 'carriage bar' on the other, with a series of private booths in which a French wine list and sophisticated bar food are available at the touch of a button.

But not all Melbourne-style bars have taken the luxuriously upholstered, exclusive-alcohol path. There is a whole subset of bars that thumbs its nose at comfort and luxury, embracing an attitudinal rock aesthetic and taking a

{*Below*} Carriage Bar at The Toff in Town

{*Opposite*} Melbourne's car park bar, Section 8

{*Following pages*} Cookie; {*far left, centre*} Camillo Ippoliti

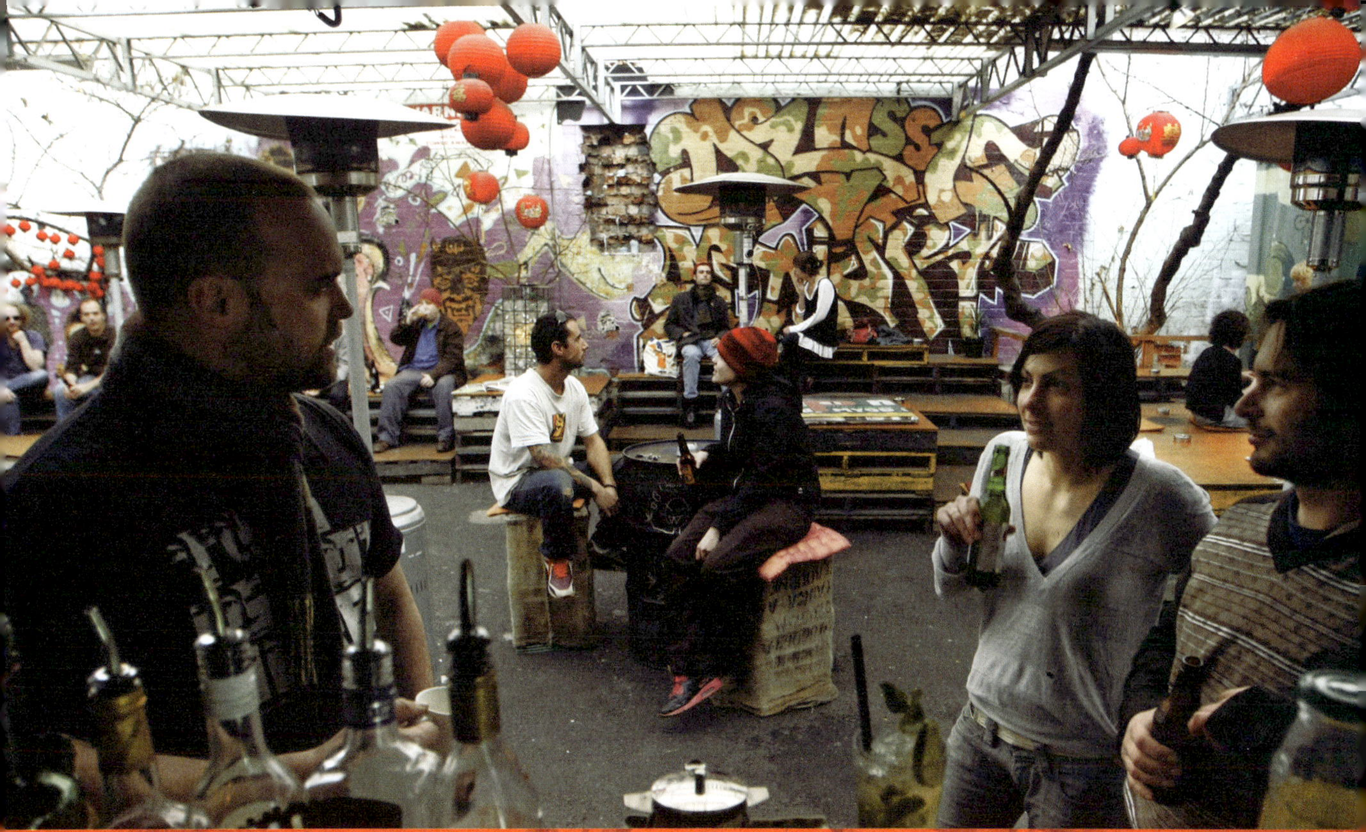

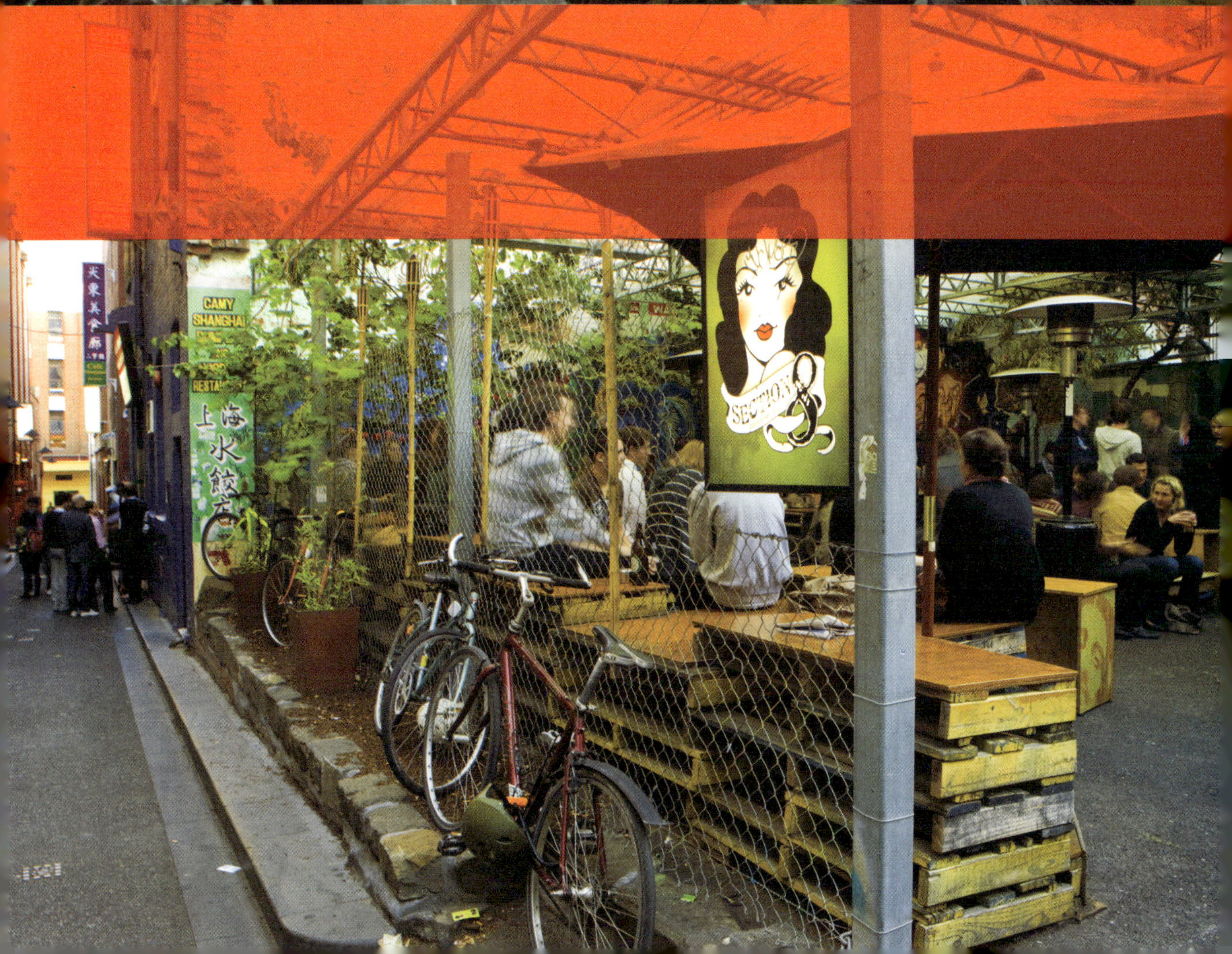
CAMY
SHANGHAI
SECTION 8

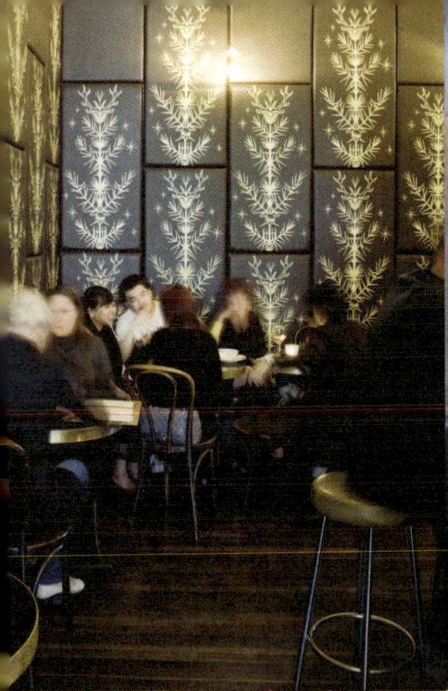

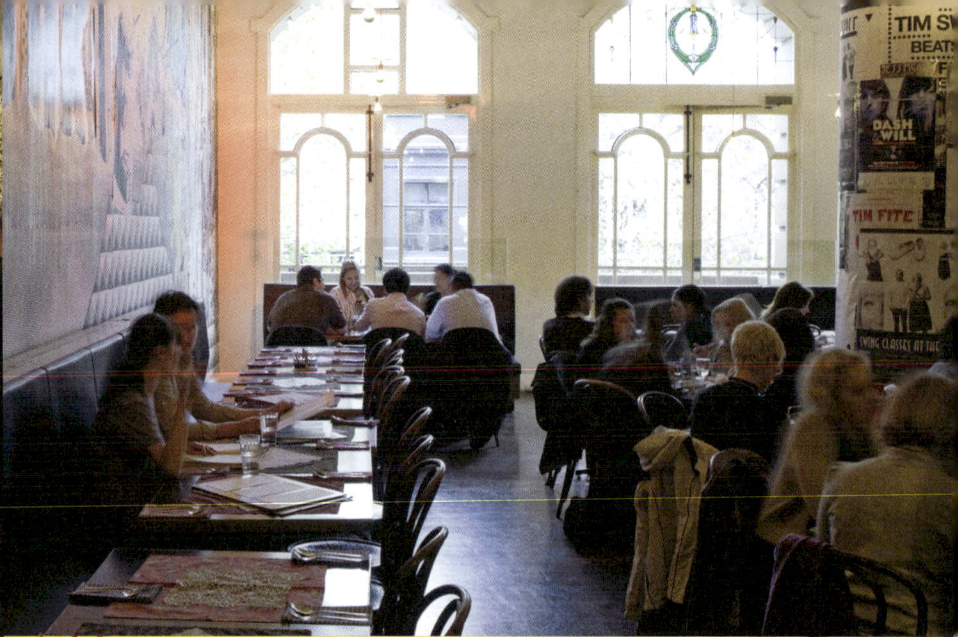
TIM FITE

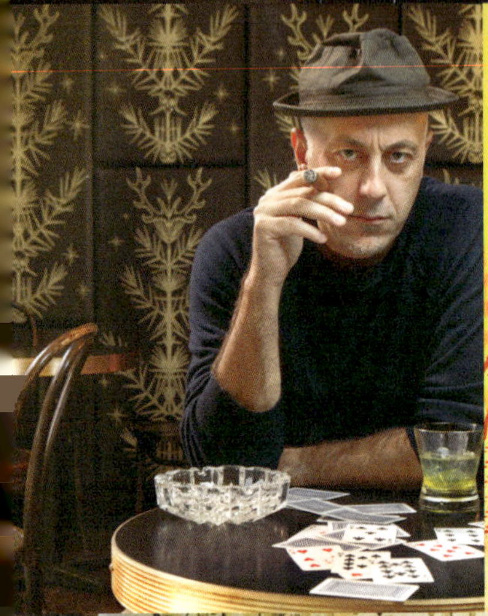

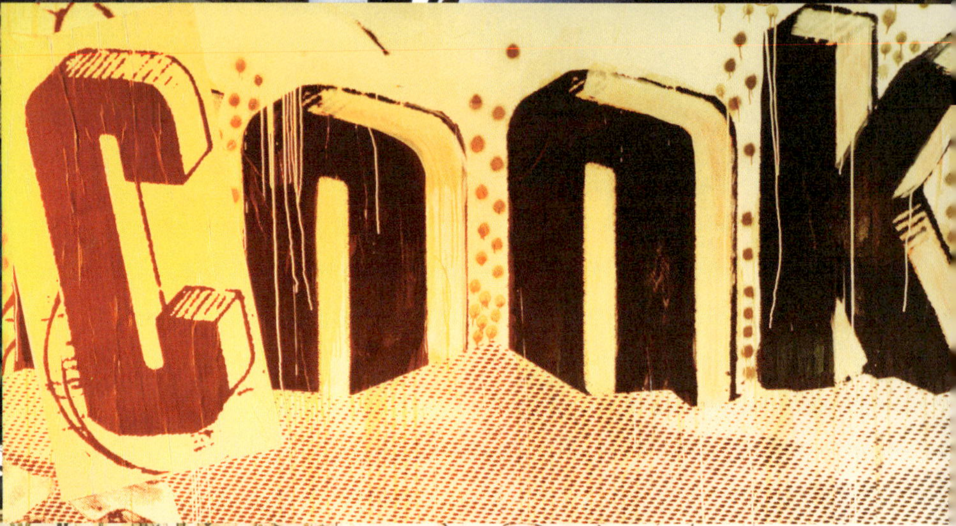

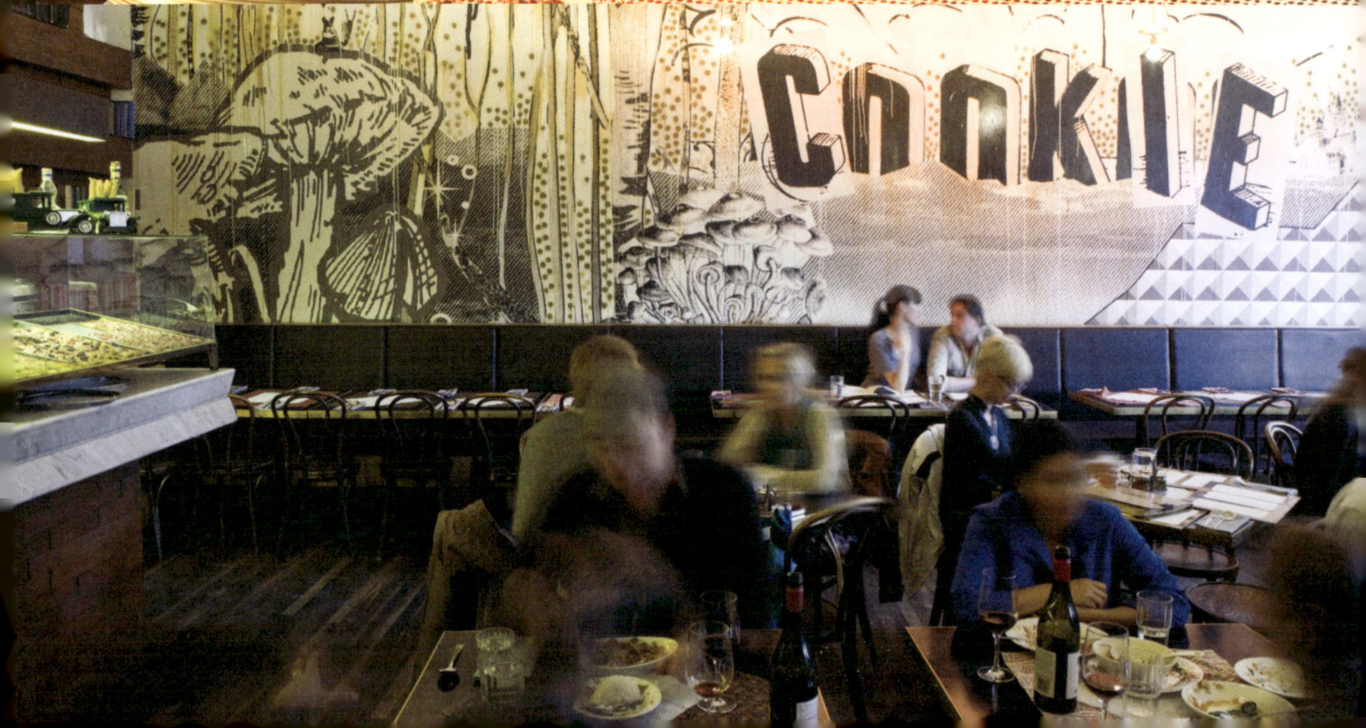
COOKIE

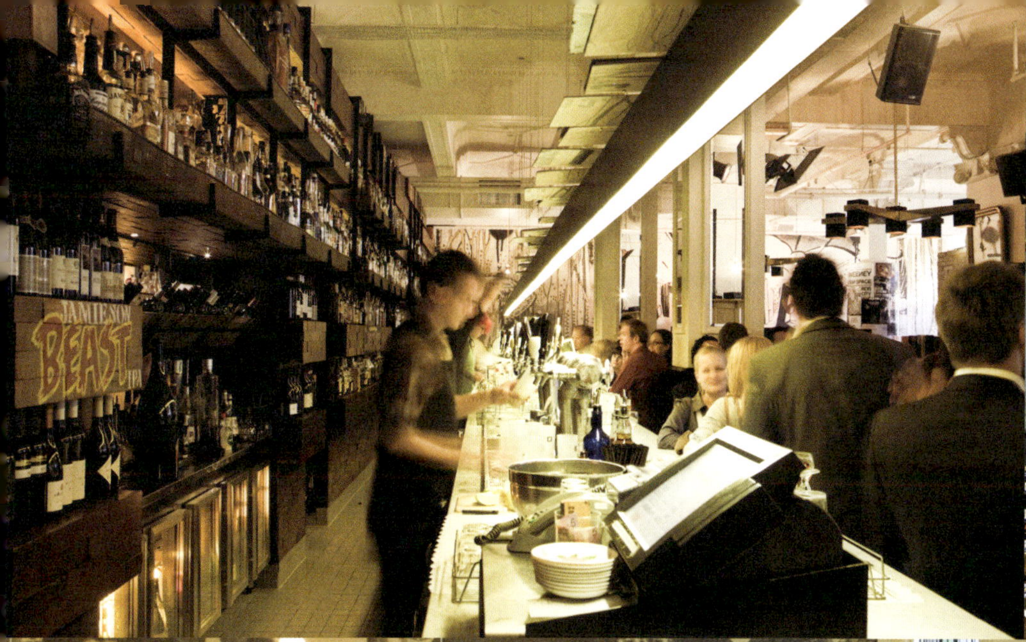
JAMIESON
BEAST

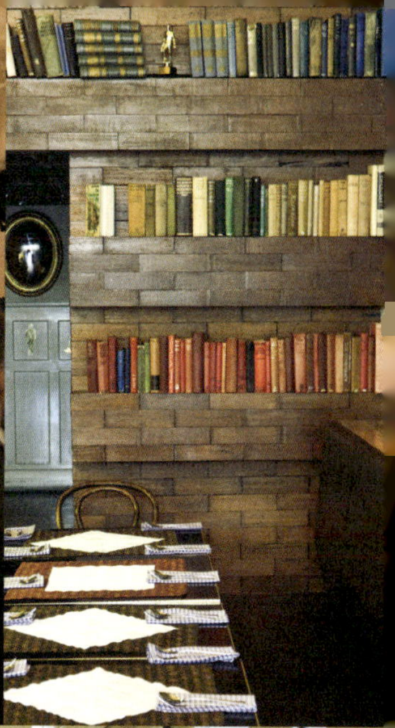

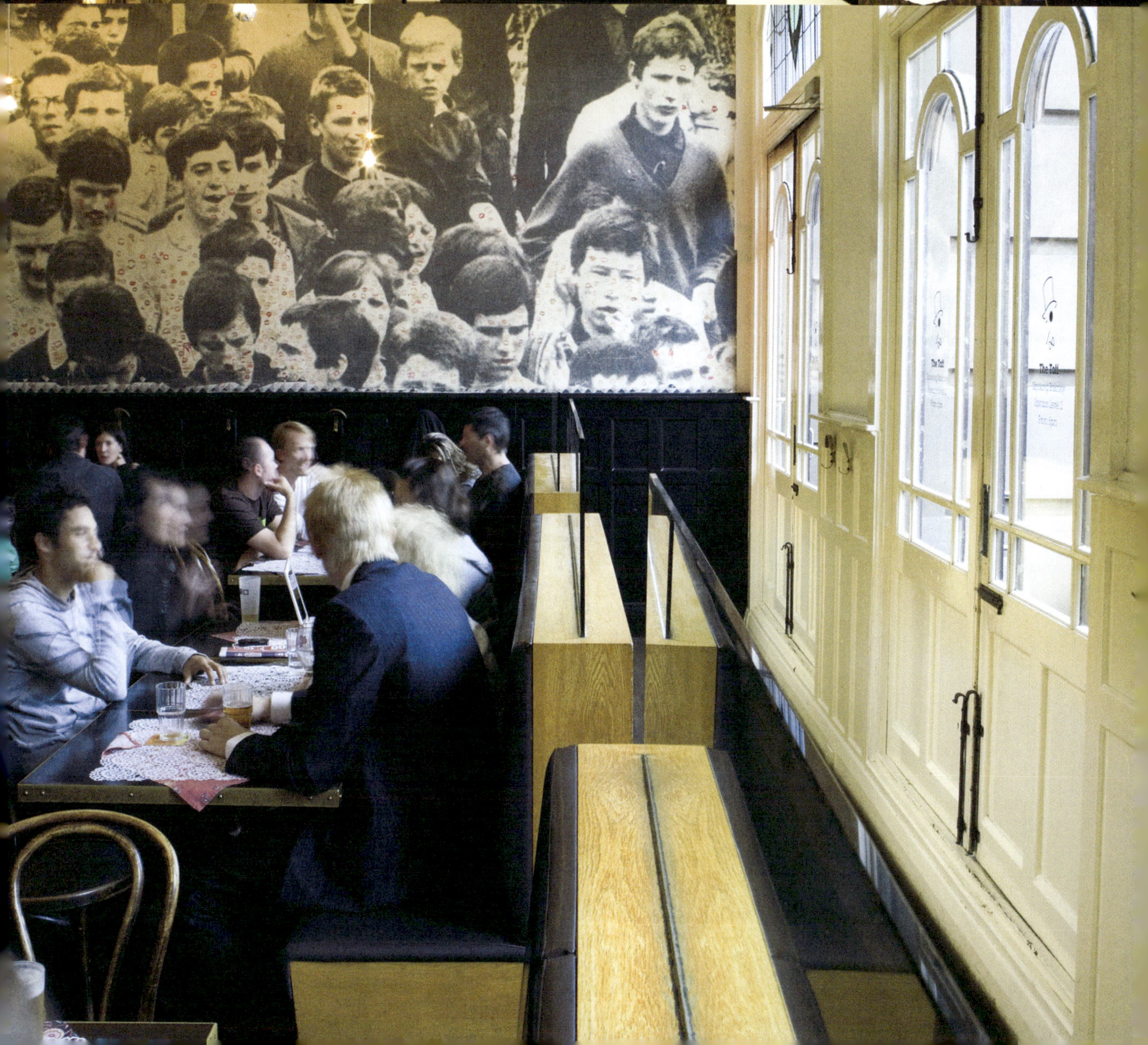

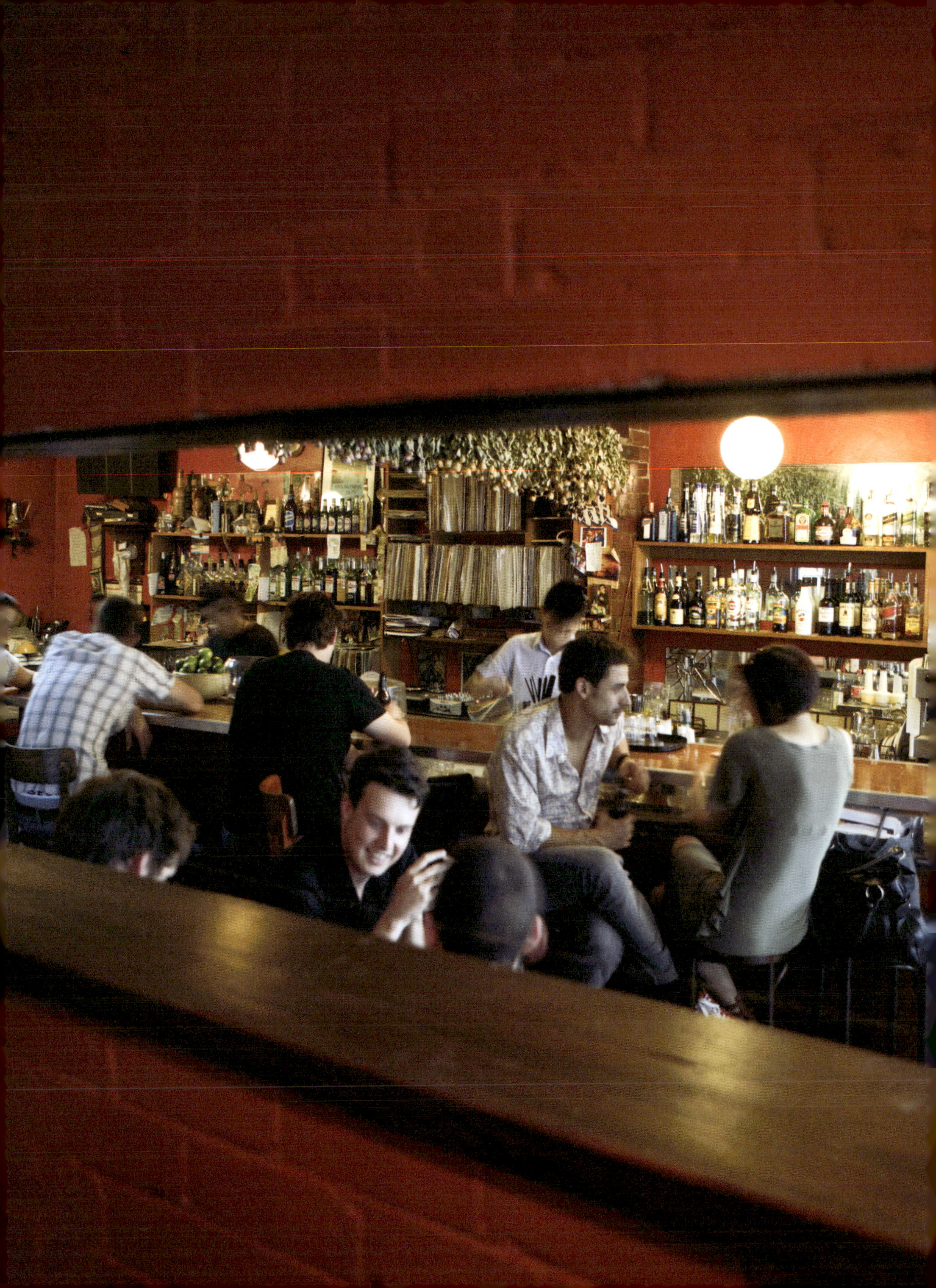

deliberately grungy, downmarket approach to late nights and pumping music. Spending the bare minimum on renovation (aside from the sound systems) is worn as a badge of honour with these places, some even eschewing bricks and mortar in order to squeeze the last drop out of street credibility. These are the temporary bars that not only set up shop down obscure, slightly whiffy laneways, but do so in places such as car parks. The first of these, called Section 8, has a shipping container that serves as the bar, forklift pallets for seating and walls decorated within an inch of their life with Melbourne's famed graffiti and stencil art. Others like it come and go, sometimes within the space of a few weeks, or even days.

But specialisation among Melbourne's watering holes has not been limited to upmarket and downmarket. Reflecting the slightly offbeat entrepreneurial spirit that Melbourne both prides and markets itself on, the bar scene has become a diverse, idiosyncratic, even cinematic screen on which the city's imagination, fantasies and hidden aspirations are played out.

There are Japanese-themed bars featuring extensive sake lists, anime nights and cult video games, gorgeous wood- and statuary-filled Old World fantasylands in former bank buildings, bars that channel 1960s Kubrick curves and others that ooze rat-pack glamour, complete with a slinky jazz soundtrack. There are places that riff on 1920s Chicago, Soviet-era Russia, Italian migrant–era Thornbury, Mao-era China, 1980s Miami, nineteenth-century Melbourne and 1960s Hong Kong. There are bars that look like science labs, like sweatshops, like airport lounges, like milk bars, like Hawaiian hotels. There are bars that have become arts hubs, presenting the work of local and international visual artists, filmmakers, architects and video artists. Some even allow poets. There are bars that are cinemas. There are bars with stupendous city vistas and others with views of trash-laden dumpsters. There are bars with video walls that change the mood and the tone of the place at the flick of a high-tech switch and others where the main choice of seating is milk crates.

It would seem to be a ludicrous proposition to try and stuff all of these disparate elements into one box with the label 'Melbourne-style bar'. Nonetheless, it is possible to classify Melbourne's bars as a particular and unique genre of watering hole. That there is a unifying style was perhaps made clearest when the bar wave began to spread beyond the basements, laneways and upper floors of the CBD and into the surrounding suburbs, colonising St Kilda and Fitzroy, Prahran and Richmond, Brunswick and Hawthorn, squeezing into former shoe shops, pizza joints, convents, churches, hippie health-food stores, European delis, factories, office buildings and furniture stores. What are the similarities between Northcote's Joe's Shoe Store, with its fencing paraphernalia and backyard *bocce* court, and the smooth concrete and plywood good looks and seriously good alcohol list at Fitzroy's

{*Opposite*} Rue Bebelon

{*Above*} Steve Miller from Handsome Steve's House of Refreshment

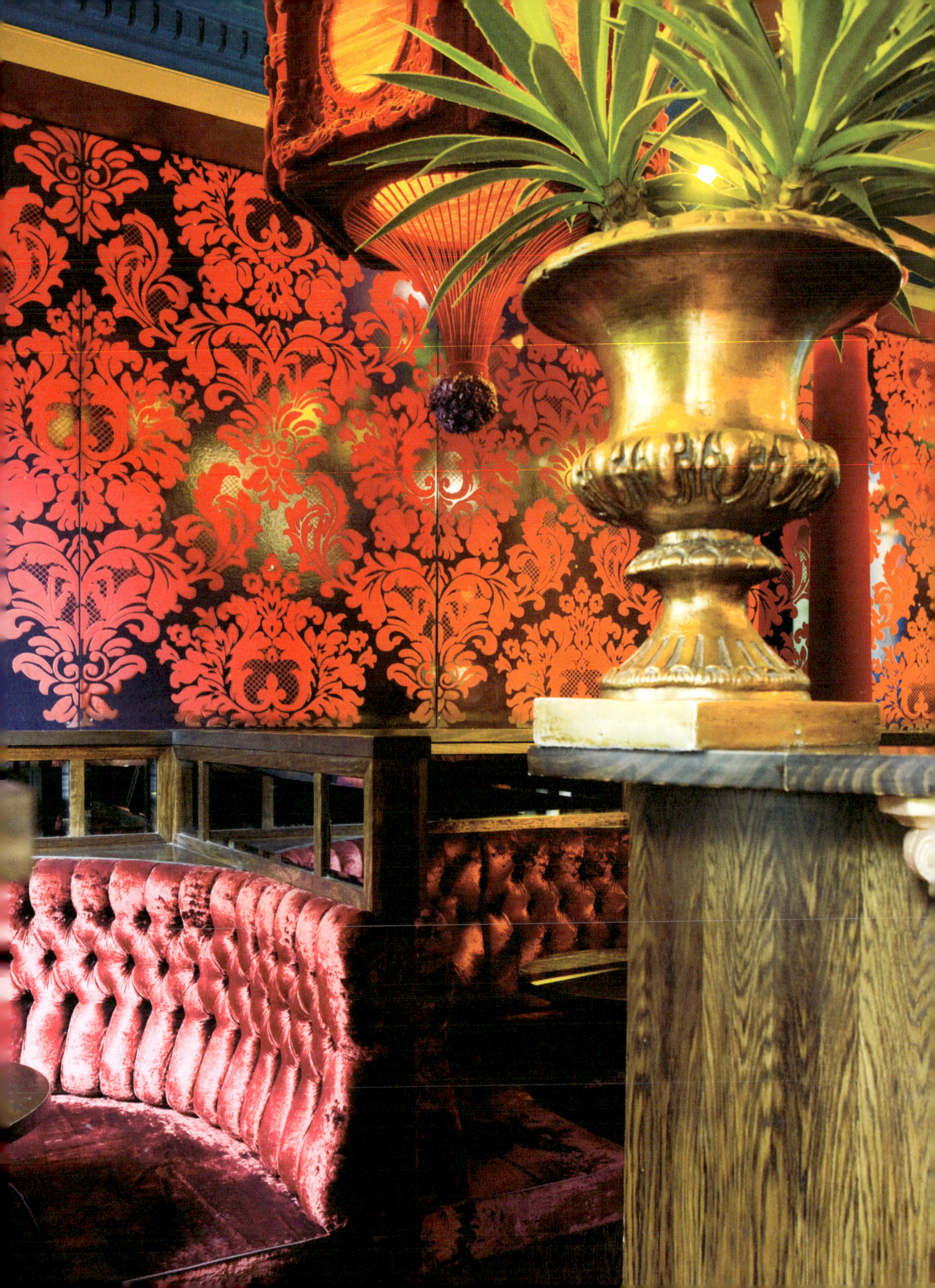

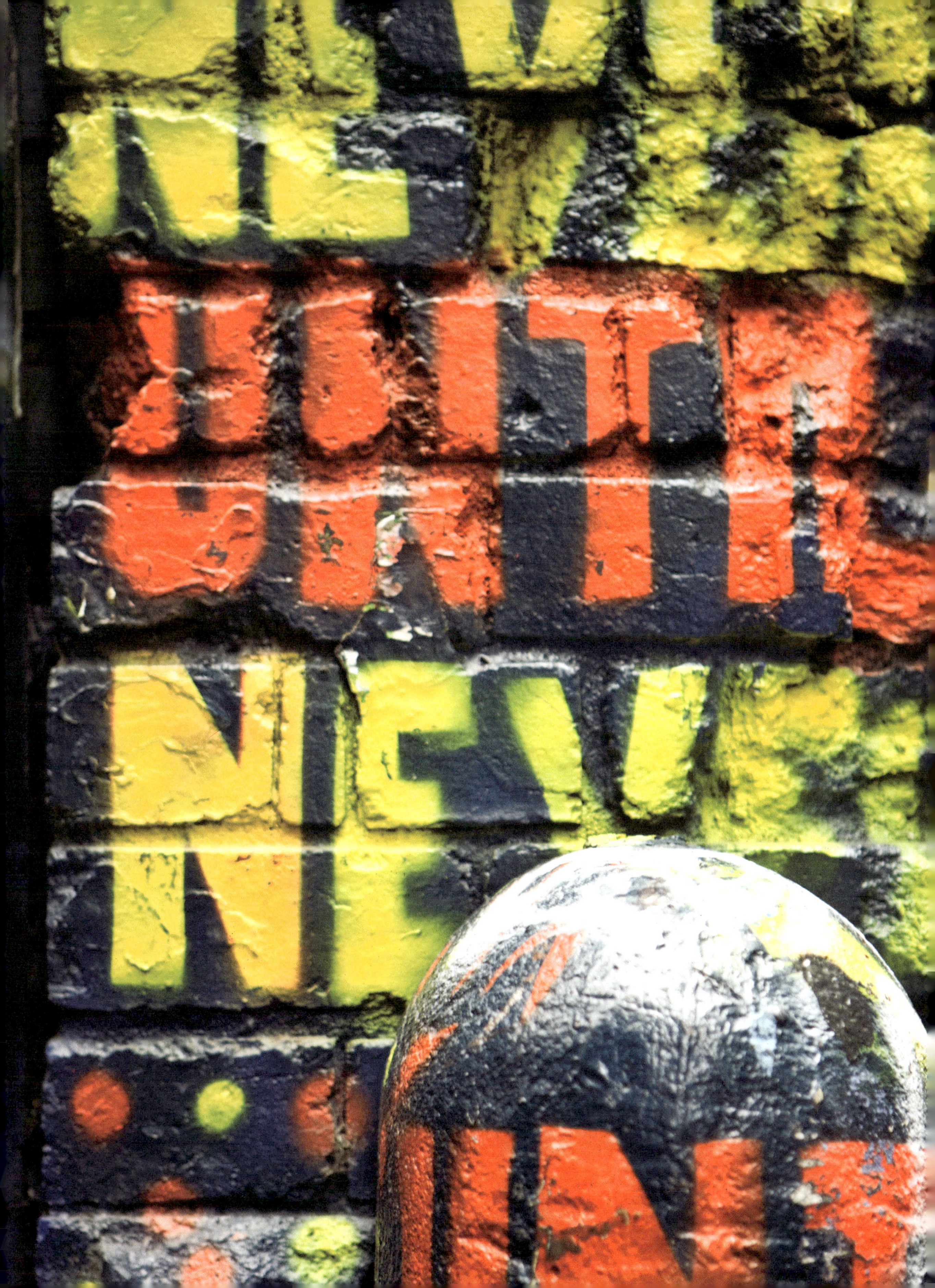

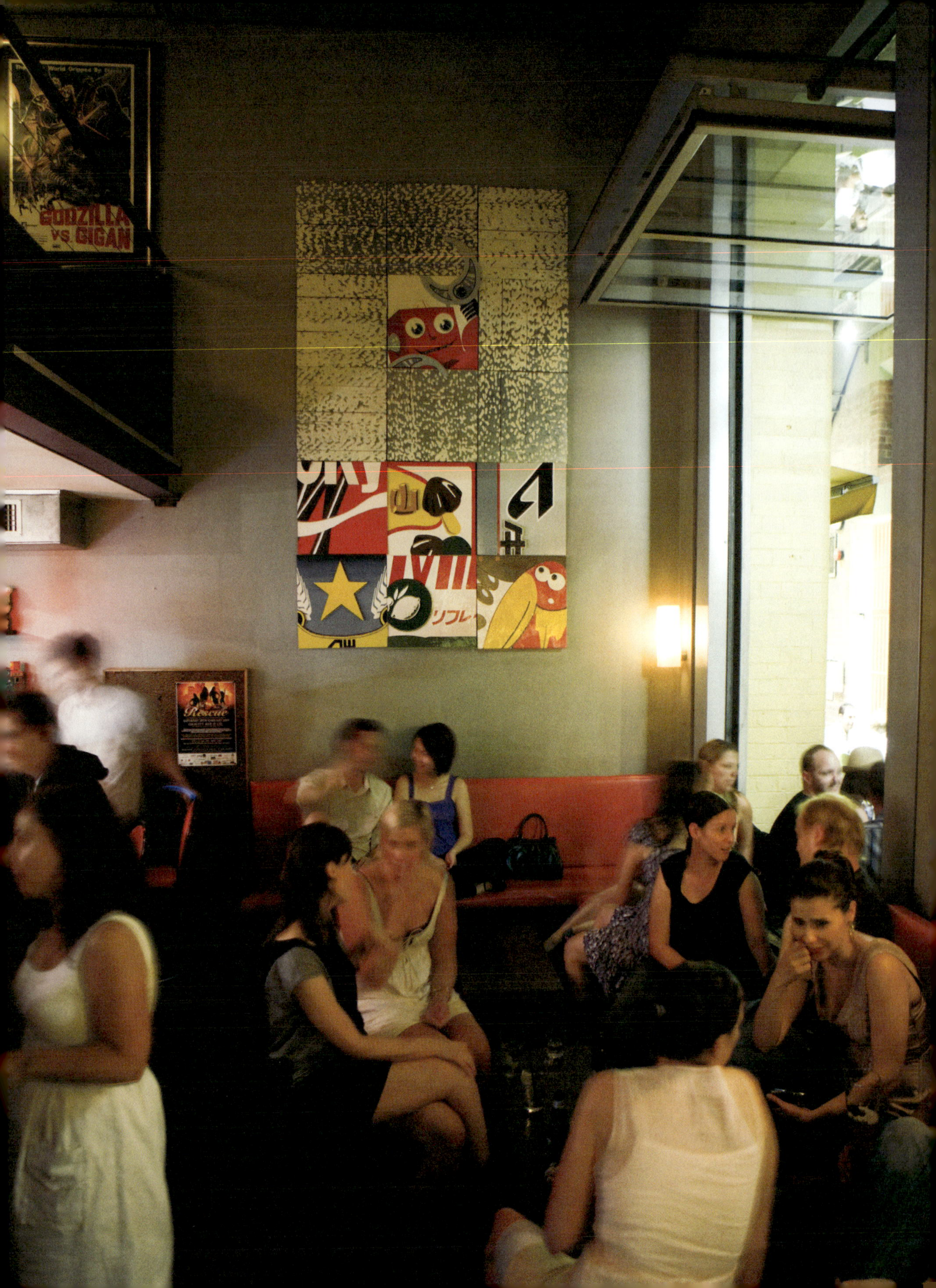
GODZILLA
VS GIGAN

Gertrude Street Enoteca? Or the retro-espresso-bar look of Handsome Steve's House of Refreshment on the first floor of the Abbotsford Convent and the moody gloom and serious cocktail expertise at Richmond's shopfront bar Der Raum? The shared elements might sometimes prove difficult to pin down but they are there, and together they define the Melbourne-style bar.

The obvious similarities run to a propensity for retro in any of its forms, a predilection for obscure spaces and an attitude that always favours substance over style. But what really pulls them together is the presence of imagination and innovation, aided and abetted by licensing laws that allowed them plenty of room to move. Ingenuity has always been present in Melbourne's hospitality scene, but until the changes to the liquor laws in 1987 and the subsequent amendments during the 1990s it had been functioning with one foot nailed to the floor. Melbourne's incredible and much-coveted bar scene has been defined by the city that nurtures it, but it flourished because the law allowed it to.

The relative freedom and versatility of the state's licensing system will continue to mark it off as one of the more enlightened places. For reformers of yesterday's system, it is a dream come true.

JOHN NIEUWENHUYSEN, 2000

Freedom of Choice

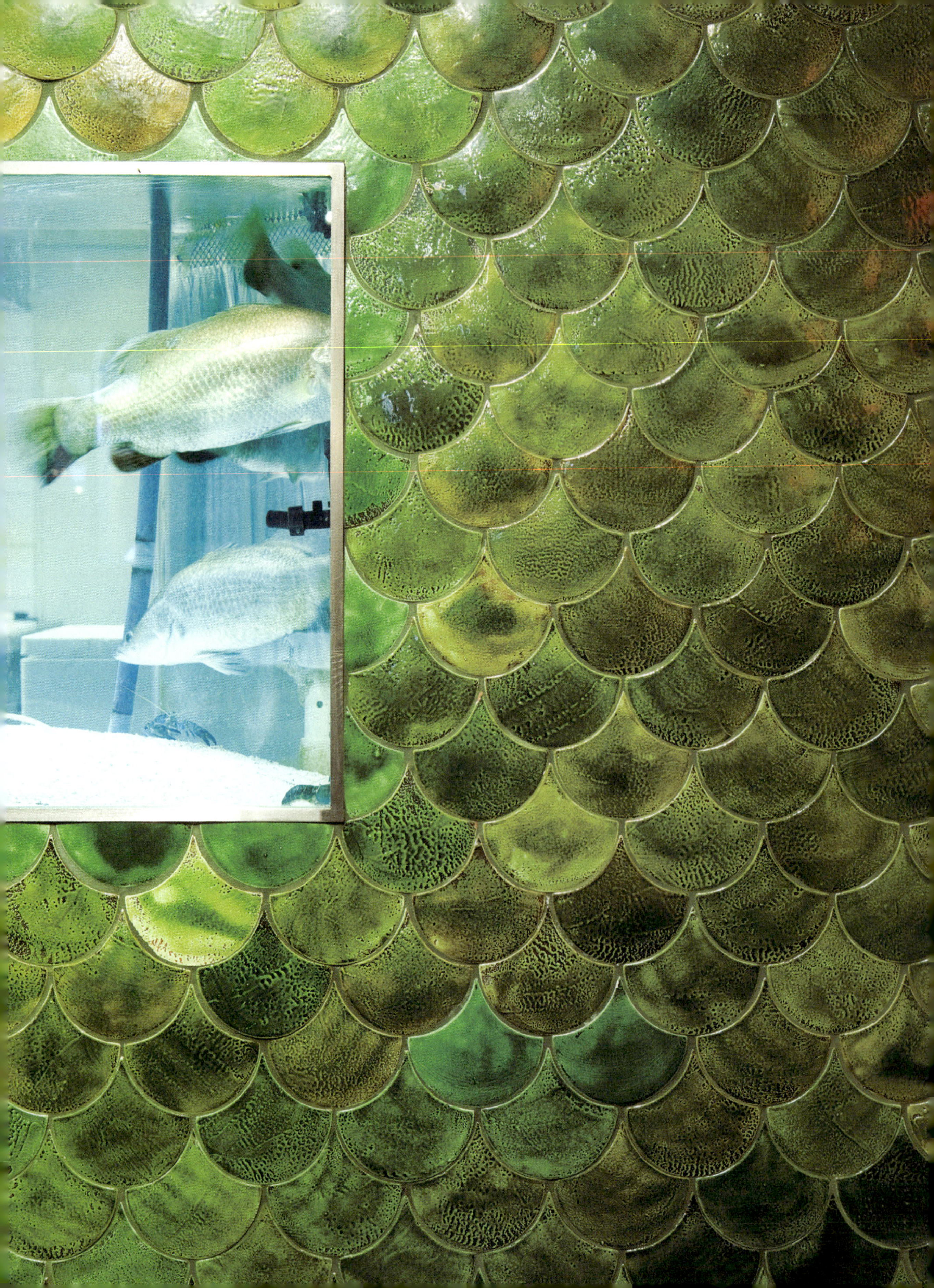

*A*lthough Victoria's food and wine scene had many signs of great potential before the changes to the state's liquor licensing laws, it would have been a far less innovative and vibrant culture had the government fudged the overhaul in the 1980s. It may not be drawing too long a bow to also suggest that Victoria generally – and Melbourne specifically – would have been less cohesive and interesting had John Nieuwenhuysen not cleared the slate and given human behaviour the benefit of the doubt. At first glance it may appear a little far fetched to imagine you could significantly alter the way a population conducts itself simply by changing the way that alcohol is made available, but if you consider the remarkable differences in Victoria's hospitality scene since its laws were changed from the most restrictive in Australia to the most liberal, the idea of a cultural shift becomes less fanciful.

By looking at the changes that followed the Nieuwenhuysen Review purely in numerical terms, the magnitude of the overhaul and its effect on society is glaringly obvious. In 1986, there were 571 businesses in Victoria with a Restaurant Licence, but by 2004 some 5136 places were operating under the post-Nieuwenhuysen equivalent, the On-Premises Licence. The increase in the number of outlets able to sell liquor in the state is even more startling, leaping from 3200 before the 1987 Act to more than 17,000 outlets twenty years later.

The growth in the availability of alcohol has been ground shifting and the figures suggest, if nothing else, that Victorians like a drink close at hand. While that may be true, if the figures are digested without any context it is easy to understand how they could be – and have been – used to suggest that there has been too much of a good thing and that the leash has been allowed to get too long. These sorts of arguments have always tended to surface whenever there is an outbreak of alcohol-fuelled violence and there is suddenly a perceived need for the government of the day to be seen to be doing something about it.

Put those same numbers in context, however, and a quite different picture emerges. When the Nieuwenhuysen Review was released, one of the most oft-repeated responses to assure those who feared the worst from a deregulated

{*Opposite*} Tiles and fishtank at Longrain

> **Prohibition in any of its forms has had little effect on the amount people drink**

industry was that there was no correlation between the consumption and the availability of alcohol. The conclusions were reached not just by looking at drinking patterns in Victoria, but by observing the results of similar experiences of loosening licensing laws in other states of Australia and overseas. The Nieuwenhuysen Review included case studies of South Australia, Canberra and Scotland, and the general conclusion from these experiments in liberalisation was that the only way the law would be able to restrict the consumption of alcohol in any effective manner would be to make restrictions so severe and heavy-handed that, according to the Scottish experience, 'No elected government could contemplate the proposition.'[1]

Simply put, prohibition in any of its forms has had little effect on the amount people drink. The case studies seemed to say that tackling the problem of alcohol abuse by restricting availability was like tackling the road toll by limiting the number of car dealerships and petrol stations. When it comes to alcohol abuse, the problem seems more rooted in human behaviour and cultural norms than in the number of bars and bottle shops on city streets.

Certainly, looking at alcohol consumption in Victoria since the 1987 Act came into force, it seems that the much-reiterated line about consumption having little to do with availability has proved to be the case. The most recent surveys show that per-capita alcohol consumption in Australia has remained relatively stable for more than a decade, with Australians placed about fourteenth in the world on the scale of alcohol consumption, a drop of seven places since the 1960s. In comparisons between Australian states and territories, Victoria consistently features as having the lowest per-capita consumption in the country, with the Northern Territory usually coming in at number one. That comparison is reached despite the almost five-fold increase in the number of liquor outlets in Victoria during the past twenty years. While the type of alcohol Australians are drinking has undergone a seismic shift – wine and spirits up, full-strength beer down – the amount being consumed still remains well under the levels of the 1960s, when more restrictive laws, including 6 pm closing, were supposedly keeping the population on the straight and narrow.

This is not to ignore the fact that alcohol is a dangerous drug and one that warrants close attention on the part of the authorities. With recent alcohol figures – the same ones showing a stable per-capita level of consumption – pointing to an increase in the number of people drinking at risky levels, there is an obvious need to keep addressing the problem. But as history has proved over and over again, whether you are talking Prohibition-era United States or home-grown restrictive policies, slamming closed the door of the pub or bar achieves little more than moving the problem elsewhere.

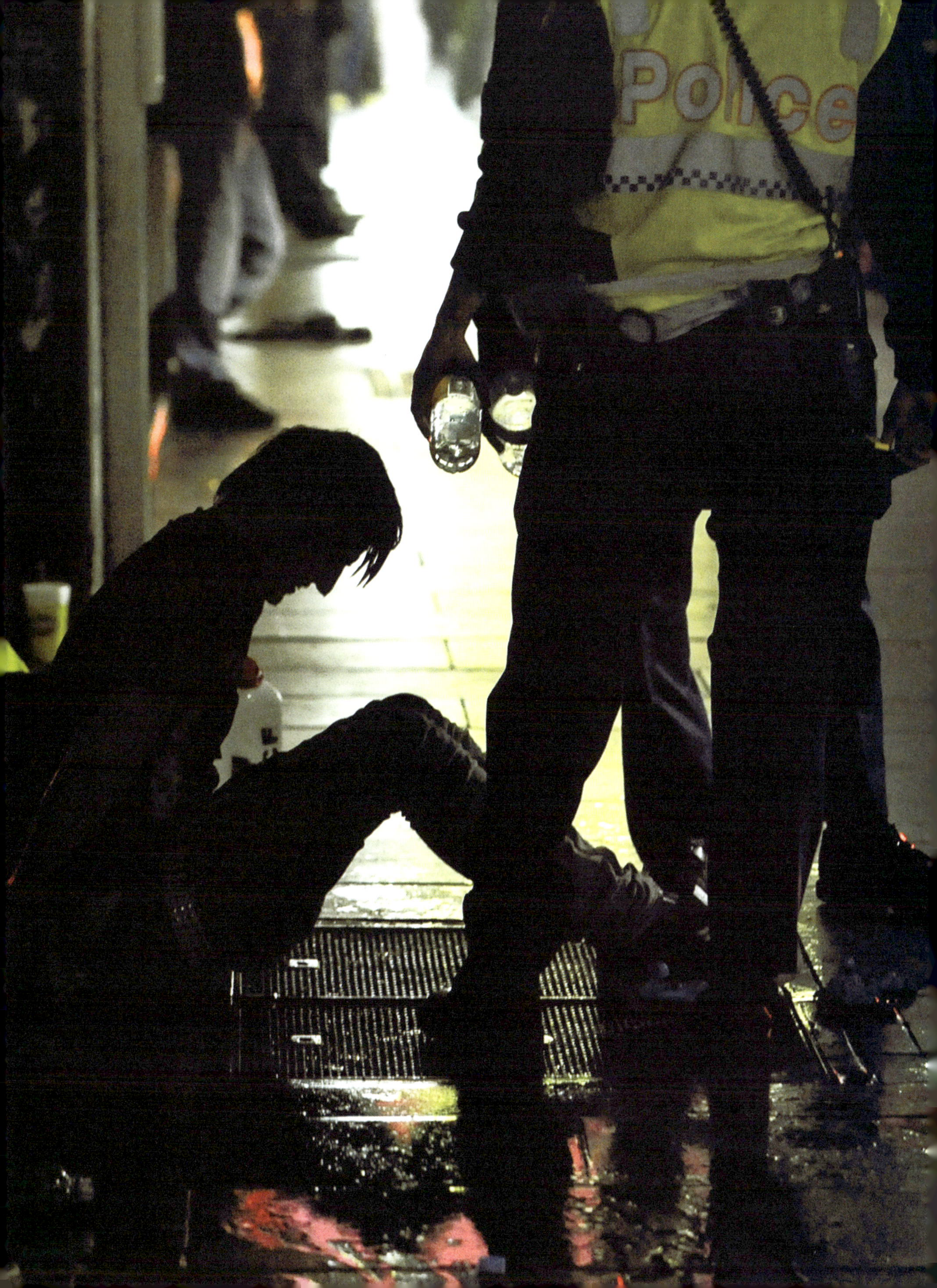
Police

> The freedom to choose to drink alcohol or not, to eat late or early in an almost endless variety of venues has become a vital part of the city's attraction

This was the point that the Nieuwenhuysen Review was pushing, especially in the nearly seventy pages devoted to spelling out the extent and effects of alcohol abuse on society and the ways of addressing the problem, apart from the proven failure of limiting availability. By allowing a greater variety of venues to serve alcohol, particularly smaller more intimate places where the emphasis on food was equal to that of booze, the review sought to substitute the monoculture of heading to the pub to get a skinful with a civil culture of consumption born out of myriad options. It created the conditions under which a different approach to drinking was not only allowed but encouraged. And while the problems of binge and under-age drinking continue to surface with wearying regularity, the rise of a culture of civilised drinking and eating in Victoria has perhaps thrown alcohol abuse into greater relief. Against a backdrop of a population that has come to enjoy imbibing in a flexible and relatively harmless fashion, the excesses become more grotesque and the solutions perhaps less black and white.

According to Erik Hopkinson, who in his public and private roles in the liquor and hospitality industries has witnessed more than his fair share of responses to liquor control, there are signs that approaches other than restricting availability to the entire population are starting to be heard and considered:

> Alcohol is a social problem but some still portray it just as a legislative liquor-licensing problem. It has been interesting to me that governments and other related authorities have promoted very strongly the responsible serving of alcohol, but there hasn't been a similar emphasis on the responsible consumption of alcohol. That's where the tide is starting to turn and there is more attention being paid to responsible consumption ... John Nieuwenhuysen has made the point that with even the ultimate regulation – prohibition – there still was abuse, so obviously the responsible serving of alcohol has a role to play. But as part of a tapestry of initiatives rather than the only one.[2]

The continuing incidence of alcohol abuse and related violence in Victoria, particularly coming from large pubs and nightclubs echoing the notorious beer barns of the 1970s, which helped create the impetus for changing the law in the first place, can make it seem that nothing much has changed. But it is easy to lose sight of just how much the sophisticated, relaxed and convivial air that Victoria projects comes from the remarkable eating and drinking culture that has grown up in the wake of the Nieuwenhuysen reforms.

Eating and drinking in the public sphere is one of the things that has become integral to the Melbourne identity. Dining publicly is a social activity – be it in a cavernous pizza joint in the suburbs, a tiny laneway cafe in the city or a high-end restaurant with water views – that helps make the city feel both welcoming and workable. The freedom to choose to drink alcohol or not, to eat late or early in an almost endless variety of venues has become a vital part of the city's attraction and, in lieu of postcard views or predictably agreeable weather, has become one of its major selling points. Flexibility and quality have become so tightly woven into the city's fabric that perhaps people have ceased to notice them and have forgotten how different the city was before the changes. The fact that the laws have been in place for more than twenty years also means that there is a generation of eaters and drinkers oblivious to any other way of life, something that John Nieuwenhuysen was confronted with when he went to have a meal in one of the city's famed laneway Italian bistros, Becco:

> I walked in the door of Becco and one of the owners came up to me and propelled me across the floor to where there was a line of waiters. He presented me to them and said: 'This is someone you should know about. If this man hadn't written his report then none of you guys would have a job here.' He explained to them what had happened, the changes to the law and so on, and one of the youngsters came up to me and asked if it had been different previously. For him – he was about eighteen – it had always been like this; he was born about the time the report was being written and so what would he know about liquor licensing reform? It had taken less than a generation.[3]

Although the spectre of complacency looms over this situation – particularly when the prospect of tightening restrictions never seems to leave the table – it is worth not only looking back to see how far we've travelled but to reflect on just how much the reform of the liquor laws has permeated and added to the lives of people living in Victoria.

John Chalker believes that Victoria has become a much better place because of the laws:

> Changing the laws brought in so many things that wouldn't have appeared otherwise. Without them we wouldn't have had the kind of wine development we have, the international varieties of grape would probably not have been grown here and we wouldn't have ever had places like the Lake House. In fact, without the changes women wouldn't have been able to come to the fore because the old system, particularly the hotels, was so blokey. It just wouldn't have been possible ... I think that Victoria has developed into a far better society now than it was thirty years ago. People are more thoughtful,

considerate, accepting, giving and intelligent and I know I am generalising terribly, but I think this change has come from the change in the laws. One of the great joys of living is the combination of food and booze and what it does for you – it is social, it lets you relax, lets you enjoy life and have a different understanding of life. When eating and drinking in a relaxed way has become such a part of life, why wouldn't it make Melbourne a better place?[4]

The eating and drinking culture that Melburnians and many regional Victorians enjoy is one that is very much in tune with the culture and the climate of the state. It is about finding places to drink espresso and red wine out of the cold in winter, or to shelter with a cold beer or Campari in some shadowy bar when the full blast of summer hits. It is a place where art and music have found fertile ground alongside Old World wine lists, and alongside bar snacks that take their culinary cues from across the globe. It is a culture where many of the old, clearly delineated lines of what role a pub, a restaurant, a cafe, a bar or a bottle shop plays have been increasingly blurred, extended and reinvented.

It is interesting to note that some of the best outcomes of the reforms have occurred in the state's pubs. Despite the Australian Hotels Association's (AHA) initial fervent opposition to a change in the status quo, it now sees that the changes were largely positive for hotels. In a 2006 interview with the *Age*, AHA Victorian CEO Brian Kearney said that while 'the Australian Hotels Association understandably opposed many of the original proposals in the 1980s ... by the mid-1990s pubs and hotels were taking advantage of the less-regulated environment and significantly re-making themselves to exploit emerging market opportunities'.[5]

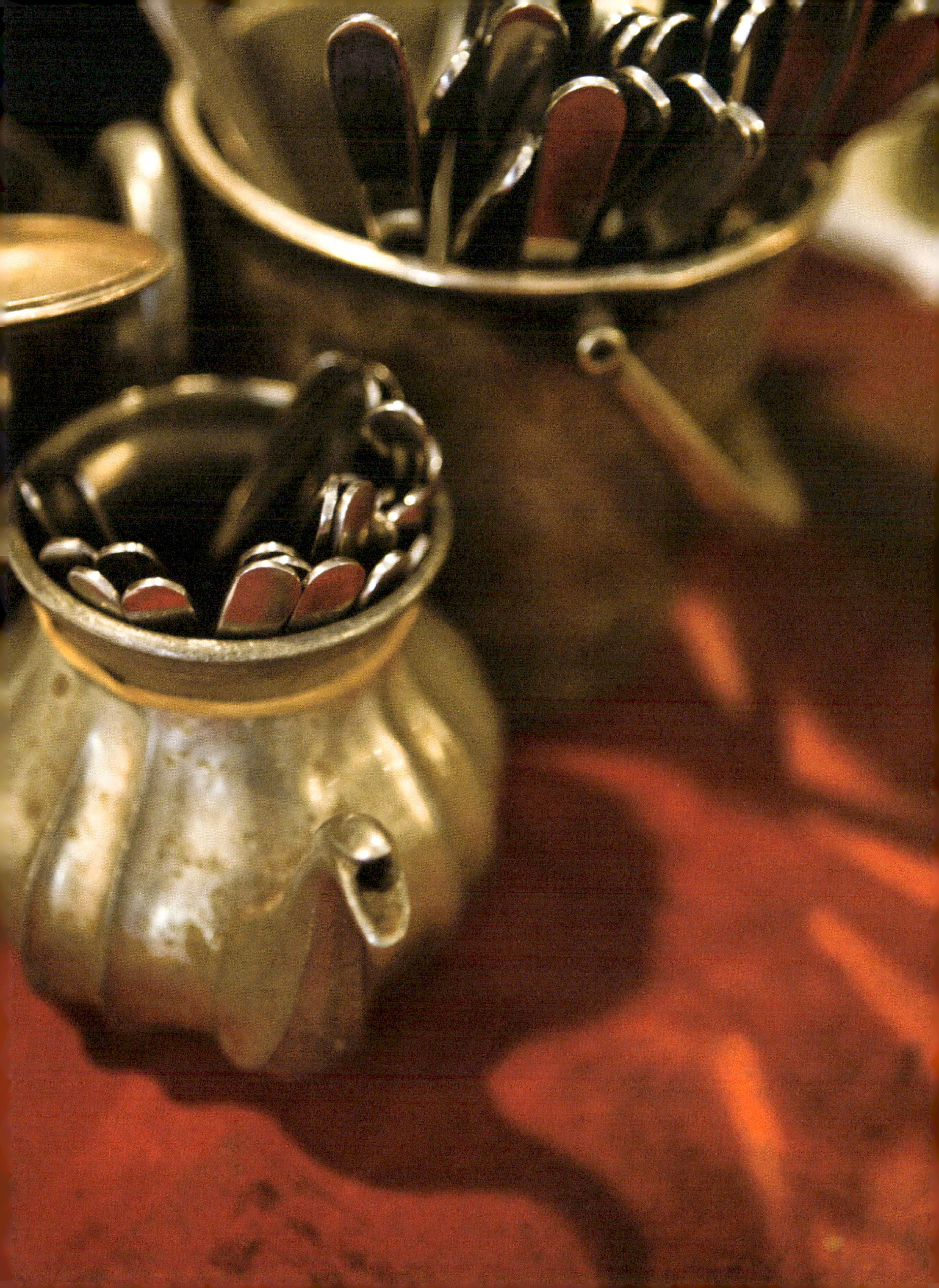

Eating Out of Town

Victoria's most highly rated regional restaurants now are found not in bigger provincial cities, but in smaller country towns, which attract food and wine lovers from Melbourne and even overseas, as well as from their own districts.

It was a little different twenty or thirty years ago, when the Copper Pot in Bendigo, La Scala in Ballarat and the Source in Geelong were the regional stars. Now the gastronomic hot spots are Daylesford and Kyneton in the central highlands, Bright and Myrtleford in the north-east alpine valleys and Mildura in the north-west. There's also good eating closer Melbourne, in the Yarra Valley and on the Mornington Peninsula, and at such destinations as Beechworth, Port Fairy, Mooroopna and Noojee, among others.

Perhaps the most heartening development is the growing awareness of 'regionality' and seasonality – an emphasis on sourcing local seasonal produce, and matching menus with a selection of the wines of the region. It is no coincidence that some of the top country restaurants are active promoters of this movement, encouraging local specialty producers and proudly naming them on their menus.

Alla Wolf-Tasker's Lake House, the internationally acclaimed restaurant and spa resort beautifully sited on Lake Daylesford, is an outstanding exponent of such regionally focused, produce-driven culinary creativity. In Bright, Patrizia Simone of Simone's Restaurant applies traditional and innovative Italian recipes to the bountiful produce of the Ovens Valley, from chestnuts and walnuts in autumn to locally bred pigeon, rabbit, goat and trout. Likewise, in Mildura, celebrity chef and author Stefano de Pieri, of Stefano's, draws on the likes of Murray cod, Mallee saltbush lamb, wild asparagus and local olive oil to give a regional flavour to his Italian-style degustation banquets.

Like eco-tourism, gastro-tourism is being strongly promoted by Tourism Victoria and regional tourist authorities, aided by the plethora of winery restaurants, cellar-door tasting rooms and outstanding good-food pubs, such as the Healesville Hotel, Daylesford's Farmers Arms Hotel and Kyneton's Royal George. Without Victoria's liberalised liquor laws, which have brought chic cafes and wine bars to country centres, they would have a much harder task, visitors would have less to attract them and country residents would be the poorer. CLAUDE FORELL

{*Opposite*} Inside the Royal George, Kyneton

Out of Town

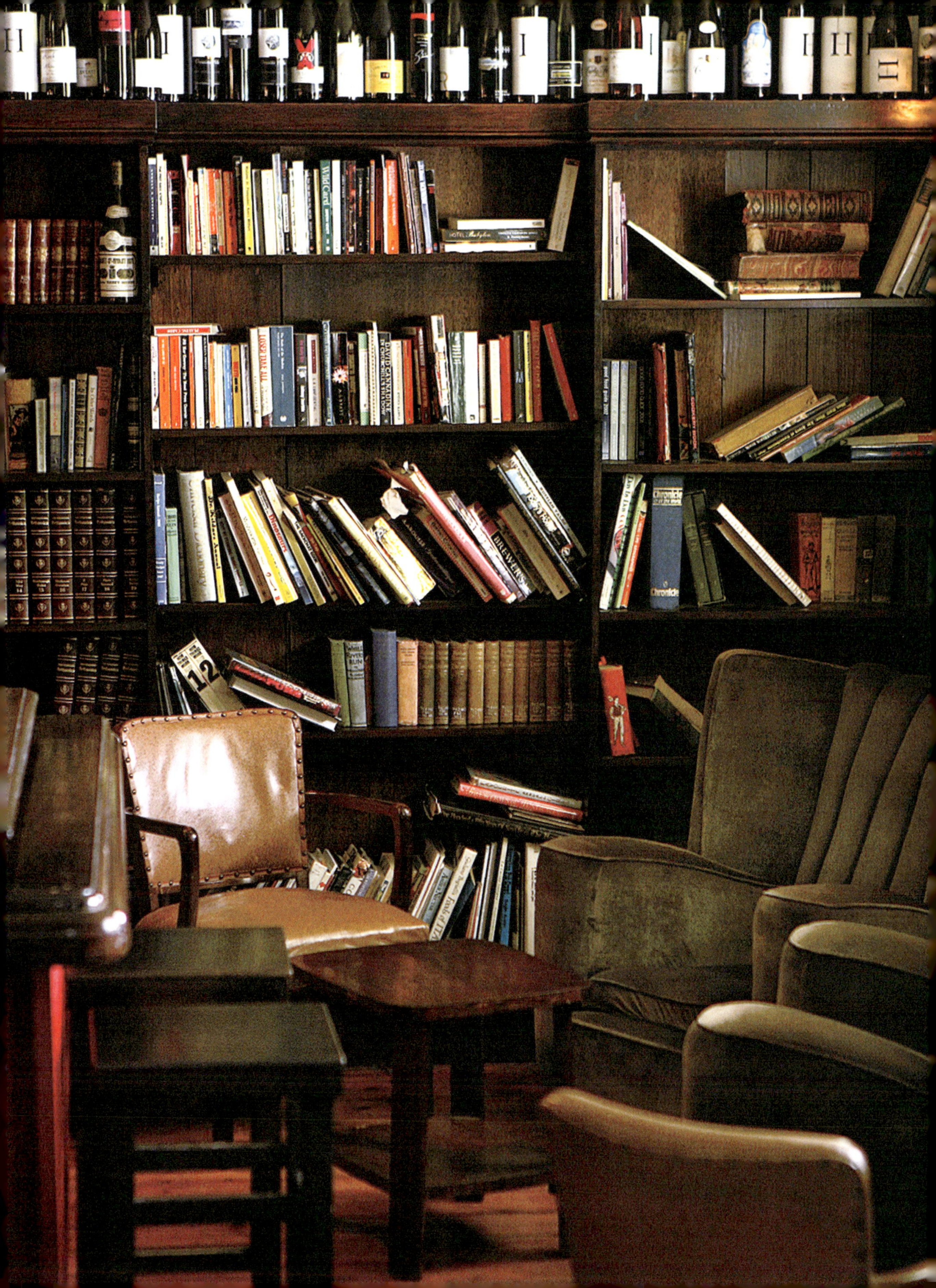

TAXI
DINING_ROOM
PUBLIC_BAR
LOUNGE_GARDEN
PUBLIC_BAR
TAXI
DINING_ROOM

Observing Victorian pubs today, it is obvious how innovative and flexible they have become since being freed from the old obligations of having to open certain hours, provide accommodation and food and sell a certain quantity of beer. This is not to say that tradition has been completely disregarded. For every sleek, expensive, designer made-over hotel with accolade-attracting food, an extensive benchmark-filled bottle shop and crack service, there is a traditional corner or backstreet pub filled with sporting memorabilia, violently patterned carpet, cheap meals, trivia nights, footy on the telly and a collection of crusty old locals propping up the bar. The freedom of choice for pub goers and owners alike is one of the great pluses of the Victorian hospitality scene.

Melbourne's newest, purpose-built hotel, the zinc- and glass-clad Transport in Federation Square, is perhaps the most obvious example of how the liquor laws have transformed pub culture. It is the sort of venue that would have given the commissioners of the old Liquor Control Commission indigestion and sleepless nights with its lack of any singular purpose: a ground-floor public bar, complete with outside drinking areas, a winter garden, a kitchen and a phenomenal list of beers, many from the boutique breweries liberally sprinkled across Victoria; a renowned second-level restaurant with impressive views and a Japanese–European menu; and a top-level late-night supper club specialising in complicated cocktails, champagne, excellent scotch, DJs and live entertainment.

{*Opposite*} Taxi and Transport at Federation Square

A 'Grand Tour' for Our Times

We go to wineries for many reasons. Sometimes the food is the attraction, or perhaps the promise of bucolic invigoration or the smart art gallery. It could be the pleasure of breathing in history and taking a great lungful of vinous air – the spicy scent of oak, the dusty aroma of earthen floors. Or maybe it's tale of the modern winemaking story from grape to glass, told through interactive computer screens, eco-trails or the chance to get your hands dirty at vintage that is seductive. And sometimes we even go to wineries for the wine. What is certain is that today we want the whole winery 'experience'.

{*Above, from left*} The cellar door at Chateau Tahbilk, north of Seymour; vista and restaurant at TarraWarra Estate in the Yarra Valley

Winery Experien

Victoria is one of the smallest wine states, with the greatest number of wineries – 687. Here, winery tourism is booming, with 75.5 per cent of wineries hosting cellar doors. Food, art and a growing interest in eco-tourism fuel the growth. On the third Sunday of each month, Yering Station in the Yarra Valley parades local food producers at the Yarra Valley Regional Farmers' Market. Also in the valley, De Bortoli has recently added a cheese factory as an adjunct to its restaurant – as has historic All Saints Estate at Rutherglen.

One of the largest private collections of modern Australian art is owned by the Besen family, and now resides in the multimillion-dollar art museum at TarraWarra Estate. Meanwhile the performing arts are played out against the dramatic backdrop of Port Phillip Bay at Scotchmans Hill, on the Bellarine Peninsula.

Wetland tours are a significant drawcard for one of the state's oldest wineries, Tahbilk, as well as one of the Mornington Peninsula's newest, Montalto.

For those seeking the ultimate wine experience – the chance to participate in making wine – you can't beat the winemaking weekends offered during vintage by Denis and Kerry Craig at Ainsworth Estate, in the Yarra Valley. 'Pinotphiles', a passionate and crazy bunch, can get their grapes off in a year-round winemaking course. The Heartbreak Grape is offered by wine man Peter Mitchell in conjunction with Tuck's Ridge on the Mornington Peninsula.

The concept of winery tourism is still new, only emerging in the late 1970s. It brought people to wine regions and has kept them there with innovative marketing ruses, such as wine festivals (the oldest of which, Rutherglen Winery Walkabout, started in 1974) and attractive cellar doors, offering food and wine.

Domaine Chandon, the multimillion-dollar Yarra Valley winery established by Champagne's Moët et Chandon in 1985, helped pioneer the cellar door we know today. In 1991, it opened its cellar door, but instead of offering free tastings, chief executive Dr Tony Jordan decided on a different approach. Wine lovers could buy a glass of Domaine Chandon sparkling wine. Revolutionary! The wine would be served at tables and consumers would be given a complimentary platter of cheese and crackers. This was unheard-of.

Many in the industry thought Jordan's approach would fail, but far from it. The seed was planted and soon others joined in. Today, around four million visitors pass through Victorian cellar doors, spending almost $290 million on wine. The total economic value of winery tourism to the state's coffers is estimated at almost $586 million. Not bad for one of Australia's smallest wine states. JENI PORT

> Melburnians don't have to suffer a place that has served them bad coffee, sub-standard food, overpriced wine or snarky attitude

In regional Victoria, too, new operators have redefined the notion of the country pub. Instead of the gloomy old places buzzing with fluorescent lights and wafting with the whiff of the deep fryer, there is a new breed of country hotel specialising in regional wine and food. They are becoming destinations in themselves on the strength of their critically acclaimed dining rooms and spruced up accommodation. These places seem light years from a relatively recent past, where many country hotels only grudgingly supplied the obligatory food and accommodation in return for the right to serve huge quantities of mass-produced beer.

Victoria's wineries, too, have embraced the flexibility of the new laws. The Yarra Valley's historic Yering Station was one of the first to understand the true potential of the post-reform freedoms when new owners, the Rathbones, bought the property in 1996. Alongside the expected vineyards, winery and cellar door, Yering Station has a produce store specialising in locally produced food, a wine bar, a cafe, an art gallery and a farmers' market. Montalto, which opened to the public in 2002 on the Mornington Peninsula, is a business with its own vineyard but with wine made at another winery. Under the old licensing regime it would never have been allowed to sell its own wine. Not only does it have a cellar door, it also has an olive grove, a restaurant, a cafe, private picnic areas and an annual sculpture competition. Elsewhere in the state there are wineries with galleries and cheese shops, produce stores and kitchen gardens, cooking classes, wood-fired pizzerias, major music events and mushroom foraging.

This is where the real strengths of Victoria's food scene lie – in the breadth, quality and flexibility of what it offers from the high to the low end, from cafes to bars and restaurants to hotels, wineries to bottle shops. Though Melbourne may not boast the same number of five-star restaurants as other states – or even that it used to – this is more a reflection of how the local scene has embraced responsiveness and dexterity rather than a lack of quality or seriousness on the part of Melbourne's restaurateurs.

One of the results of relaxing the state's licensing laws has been that going out to eat has become a commonplace activity and, in making eating out a part of everyday life rather than something reserved for a special occasion, the default setting for many eateries is relaxed and casual rather than flash and dazzle.

Some commentators believe this has not necessarily worked in the favour of Melbourne's restaurant scene. Commenting on the legacy of the Nieuwenhuysen reforms in the *Age* in 2006, food writer and critic John Lethlean commented on how the explosion in the number of On-Premises Licences had led to an extraordinarily competitive market dominated by a mindset more about survival than creativity:

> Freedom to enter the restaurant industry has brought Australia some of its great chefs and restaurants – people such as Stephanie Alexander, for whom

the barriers to entry were not so high she gave up at the first hurdle. However, I believe the free-for-all with liquor licences has produced an almighty surfeit of places that call themselves restaurants and few are motivated by culinary ambition. Standards of food and wine have come down as every operator aims for the same, safe dollar. I think the freedom to gain a licence and open a restaurant here, over the past 10 years particularly, has forced a bistro mentality on Melbourne the likes of which we haven't seen before. There is a dismal, blanket sameness about so much that is on offer.[6]

While there may be too many businesses treading the same ground, the increased number of choices generally has seen a corresponding growth in the expectations and education of diners. When a population views eating out regularly and well as an important part of city life, it tends to become more discerning. With so many alternatives available, Melburnians don't have to suffer a place that has served them bad coffee, sub-standard food, overpriced wine or snarky attitude. A certain standard is expected and those that don't meet it soon pay the price.

There are many fine, modest bistros in Melbourne that serve as the foundation of its 'food city' credentials – just as other great food cities around the world have their renowned restaurants resting on a bed of good-quality, low-key bistros – but the local industry also continues to produce innovative, artistic players who continue to push boundaries, challenge traditional definitions and are constantly on the lookout for new ways of doing things. People such as Andrew McConnell, Geoff Lindsay, Guy Grossi, Rita Macali, Ben Shewry, George Calombaris, Greg Malouf, Shannon Bennett, Cath Claringbold, Joseph Abboud, Paul Wilson, Frank Camorra, Teage Ezard and Karen Martini have kept the drive for Melbourne's signature style changing and evolving. They challenge complacency by always searching for new and interesting venues in which to nourish their patrons in new and interesting ways. They are aware of and acknowledge Melbourne's food history without being in its thrall. They are the ones who have fully realised and explored the freedoms and potentials of the Nieuwenhuysen reforms and the several versions of the Liquor Control Act that followed.

Even at the top end of Melbourne's dining scene there are plenty of signs of this constant desire to explore new ways for the locals to eat and drink. There are traditional grand fine diners like Flower Drum and Grossi Florentino that reinvent themselves every day, with superb produce and consistently brilliant cooking. But then places like Vue de Monde and Jacques Reymond put a Melbourne spin on the fine-dining concept, doing away with traditionally structured meals, experimenting with ingredients and operating from dining rooms that, in typical Melbourne style, celebrate the history of their buildings while overlaying it with thoroughly modern style.

{*Above*} Guy Grossi

{*Following pages*} Frank Camorra's Movida

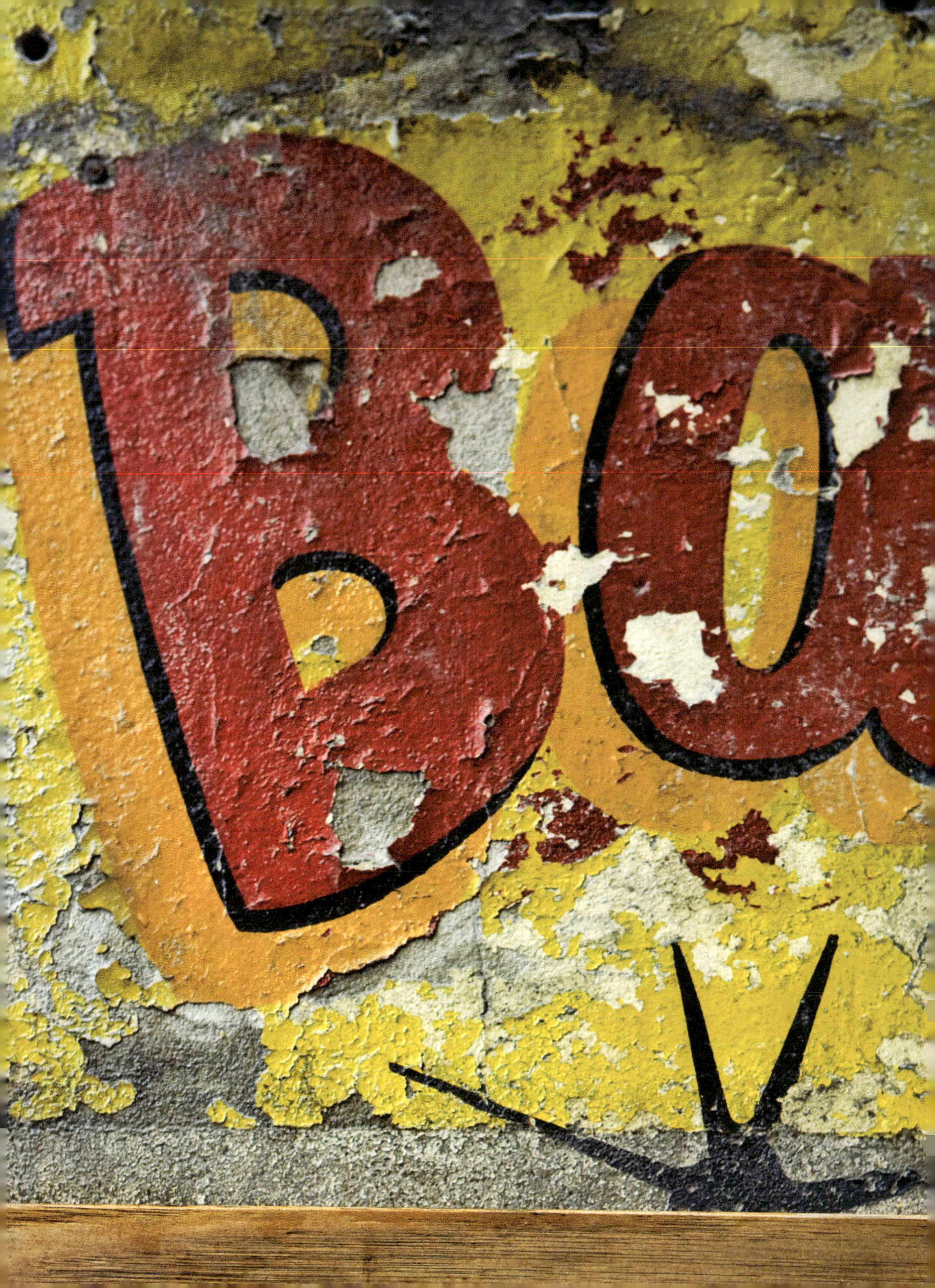

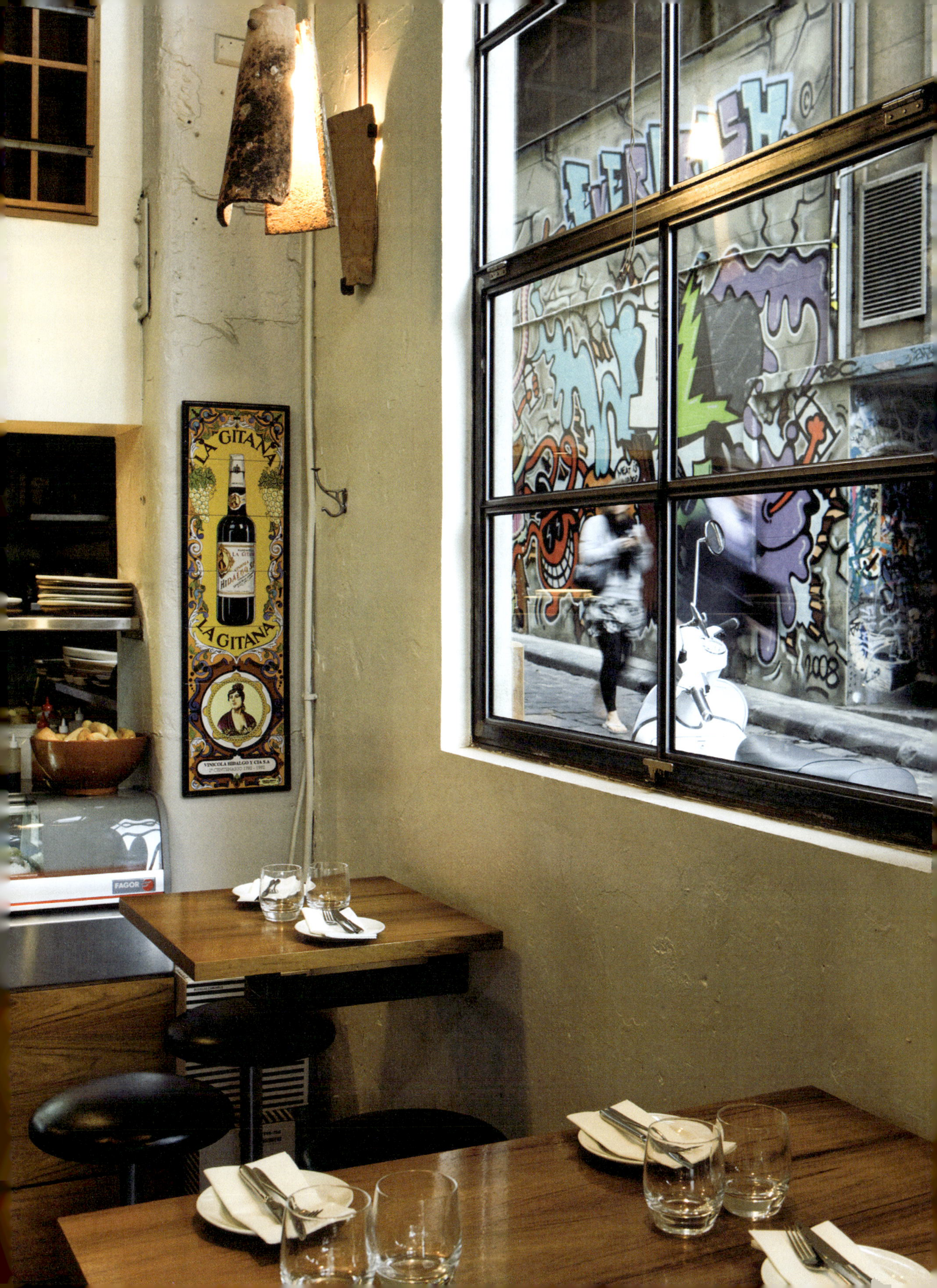
LA GITANA
LA GITANA
VINICOLA HIDALGO Y CIA S.A
FAGOR

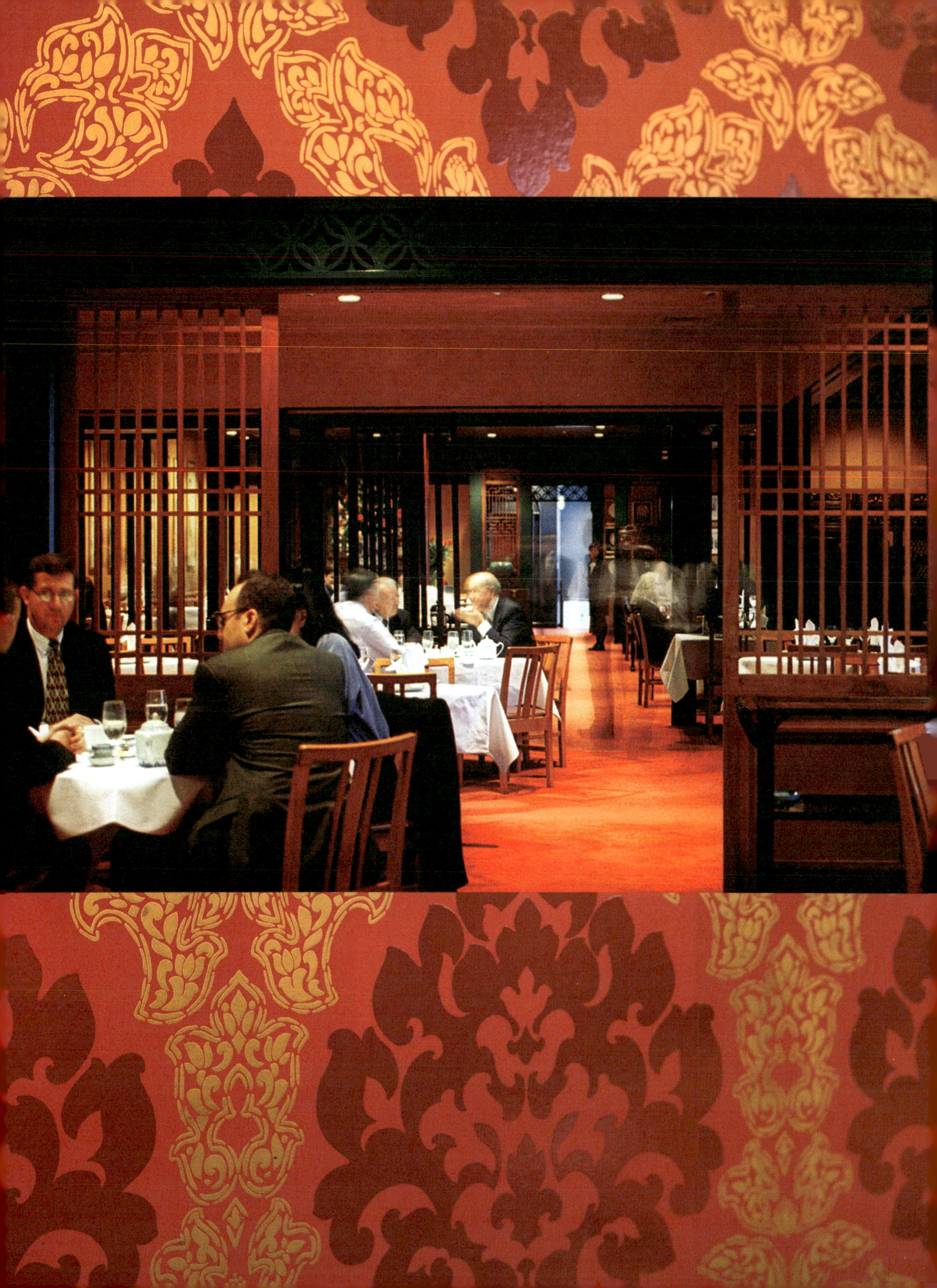

Perhaps the best place to look for quintessential Melbourne-style dining is among those places that increasingly blur the lines between all the existing models of eating and drinking venues to create an entirely new contender. These are places that are taking the entrepreneurial spirit that pervaded the city in the wake of the Nieuwenhuysen Review to another level and another generation. They are run by people who have experienced more than a decade of Melbourne's bar culture and have begun to blend the sensibilities and aesthetics of the small quirky bar with the solid traditions of skilled, authentic cooking that would more usually be associated with a restaurant: places like the Gertrude Street Enoteca, which operates as a bottle shop, a bar and a cafe, but could not be comfortably fitted into any of those boxes alone; or Bar Lourinha, which takes its flavour and design cues from the tapas bars of Spain and Portugal, but does so in a laneway space that makes it appear like the quintessential Melbourne bar; or Gerald's Bar in North Carlton, a bar that channels a small-town Italian cafe (complete with net half-curtains) and dishes up great rustic food from a menu that changes according to what is available at the market that day; or Journal Canteen, which operates as a Sicilian cafe during the day and as a demonstration kitchen for aspiring cooks at night. These are the type of places where you have an invigorating freedom of choice about how and when you eat, where you can always get a snack or assemble a meal from a number of snacks. They not only have well-considered wine lists that take in both the Old and the New Worlds, but they choose all their alcohol carefully, be it sherry or gin, whisky or beer, cognac or grappa. They are places where you expect to find something – wine or food – that you have never heard of or tried before, where you are just as likely to observe cooks shucking oysters or flaming pans as you are to watch bartenders working espresso machines or muddling cocktails. They are places where traditional boundaries and old ways of doing things are points of reference rather than ironclad templates.

{*Opposite*} Flower Drum

{*Below*} Vue de Monde

{*Following pages*} Journal Canteen

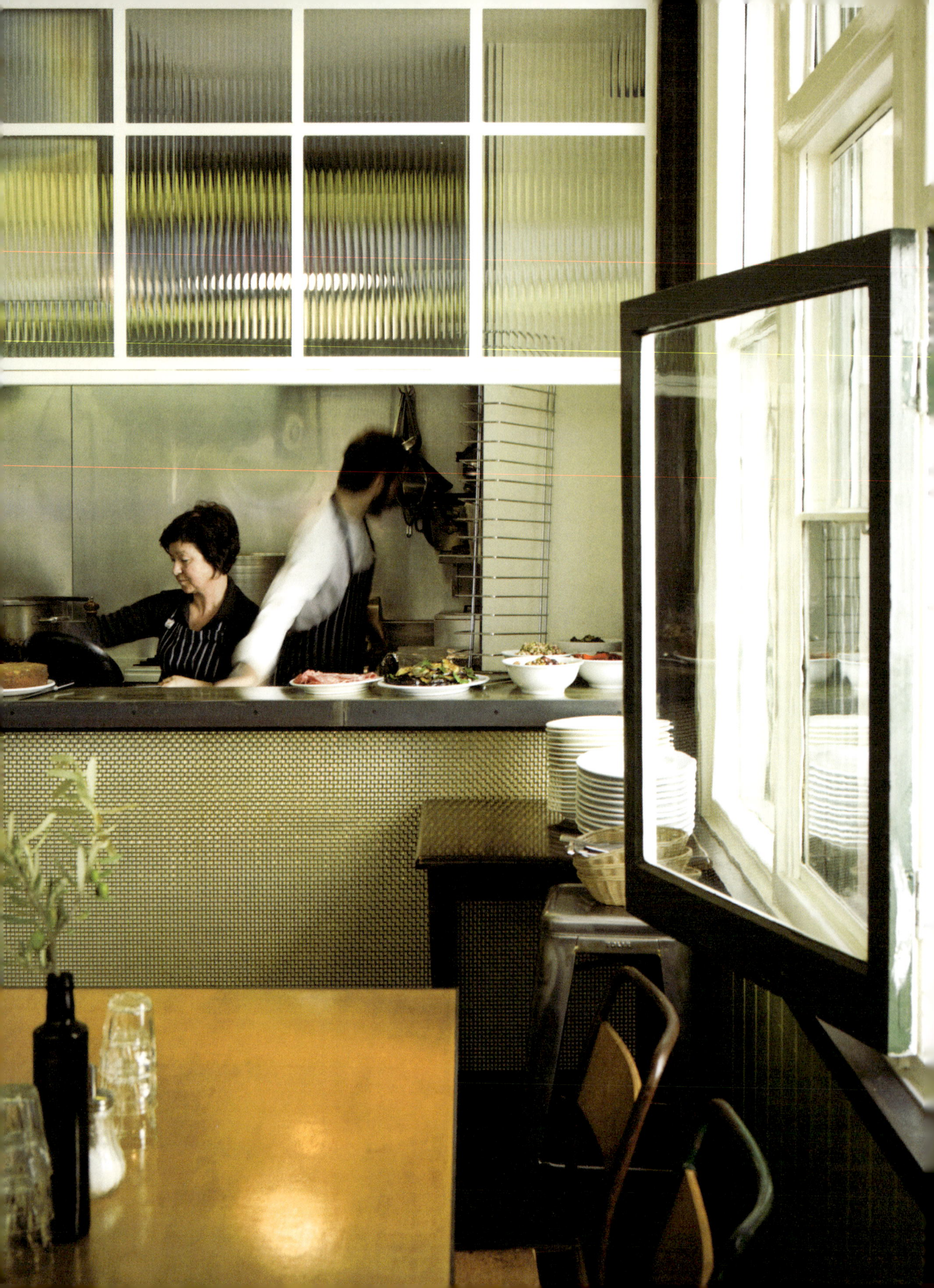

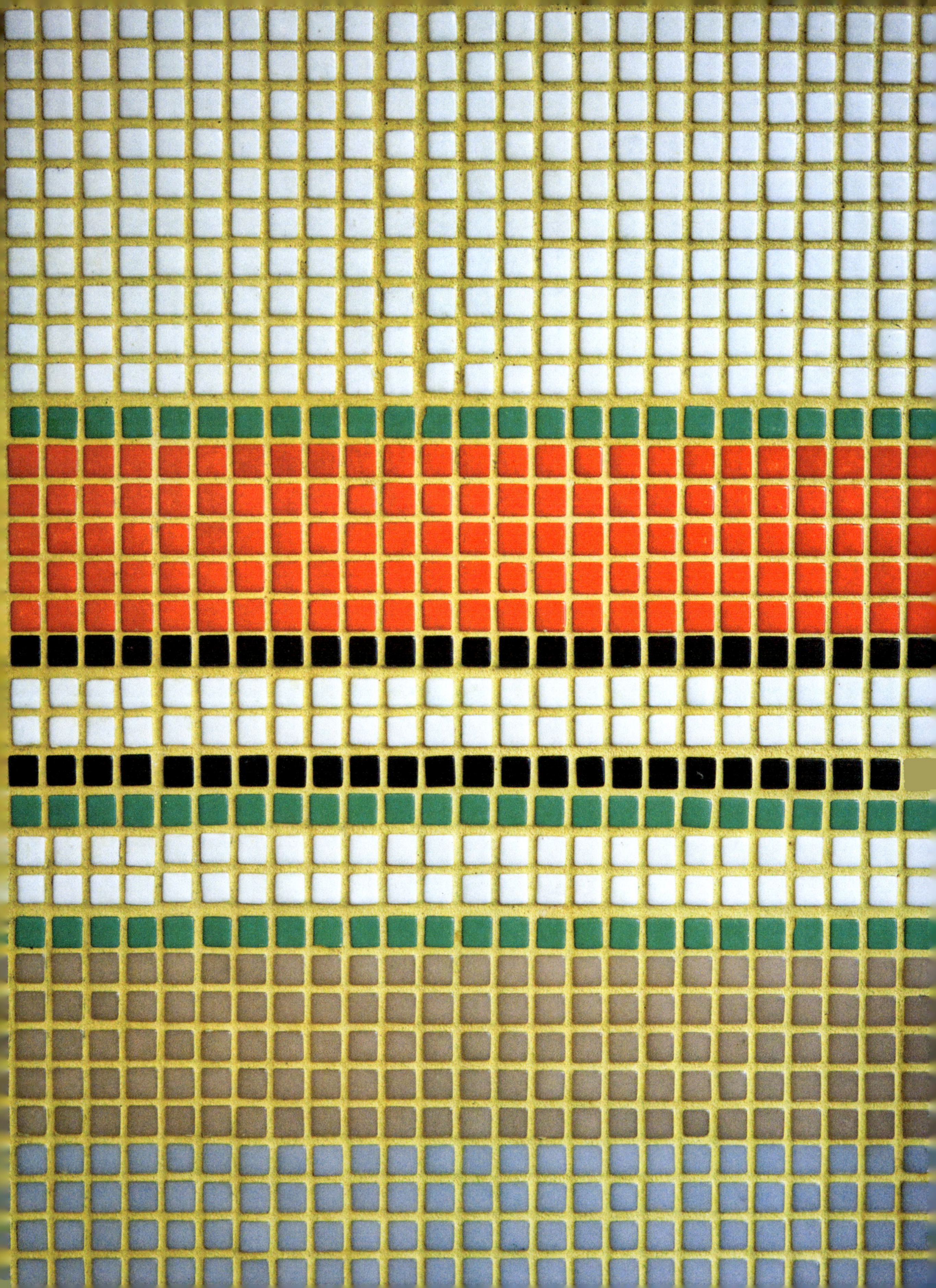

> How much poorer and less interesting the state would be without these places where all its citizens can gather together

{*Below, left*} Wall Two 80 in Balaclava

{*Opposite*} Journal cafe

{*Following pages*} Riverland, on the banks of the Yarra

Then there are the art galleries with bars, the hairdressers where you can get a glass of champagne or a beer while you're being coiffed, the bookstores where you can crack the spine of your latest purchase over a glass of wine, the jewellery and clothing stores where you can contemplate expanding your credit-card debt over a coffee or a gin, and bottle shops where you can have a glass of wine and a panini while perusing the shelves, chatting with people fascinated with obscure Italian grape varietals.

A culture has been created through Victoria's unique, and wonderfully idiosyncratic eating and drinking places, and how much poorer and less interesting the state would be without these places where all its citizens – men and women, old and young, stylish and scruffy, rich and poor, drinker and teetotaller, night owl or early bird – can gather together to eat and drink in a communal fashion. So many people eating together in public every day and night surely can only lead to a more cohesive and inclusive society. Sporadic outbreaks of alcohol-fuelled violence are universal and will probably always be with us, but the bad story should not be allowed to overshadow the good. A thriving and unique dining and drinking scene like the one that has been nurtured by law and creativity and circumstance in Melbourne is perhaps the best way to ensure that this happens.

| Charing Cross Road |
| Waterloo Elephant |
| Bermondsey Deptford |
| Lewisham Catford |
| |
| Woolwich Blackheath |
| Lewisham Catford |
| Beckenham Junction |
| Elmers End Croydon |
| |
| Charlton Blackheath |
| Lee Green Catford |
| Sydenham Penge |
| Norwood Junction |
| |
| Lee Green Grove Park |
| Burnt Ash Lane |
| Bromley Southborough |
| Petts Wood Station |
| |
| Catford Lewisham |
| Greenwich Woolwich |
| Plumstead |
| Abbey Estate |
| |
| Griffin Road Woolwich |
| Eglington Hill |
| Shooters Hill Road |
| Blackheath |
| |
| PRIVATE |

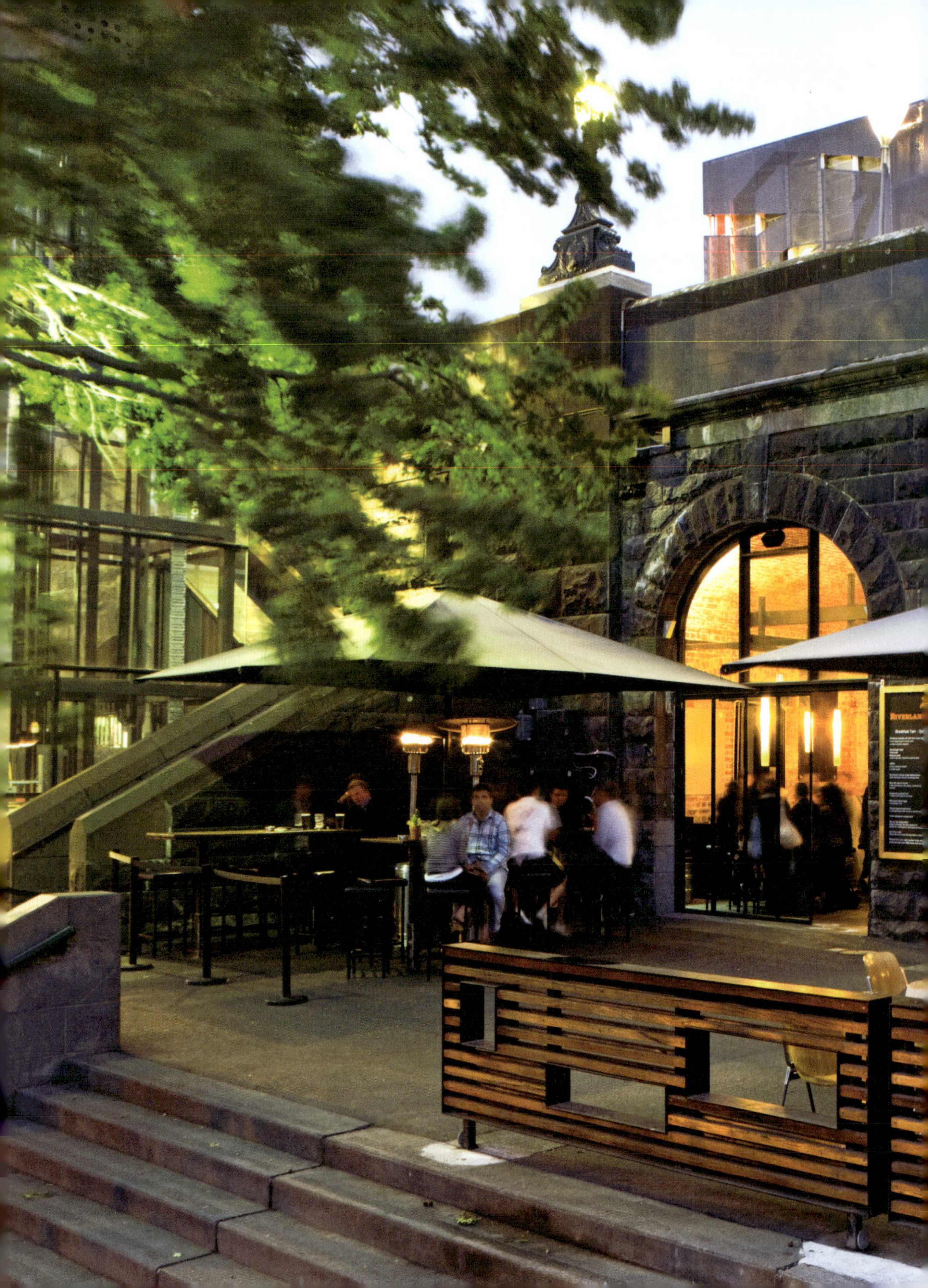

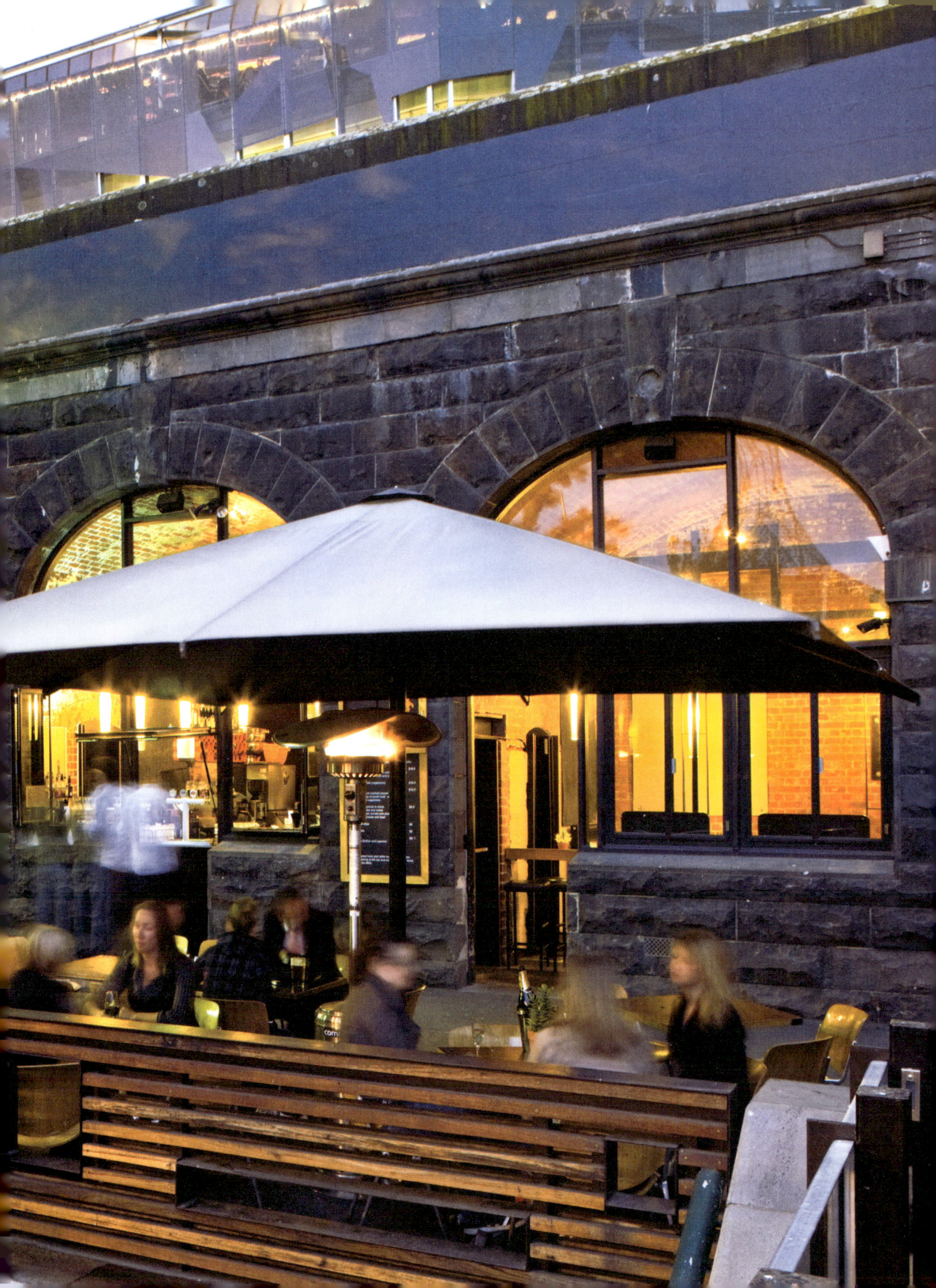

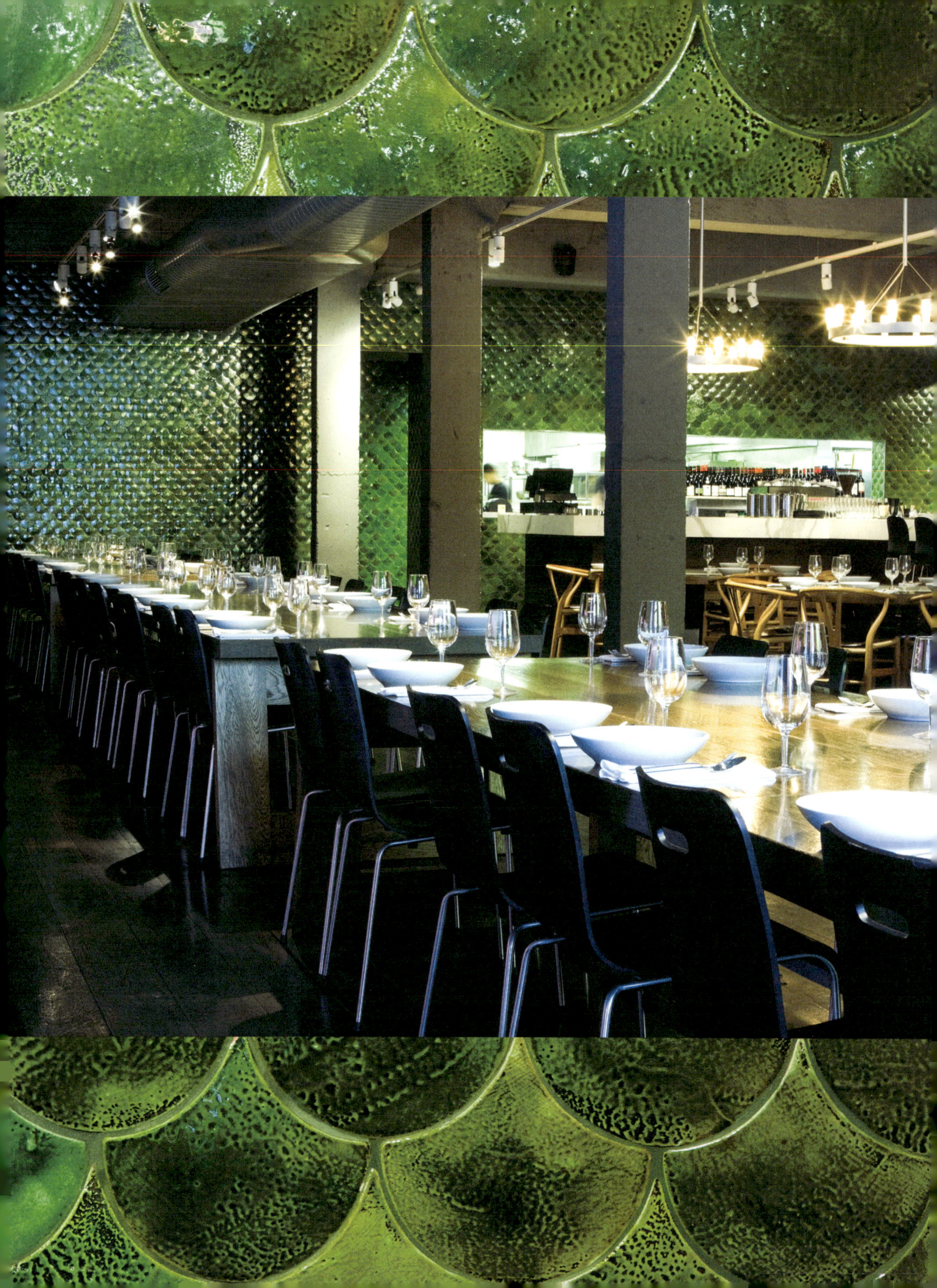

John Nieuwenhuysen's trust in the Victorian people's maturity has been rewarded. In the two decades since his recommendations were accepted by government and made into law, both the public and the industry have responded to the freedom of choice the reforms gave them with a particularly satisfying gusto. Things are not perfect, and nor is the Liquor Control Reform Act a document to stand untouched for all time. Alcohol is, after all, a slippery beast that is constantly in need of checking. But, as the Nieuwenhuysen reforms have shown, if the right checks and balances are applied, it can be a very endearing beast indeed.

{*Opposite*} Longrain

{*Following pages*} Cookie

JAMIESON
BEAST
IPA

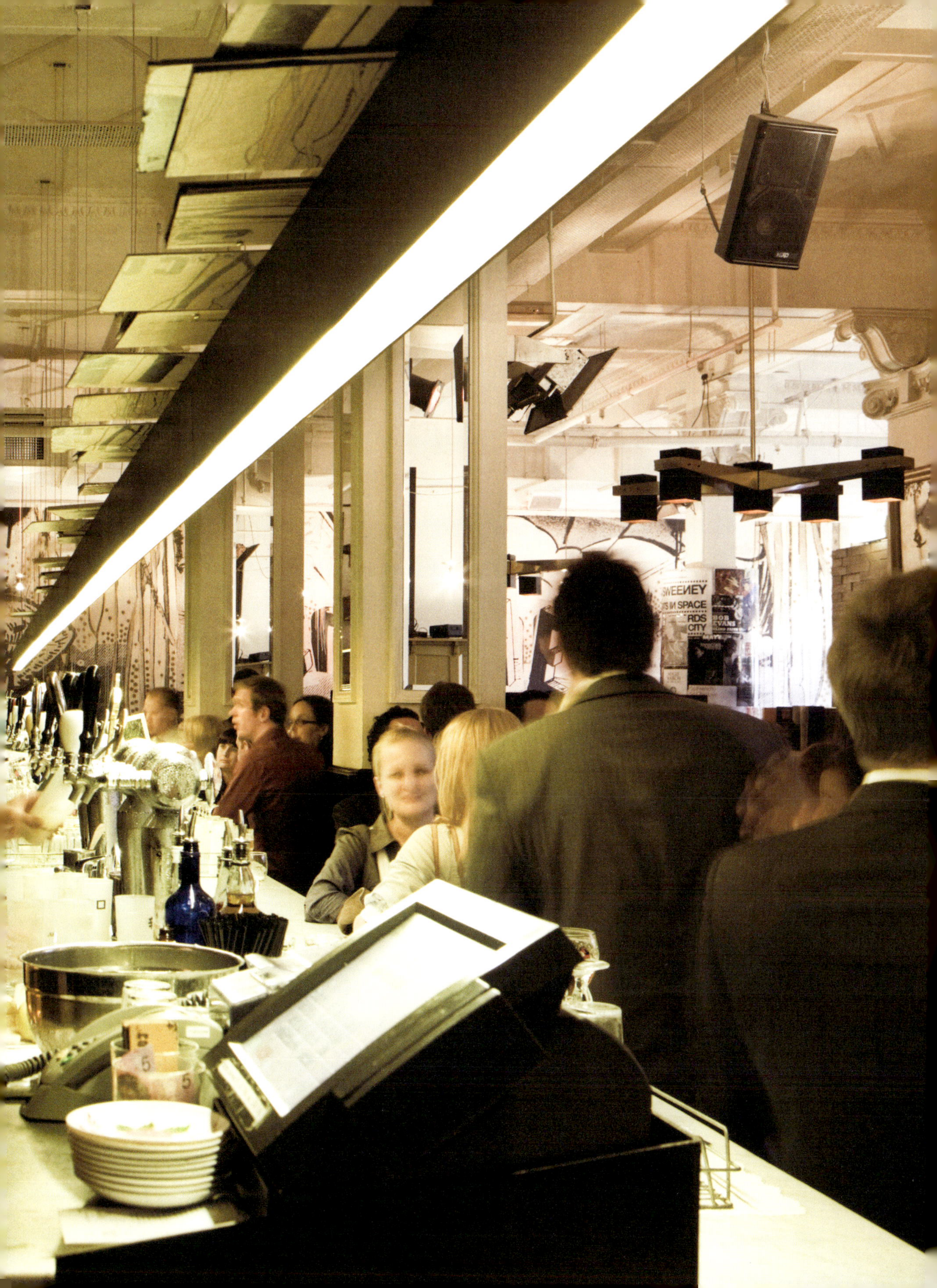
SWEENEY
SPACE
RDS
CITY

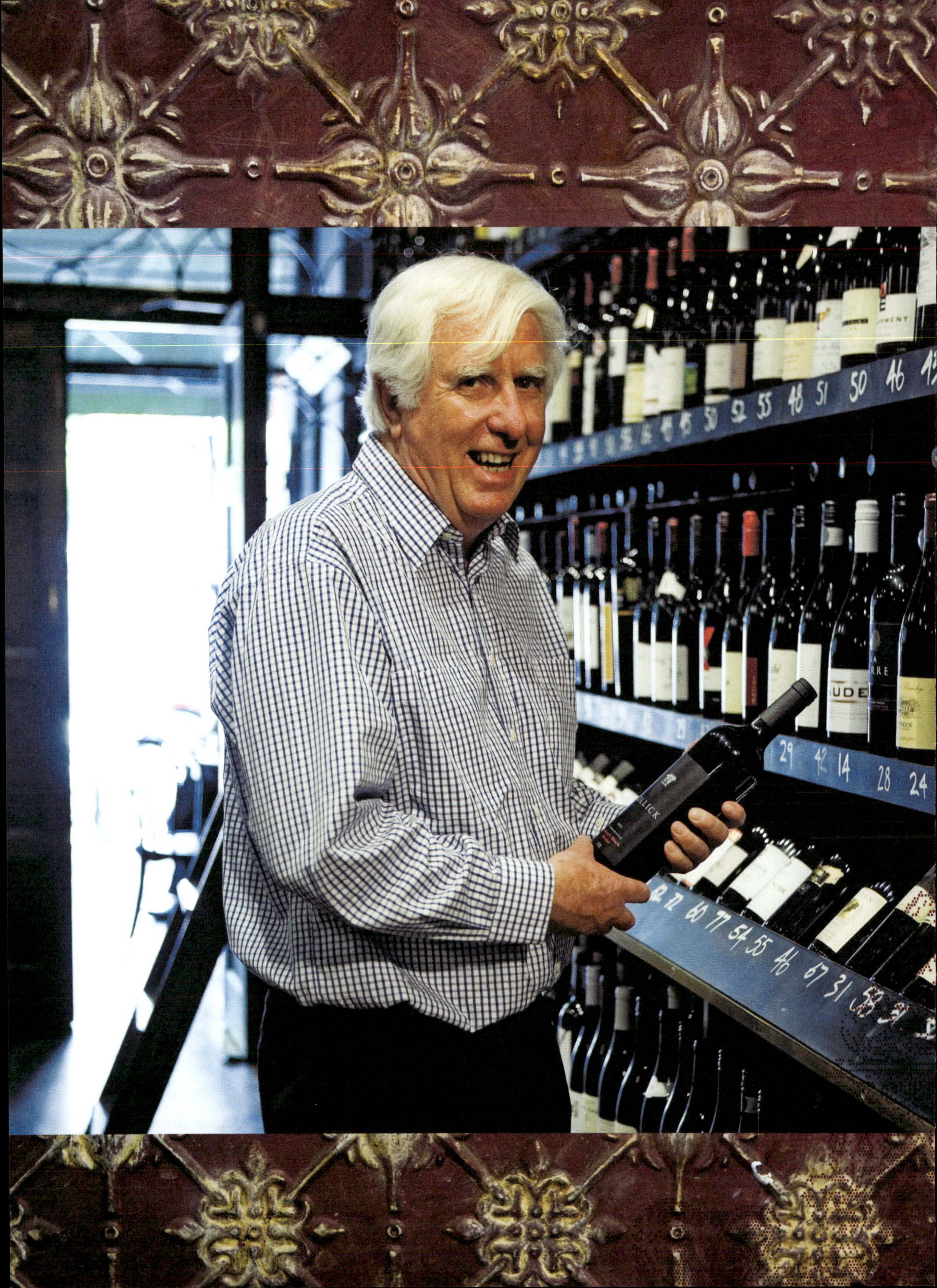

Afterword

The miserable, grey September 1963 day when I came as a migrant to take up a lectureship in economics at Melbourne University reflected my sad mood. Being driven from Essendon Airport through an unfamiliar landscape to my digs at Queen's College, everything felt extremely alien. I had left exciting, friend-filled student days in London for what seemed the back of beyond in 'the last of lands'.

On my second evening at (Methodist) Queen's College, a clandestine, presumably illegal thimbleful of sherry was dispensed to me from a tutor's locked cupboard store. Australia was then a society whose pubs (some resembling butcher shops with sawdust on the floor) closed at 6 pm.

I never dreamed then, however, that the dismal drink culture of Melbourne in 1963 would become a major preoccupation of mine twenty years later with the invitation by John Cain's reforming Government in 1984 to review the 1968 Victorian Liquor Control Act. Indeed the invitation came as a surprise. In 1982–83 I had chaired a difficult Inquiry on Victorian Revenue Raising for the Cain Government but I knew little if anything about the intricacies of the State's liquor laws, apart from my limited experience as a customer of the odd licensed restaurant and of Jimmy Watson's wine bar (whose waiters kicked the chairs of drinkers to encourage them to leave at 6.10 pm precisely). Basically I had avoided the male-dominated pubs and their ice cold VBs. Nonetheless, in the belief that when a good opportunity knocks one should open the door, I had no hesitation in accepting the invitation to review the Liquor Act, and my employer, the University of Melbourne, encouraged this participation, and gave me leave of absence.

Chairing a major State Inquiry is both a heavy responsibility and a tremendous opportunity. A State Inquiry is such a powerful vehicle compared with, for example, the privately engineered and executed academic publication. For a State review, there are terms of reference which, if properly dealt with, can lead to new legislation. There is also the assurance of publicity and the backing of the great financial resources of government. This presents a scale of activity and potential policy impact which is a far cry from the private academic exertion I was more familiar with.

The process of planning the research, consultation and combining and finally writing up all the material, as well as being the public face of the review, were my main responsibilities as chair. This was an enormously hard and stressful task, especially because of the intense media, community and industry interest in the issue. I would often work all weekend in my study at home.

During the last months, following the enormous research effort, the review team discussed and sharpened every sentence of the report, and there were on average eight redrafts of each chapter. The members of the review team were outstanding in every stage of the work, and it is important that their part in this story be acknowledged. My name is associated with the report, but it was a joint effort with great colleagues.

This sustained research and writing effort was not easy to reconcile with the calls on my time of family, house and garden. Indeed the pressure of the report and the duties of parenthood on one occasion collided in a way that could have spelled calamity for the review. Driving my daughters Sarah and Anna to school one morning, I exited the dark home garage unaware that, in the haste of departure, the full advanced draft of the report had been left lodged on the top of the car boot. Arriving at work, I was puzzled that I could not find it in the boot, where I thought it was, and concluded that it was still at home. At about ten o'clock, however, I received a phone call telling me that the report had been discovered in the middle of Kooyong road. The caller was the director of the large Moral Rearmament Movement Centre in that street. He could have had a field day, had he wished, releasing the report to the media, and I am ever grateful for his integrity and beneficence in returning it to me.

The Herculean effort and energy of the review team could not have been inspired without a passion for the subject, derived from the strong evidence that the 1968 Act was illogical and created inequity. In particular, it was seen as economically and administratively obtrusive in ways which had little or no bearing on a policy of restraining alcohol abuse. The Act appeared to serve mainly the purpose of dividing business among current licence holders – those who had in effect persuaded earlier governments to legislate for the benefit of current industry members rather than the public, or the proper purpose of liquor laws.

Both when the report was released by the Cain Government in March 1986 to favourable media responses, and when, some fifteen months later, its decision to accept the great majority of the recommendations was announced, my colleagues and I felt that our efforts were well rewarded. Perhaps the most satisfying event was when at a Carlton restaurant, Masanis, the Government arranged a lunch to announce to the media the details of the new reformed Act.

A further pleasure came in 1996 when the Melbourne Food and Wine Festival awarded me the title of a 'Special Legend' in the industry. That was a great day – the then Premier, Steve Bracks, presented the certificate in the new Melbourne Museum forecourt. And a comrade in arms, Claude Forell, of the *Age*, was a fellow recipient. Another champion of the cause was also there. She, like Claude, whose articles and editorials in the *Age* had been crucial in gaining acceptance for the report, was Mietta O'Donnell, and her influence was enormously important for the review's success. Without the enthusiasm of Claude, Mietta, her partner Tony Knox, and many others in the media and industry, such as Richard Frank, the report would not have succeeded. And of special and key importance was Brian Bourke, author of *Bourke's Liquor Laws of Victoria*, who served as legal counsel to the review, thoroughly checking and wisely advising on every interpretation which the report made of the Act and decisions under it.

Like Claude, Mietta and Brian, I contended that the public was ready and perfectly mature enough to adapt to the change to European-style premises which the report envisaged. But I had no idea how extensively and thoroughly the lifting of restrictions would over time transform the drinking culture of Victoria – notably in the amazing rise of the multitude of smaller bars, the extension of restaurant and cafe life, and the grasping of new opportunities under the reformed vigneron licence.

Little of this could have happened in the absence of new planning regulations. But, unfortunately, one major mistake has been made by the authorities over the past twenty-two years, and this has darkened the generally very high and leading edge reputation of Victoria's laws in this field. I refer to the new drinking coliseums – the gargantuan nightclubs in the CBD and elsewhere. The thrust of the report in 1986 – and the Cain Government's intentions – was to move away from the big 'beer barns' of old, with the problems which large size inevitably creates. Thousands of (mostly young) customers are congregated in one place and it is exceedingly difficult for those in charge to ensure that drunkenness does not ensue. The violence and public anti-social behaviour surrounding the nightclubs have aroused much protest, and rightly so. A solution needs to be found. Moreover, a new hazard is the combined intake of alcohol and a variety of other drugs, effective control of which is even more intractable.

But as I walk down, say, Brunswick Street in Fitzroy, or dine in an upgraded pub, or see the myriad new innovative small bars in the city, or select a wine from the brilliant vast range available in expanded or boutique retail outlets, or have lunch and sample wines at a vineyard, or choose from the great array of restaurants and cafes now enabling dining in an atmosphere and milieu far removed from conditions of the past, I say 'Cheers'.

Professor John Nieuwenhuysen, AM

DESSE
HURROS - RICH
LAN - CREME
ANACHE - HOT GA
LADOS - HOMEM
EPALOS - CHILL
UESO - CHEES

...DRINKING...
...CARAMEL SERVED W/...
...ACHE PUDDING W/ VANILLA BEAN ICE-CREAM &...
...E ICE-CREAMS W/ FIG BREAD $12.50
...CITRUS & MINT SOUP W/ CINNAMON DUMPLINGS & ME...
...OF THE DAY $21

Notes

Before and Beyond the Swill, pages 1–31

Opener quote: John Nieuwenhuysen, *Review of the Liquor Control Act 1968*, vol. 1, Government Printer, Melbourne, 1986, pp. 73–4.

1. Nieuwenhuysen, *Review of the Liquor Control Act 1968*.
2. Keith Dunstan, *Wowsers: Being an account of the prudery exhibited by certain outstanding men and women in such matters as drinking, smoking, prostitution, censorship and gambling*, Cassell Australia, Melbourne, 1968, p. 71.
3. Archibald M. Fraser, *Report on Visit Overseas to Examine Liquor Laws and Their Operation*, Mimeo, 1960, p. 5.
4. Reg Leonard, *Sun News Pictorial*, 21 March 1956.
5. Milton Lewis, *Rum State, Alcohol and State Policy in Australia, 1788–1988*, AGPS, Canberra, 1992, p. 82.
6. Cited in Nieuwenhuysen, *Review of the Liquor Control Act 1968*, vol. 1, p. 80.

The Laws of Dining, pages 32–57

Opener quote: Mietta O'Donnell and Tony Knox, Submission to the *Nieuwenhuysen Review of the Liquor Control Act 1968*, May 1986.

1. Michael Symons, *One Continuous Picnic: A gastronomic history of Australia*, Melbourne University Publishing, Carlton, Vic., 2007, p. 129.
2. Nando Donnini, interview with the author, 17 September 2007.
3. Hermann Schneider, interview with the author, 30 June 2008.
4. Richard Frank, interview with the author, 16 June 2008.
5. Mietta O'Donnell, Submission to the *Nieuwenhuysen Review of the Liquor Control Act 1968*, May 1986.
6. Frank interview, 16 June 2008.
7. Schneider interview, 30 June 2008.
8. Liquor Control Commission, Report on the application by the Weathercock, Carlton, May 1976, p. 3.
9. Liquor Control Commission, Report on application by the Culloden Castle, Geelong, November 1976, p. 5.
10. Peter Ryan, 'With respect', *The Age*, 29 June 1986.
11. John Nieuwenhuysen, interview with the author, 8 April 2008.
12. John Chalker, interview with the author, 24 June 2008.
13. Rod Usher, 'Licensing lunacy', *The Age*, 12 June 1984.

Revolution Not Evolution, pages 58–77

Opener quote: John Cain, Premier of Victoria 1982–90, unpublished writings, 1990–92.

1. John Nieuwenhuysen, interview with the author, 8 April 2008.
2. John Cain, unpublished writings, 1990–92.
3. John Cain, interview with the author, 23 June 2008.
4. John Cain, unpublished writings, 1990–92.
5. John Nieuwenhuysen, interview with the author, 14 May 2008.
6. Nieuwenhuysen interview, 8 April 2008.
7. Nieuwenhuysen interview, 8 April 2008.
8. Nieuwenhuysen interview, 8 April 2008.
9. Erik Hopkinson, interview with the author, 24 June 2008.

Hopes, Fears and the Word Made Law, pages 78–101

1. *Daily Advertiser*, November 1985.
2. Claude Forell, 'Scrap liquor controls and start again', *The Age*, 22 January 1986.
3. John Nieuwenhuysen, interview with the author, 14 May 2008.
4. Australian Hotels Association, *'Hogwash': Evolution or Revolution?*, brochure, AHA Victoria, Melbourne, 1986.
5. John Nieuwenhuysen, interview with the author, 8 April 2008.
6. Nieuwenhuysen interview, 8 April 2008.
7. Richard Frank, interview with the author, 16 June 2008.
8. Mietta O'Donnell and Tony Knox, Submission to the *Nieuwenhuysen Review of the Liquor Control Act 1968*, May 1986.
9. John Chalker, interview with the author, 24 June 2008.

10 John Cain, unpublished diary, 1990–92.
11 John Cain, interview with the author, 23 June 2008.
12 Don Hayward, interview with the author, 25 June 2008.
13 John Nieuwenhuysen interview, 8 April 2008.

The Taste of Freedom, pages 102–137

Opener quote: Jeni Port, 'The great reformation', *The Age*, May 1988.

1 Port, 'The great reformation'.
2 Richard Frank, interview with the author, 16 June 2008.
3 Claude Forell, interview with the author, 24 June 2008.
4 Mietta O'Donnell and Tony Knox, Submission to the *Nieuwenhuysen Review of the Liquor Control Act 1968*, May 1986.
5 Erik Hopkinson, interview with the author, 24 June 2008.
6 Maria Bortolotto, interview with the author, 2 July 2008.
7 Hopkinson interview, 24 June 2008.
8 Rinaldo Di Stasio, interview with the author, 14 July 2008.
9 Stephanie Alexander, *Stephanie's 21 Years of Fabulous Food*, Stephanie's, Melbourne, 1998, p. 4.
10 Con Christopoulos, interview with the author 15 July 2008.
11 John Ellis, interview with the author, 22 July 2008.
12 Peter Rowland, interview with the author, 16 July 2008.

Raising the Bar, pages 138–175

Opener quote: Clover Moore, MP NSW Parliament, introducing the Liquor Amendment (Small Bar and Restaurant) Bill to the NSW Legislative Assembly, September 2007.

1 John Nieuwenhuysen, interview with the author, 8 April 2008.
2 John Thorpe, in Sunanda Creagh, 'Don't inflict effete Melbourne ways: hotels', *Sydney Morning Herald*, 4 August 2007.
3 John M. Freeland, *The Australian Pub*, Melbourne University Press, Carlton, Vic., 1966, pp. 192–3.
4 Con Christopoulos, interview with the author, 15 July 2008.
5 Carlo Colosimo, interview with the author, 17 July 2008.

Freedom of Choice, pages 176–205

Opener quote: John Nieuwenhuysen, *Mietta's Eating and Drinking in Melbourne*, 2000.

1 C. Clayson, *Licensing Law and Health: The Scottish Experience*, Action on Alcohol Abuse Policy Forum, London, December 1984, p. 2.
2 Erik Hopkinson, interview with the author, 24 June 2008.
3 John Nieuwenhuysen, interview with the author, 4 July 2008.
4 John Chalker, interview with the author, 24 June 2008.
5 Necia Wilden, 'Here's cheers after 20 Years', *The Age*, 21 March 2006.
6 Wilden, 'Here's cheers after 20 Years'.

Photography Credits

All photographs not acknowledged below are by Dan Magree. All matchboxes are courtesy of Neil Abbot.

Before and Beyond the Swill, pages 1–31

pages xiv–1: MCG bar 1983 © Rennie Ellis Photographic Archive

page 2: Pictures Collection, State Library of Victoria

pages 5–6: illustrations from the Pictures Collection, State Library of Victoria

page 7: courtesy of Rare Printed Collections, State Library of Victoria

page 8: The Herald and Weekly Times Photographic Collection

pages 10–11: The Herald and Weekly Times Photographic Collection

page 13: (above) Fred M. Day, Pictures Collection, State Library of Victoria; (below) Fairfaxphotos.com

page 15: Fairfaxphotos.com

page 16: The Herald and Weekly Times Photographic Collection

pages 18–19: © Rennie Ellis Photographic Archive

page 20: menu detail from Chris Suhr's menu collection

page 21: photograph by Wolfgang Sievers / Pictures Collection, State Library of Victoria; menu from Chris Suhr's menu collection

page 24: Wolfgang Sievers / Pictures Collection, State Library of Victoria

page 27: National Archives of Australia: A6180, 29/5/79/9

pages 28–29: Fairfaxphotos.com

The Laws of Dining, pages 32–57

page 34: The Herald and Weekly Times Photographic Collection

page 38: (above) Neil Newitt / Fairfaxphotos.com; (below) The Herald and Weekly Times Photographic Collection

page 39: (above) Bruce Magilton / The Herald and Weekly Times Photographic Collection; (below) Philip Castle / Fairfaxphotos.com

pages 40–41: Fairfaxphotos.com

page 43: Wolfgang Sievers / Pictures Collection, State Library of Victoria

page 44: (above) The Herald and Weekly Times Photographic Collection; (below) The Herald and Weekly Times Photographic Collection

page 46: (left) Fairfaxphotos.com; (right) © Rennie Ellis Photographic Archive

page 48: menu from Chris Suhr's menu collection; photograph from The Herald and Weekly Times Photographic Collection

page 49: The Herald and Weekly Times Photographic Collection

page 50: Top of the Town ephemera courtesy of Richard Frank

page 54: Eddie Jim / Fairfaxphotos.com

page 56: (left) Dan O'Brien / The Herald and Weekly Times Photographic Collection; (right) Fairfaxphotos.com

Revolution Not Evolution, pages 58–77

page 60: courtesy of John Nieuwenhuysen

page 63: Martin Kantor / Fairfaxphotos.com

page 68: Cameron L'Estrange / The Herald and Weekly Times Photographic Collection

page 70: (above) courtesy of the family of Catherine James; (below) courtesy of Brian Bourke

page 71: Mike Martin / Fairfaxphotos.com

page 75: clipping courtesy of The Herald and Weekly Times

page 76: courtesy of Erik Hopkinson

Hopes, Fears and the Word Made Law, pages 78–101

page 80: courtesy of *The Age*

page 83: courtesy of John Nieuwenhuysen

page 89: courtesy of *The Age*

page 91: courtesy of The Herald and Weekly Times

page 92: Darryl Gregory / The Herald and Weekly Times Photographic Collection

page 93: courtesy of Richard Frank

page 94: Virginia Vlatko-Rulo / The Herald and Weekly Times Photographic Collection

page 95: (above) Craig Borrow / The Herald and Weekly Times Photographic Collection; (below) Fiona Hamilton / The Herald and Weekly Times Photographic Collection

page 97: courtesy of the Herald and Weekly Times

page 99: courtesy of John Nieuwenhuysen

The Taste of Freedom, pages 102–137

page 108: Richard Cisar-Wright / The Herald and Weekly Times Photographic Collection

page 112: (above) Fairfaxphotos.com; (below) Fairfaxphotos.com

page 113: (left) Norm Oorloff / The Herald and Weekly Times Photographic Collection page 116: photograph by Lucy Swinstead / The Herald and Weekly Times Photographic Collection; menus courtesy of Mario De Pasquale and Mario Maccarone

page 117: (above) collage by Massimo di Sorta; (below) Rob Baird / The Herald and Weekly Times Photographic Collection

page 118: (above) Neale Duckworth / Fairfaxphotos.com; (below) Mike Martin / Fairfaxphotos.com

page 122: Gary Medicott / Fairfaxphotos.com

page 123: Robert Banks / Fairfaxphotos.com

page 124: (above) David Caird / The Herald and Weekly Times Photographic Collection; (below) courtesy of the Tony Chapman collection

page 125: Ben Swinnerton / The Herald and Weekly Times Photographic Collection

page 127: (above) Rob Baird / The Herald and Weekly Times Photographic Collection; (below) Alex Coppel / The Herald and Weekly Times Photographic Collection

page 128: Marina Oliphant / Fairfaxphotos.com

page 129: Simon Schulter / Fairfaxphotos.com

page 130: (above) Nicole Emanuel / The Herald and Weekly Times Photographic Collection; (below) Alex Coppel / The Herald and Weekly Times Photographic Collection

page 131: Manuela Cifra / The Herald and Weekly Times Photographic Collection

page 134: (above) Andrew Tauber / The Herald and Weekly Times Photographic Collection

page 135: Craig Sillitoe / Fairfaxphotos.com

Raising the Bar, pages 138–175

page 143: Kelly Barnes / The Herald and Weekly Times Photographic Collection

page 144: Manuela Cifra / The Herald and Weekly Times Photographic Collection

page 146: Kelly Barnes / The Herald and Weekly Times Photographic Collection

page 150: (above) Jason Childs / Fairfaxphotos.com; (below) Fairfaxphotos.com

page 151: Darryl Gregory / The Herald and Weekly Times Photographic Collection

page 154: Rob Baird / The Herald and Weekly Times Photographic Collection

page 155: Rob Baird / The Herald and Weekly Times Photographic Collection

page 158: (top left) Nicki Connolly / The Herald and Weekly Times Photographic Collection

page 159: (bottom left) Darryl Gregory / The Herald and Weekly Times Photographic Collection

page 160: (left) Darryl Gregory / The Herald and Weekly Times Photographic Collection; (right) Nicole Cleary / The Herald and Weekly Times Photographic Collection

page 165: (left) Zhenshi Van Der Klooster / The Herald and Weekly Times Photographic Collection; (right) Cameron Tandy / The Herald and Weekly Times Photographic Collection

page 167: (above) Justin McManus / Fairfaxphotos.com

page 168: (far left, centre) portrait of Camillo Ippoliti by Simon Schulter / Fairfaxphotos.com

page 171: Darryl Gregory / The Herald and Weekly Times Photographic Collection

Freedom of Choice, pages 176–205

page 181: Michael Keating / The Herald and Weekly Times Photographic Collection

page 183: Andrew Batsch / The Herald and Weekly Times Photographic Collection

page 184: (right) Greg Scullin / The Herald and Weekly Times Photographic Collection

page 187: Darryl Gregory / The Herald and Weekly Times Photographic Collection

page 190: (left) Mike Keating / The Herald and Weekly Times Photographic Collection; (centre and right) courtesy of TarraWarra Estate

page 193: Simon O'Dwyer / Fairfaxphotos.com

page 196: Robert Banks / Fairfaxphotos.com

page 197: (left) Rodger Cummins / Fairfaxphotos.com; (right) Norm Oorloff / The Herald and Weekly Times Photographic Collection

page 200: (left) Nicki Connolly / The Herald and Weekly Times Photographic Collection

Afterword, pages 208–211

page 208: photograph by Mark Rogers

Every effort has been made to contact copyright holders for material used in this book. Please contact the publishers if you have any queries regarding copyrighted material.

Acknowledgements

Much of the energy that brought this book into being came from the frank and fearless Kate Latimer. With her sharp eye for detail, excellent sense of the ridiculous and astonishing ability to get things done in the shortest time possible she was both a force to be reckoned with and a joy to work alongside. To her I say: Cheers!

I would also like to thank John Nieuwenhuysen, not just for helping Melbourne become one of the world's great eating and drinking cities, but for being so generous with his time, advice, encouragement, humour and memory.

I am very grateful to John Cain for sharing the stories and information that were integral to this book's tale, for his comments on initial drafts and for agreeing to be part of the book through writing the foreword.

Many thanks also to Claude Forell and Jeni Port for bringing their insight and experience to the table and to Sahar Sana who helped smooth the way on numerous occasions.

Thanks to the team at Hardie Grant, especially Catherine Cradwick and Mary Small, both of whom were integral in keeping this sometimes unruly project on course in a perpetually calm and positive way.

To Trisha Garner, the designer, who has worked her usual magic to make this book look so beautiful, thanks for the talent and the sunny attitude.

A heartfelt thank you to the following people for sharing their time, photos, stories, expertise, memorabilia and passion for Melbourne's eating and drinking culture:

Erik Hopkinson, Brian Bourke, Don Hayward, Richard Frank, John Chalker, Hermann Schneider, John Ellis, Peter Rowland, Ronnie Di Stasio, Chris Lucas, Con Christopoulos, Mario De Pasquale, Mario Maccarone, Carlo Colosimo, Neil Abbott, Christopher Suhr, David Cousins, Necia Wilden, Frank Wilden, David Cousins, Heather Kelly, Nino Pangrazio, Six Degrees, TarraWarra Estate, Roger Fowler, Hilary Ericksen.

I would also like to acknowledge the organisations that generously sponsored this project: The City of Melbourne, Monash University and Tourism Victoria.

And to my beautiful daughter, Michaela Teschendorff Harden: thanks again for being so patient and helping me to get the job done. You're a truly special kid.

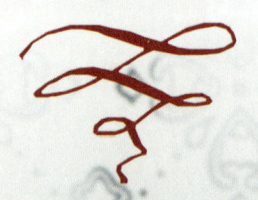

Index

Page numbers in italics refer to illustrations.

Abbotsford 175
Abboud, Joseph 193
Acland Street 22, 119
Ainsworth Estate 191
Albert Park 122, 148
alcohol abuse 74, 76, 86, 87, 92, 180, 182
alcohol-related violence 179, 182, 200
Alexander, Stephanie 57, 109, *124*, 125, 128, *128*, 129, 192–3
All Saints Estate 191
Antonio's 50
Arthurs Seat restaurant 47
Asiana 157
Australia Hotel 42
Australian Club 36, *37*
Australian Hotels Association 56, 69, 81–2, 86–7, 90–1, 92, 126, 141, 184

Balaclava 200
Ballarat 186
Bank Place 131
Bar Lourinha 156, 197
Becco 160, 183, *183*
Beechworth 186
beer gardens 147
Bellarine Peninsula 191
Bendigo 135, 186
Bennett, Shannon 193
Besen family 191
Bilson, Tony 57
Birrell, John 25
Black Cat cafe *112*, 113
Block Place 131
Bortolotto, Maria 110
bottle shops 74
Bourdain, Anthony 72
Bourke Street 42, 148, 151
Bourke, Brian 70, *70*, 210–11

bowling alley restaurants 93
Boyd, Robin 146
Bracks, Steve 210
Bridge Road Club 151
Bright 186
Brunswick 171
Brunswick Street 42, 56, 109, 113, 116, 125, 131, 211
BYOs 20, 25, 50, 57, 92, 93, 95, 98

Café Balzac 48
Cafe Di Stasio *118*, 126
Cafe D'Italia 42
Cafe Florentino 38, *38*, 39, 42, 45, 145
Cafe Segovia 131
Café Sport 113
Caffè e Cucina 126, *127*
Cain, John 58, 62, *63*, 64–5, 82, 96, 100, 209
Calombaris, George 193
Camorra, Frank 193
Campari bistro 113
Campton, John 87
Caprioli, Giancarlo and Beverly 95–6, *97*
car park bars *167*, 171
Carlton 20, 30, 42, 113, 125, 128, 142, 145, 146, 147, 210
Carlton and United Breweries 9
Carriage Bar *166*
Carter's 93
Casa Virgona 40–1, *42*
casinos 64
Cathie, Ian 62
Cellar Bar 42, *144*, 145
Chalker, John 56, *95*, 96, 183–4
Chalker, Vernon 160, *160*, 165
Chalkies 56, 96
Chapel Street 126, 166
Chateau Tahbilk *190*
Chevron Hotel *44*, 45

Chinatown 35, 45, 54
Chlebnikowski, Nick 30, 68, *68*
Chlebnikowski, Vic 68
chop houses 36
Christopoulos, Con 131, 151, 165, *165*
Circa, The Prince 131, 157
City Wine Shop *164*, 166
Claringbold, Cath 193
Clayton, Louise 69–70, *71*
Clichy 95
coffee (liquor) haunts 22
Collingwood 95, 122, 128, 148
Collins Quarter 165
Collins Street 93
Colosimo, Carlo 151–2, *151*, 155
Commercial Club Hotel 56
Cookie 166, *168*–9, 206–7
Copper Pot 186
country hotels 192
Cousins, Dr David 70, *71*
Coverlid Lane 160
Craig, Denis and Kerry 191
Crittenden's 30
Crown Casino 155
Crystal Café 36
Curtin House 166
Cushing, Bill 62

Dan Murphy's 30, 135
Dara, Dur-e *124*, 125
Daylesford 186
De Bortoli 191
De Pasquale, Mario 116, *117*
Degraves Espresso *130*, 131
Degraves Street 131
Delgany Country House 47
Demetry, Sarmita *71*
Der Raum 175
di Pieri, Stefano 186

Di Stasio, Ronnie 118, 119, 126
Dogs Bar 119, 122, *123*
Domaine Chandon 191
Doncaster 30, 68
Donnini, Nando 45
Duke and Moorfield 30
Duke, Ross 30
Dunn, Jean *71*
Dunstan, Keith 12

East Melbourne 48
Edwards, Toni 113, *113*
Ellis, John 132, 135, *135*
Empress of China 54
espresso bars 20, 42, 57, 113, 119
Exhibition of Victorian Winemakers 31
Exhibition Street 42
Ezard, Teague 193

Fan Court 93
Fanny's 47, *48*, 57, 110, 120
Farmers Arms Hotel *184*, 186
Fasoli's 39
Federation Square *188*, 189
Ferdi's Bistro 147
Fink, Max 131
Fitzpatrick, Donlevy *118*, 119, 122, 131, 148
Fitzroy 42, 56, 109, 113, 116, 125, 128, 131, 171, 175, 197
Fitzroy Street 126
Fleyfel, Louis 93
Flinders Lane 119
Flower Drum 54, 193, *196*
Fordham, Robert 77, 81, 85
Forell, Claude 82, 106, 210, 211
Foster, Will 70, *71*
France-Soir 157
Frank, Richard 48, 50, 55, 92, 93, *93*, 106, 210
Fraser, Archie 17, 48

free counter lunches 36
Freeland, J.M. 147

Geelong 51, 186
George Hotel 131
Gerald's Bar 197
Gertrude Street Enoteca 175, 197
Gesualdi, Piero 119
Gin Palace *140*, 160, *161–3*, 165
Glo Glo's 47, 57, 120
Greasy Joe's 107, 110
Great Australian Bite 55
Greek men's clubs 113
Greville Street 50
Grossi Florentino 39, 193
Grossi, Guy 193, *193*
Gude, Phil 82
Gypsy Bar 131

Handsome Steve's House of Refreshment *171*, 175
Hanging Rock Winery 132
Hard Times 151
Hardware 151
Hartwell 57
Hawthorn 125, 128, 171
Hayward, Don 100–1
Healesville Hotel 186
Heathcote 135
Herscu, George 68
Hewitson, Iain 95
Hopkinson, Erik 76, *76*, 93, 107, 111, 113, 182
hotel bar/lounges 20, 142
hotel dining rooms 42, 45

Il Bacaro 126, *127*
Il Bistro 42, 45, 145
International Club 22
Ippoliti, Camillo 166, *168*

Italian bistros 113, 126
Italian Waiter's Club 22

Jacques Reymond 93, 193
Jamaica House 125, 128
James, Catherine 70, *70*
Jimmy Watson's wine bar 42, 142, *143*, 145, 147, 209
Joe's Garage 131
Joe's Shoe Store 171
Jordan, Dr Tony 191
Jorgensen, Sigmund 57, 95, *95*
Journal Canteen 197, *198*, 201

Kearney, Brian 184
Kennett, Jeff 101, 155
King Street 93
King Valley 135
King and Godfree 30
Knox, Tony 56, 95, 109, 210
Kratzner, Gerd 61
Kyneton 186

La Mascotte 36
La Scala 186
Lager Bar 107, 110
Lake House 186
laneways 119, 131, *136*, 152, 155, 160, 171
Lau, Gilbert 54, *56*, 57
Lau's Family Kitchen 54
Lazar's 93
LCC (Liquor Control Commission) 25–6, 35, 51, 55–6, 61, 105, 107
Le Monde 148, *150*, 151, 152
Leonard, Reg 17
Les Halles 22
Lethlean, John 192–3
Lewis, M.J. 25
Lindsay, Geoff 193
Liquor Union 87, 96

Little Bourke Street 36, 45, 54
Little Collins Street 93
Little Lonsdale Street 160
Longrain *178*, *204*
Lonsdale Street 39, 93
Lounge 151–2, 155
Lucas, Chris 126
Lygon Street 42, 45, 56, 57, 76, 95–6, *97*, 99, 125, 142, 146

Maas, Henry 113, *113*
Macali, Rita 193
McCallum, Norman 25
Maccarone, Mario 116, *117*
McConnell, Andrew 193
Macedon Ranges 135
Madame Brussels 160, 165
Maison Dorée 36
Malouf, Greg 193
Maria and Walter's 110
Mario's 42, 45, 50, 109,
Marios 116, *116*, *117*, 131
Market Lane 160
Martini, Karen 193
Masanis 210
Mathis, Paul 131
Matteo's 109
Max, Gary 70, *71*
Maxim's 45, 48, 50, 110
Melbourne Supper Club 165–6
Melbourne Wine Room *118*, 126, 131, 157
Menzies Hotel 24, *34*, 42, 45, 142
Meyers Place *154*, 155, *155*, 160
Mietta's 56, *94*, 95, 109, 116, 148
Mildura 186
Miller, Steve *171*
Mitchell, Peter 191
Molina's 42
Montalto 191, 192

Moorfield, Roy 30
Mooroopna 186
Mora, Georges and Mirka 42, 48, *49*
Mordialloc 93
Mornington Peninsula 135, 186, 191, 192
Movida *194–5*
Murphy, Dan 68, 98
Myrtleford 186

Naval and Military Club 95, 109, 148
New Paris Nightclub 22
Nick's Wine Merchants 30, 68
Nieuwenhuysen, John ix–x, 55, 60, 62, 65–77, *71*, *75*, 85, 87, 89, 90–2, 100, 101, 106, 141, 179, 183, *205*, *208*, 209–11
Nieuwenhuysen report 3, 35, 62, 65–77, *75*, 80, 81, 82, *82*, 85, 89, *89*, 92, 95, 96–7, 100–1, 122, 132, 135, 137, 179–80, 182, 192, 210
nightclubs 25
Noojee 186
North Carlton 197
North Fitzroy 95
North Melbourne 30, 42
Northcote 171
Nudel Bar 125

O'Donnell, Mietta 50, 56, 57, *94*, 95, 107, 108–9, *108*, 125, 210, 211
Order of Melbourne 165
oyster saloons 36

Page, Eric 57
Paris Follies Nightclub 22
Paris Nightclub 22
Pellegrini, Leon and Vildo 42
Pellegrini's Espresso Bar 42, *44*, 45, *112*, 113, *113*, 151, 155
Petty Sessions 93
Phillips, Sir Phillip D. 20, 85
Phillips inquiry 25

pizza houses 51
Poliness, Grania 146
Port Fairy 186
Prahran 30, 50, 166, 171
Prince of Wales 131
Prince's Bridge Hotel 28–9
Provincial Hotel 131
Purple Cow 22

Quarter Sessions 93
Queen Street 48, 50, 93
Queenscliff Hotel 92, 95, 109

Rathbone family 192
Razor 151
Red Eagle 148
Restaurant and Catering Association 92, 93
restaurant guides 57, 82, 110
Retail Liquor Merchants' Association of Victoria 87
Review of the Liquor Control Act 1968, see Nieuwenhuysen report
Revolver 166
Reymond, Jacques 56, 57, 93, 109, 120
Rhine Castle Cellars 48, 50, 93
Rhumbarella 113
Richmond 22, 30, 125, 151, 171, 175
Richmond Hill Cafe & Larder 125, 128
Richmond Hill Cellars 30
Rick's 48, 50, 93
Riley, Lincoln 157
Rinaldi's Wine Hall 39
Riverland 202–3
Roesti Bistro 47
Rogalsky's 110
Rosati 119, 126, 151
Rowland, Peter 137
Royal George 186, *187*
Rubenstein, Linda 96
Rue Bebelon 160, *170*

Russell Place 160
Russell Street 160
Rutherglen 145, 191
Ryan, Tony 105

Sadie's 160
St Kilda 20, 22, 42, 54, 107, 110, 113, 119, 122, 126, 131, 171
Savoy Plaza Hotel 43, 45
Schneider, Hermann 45, 46, *46*, 47, 50, 51, 55
Scotchmans Hill 191
Seabrooks 47
Section 8 *166*, 171
Shewry, Ben 193
Shield, Mark 68
Siglo *165*, 166
Simone, Patrizia 186
Simone's Restaurant 186
Six Degrees 155
six o'clock swill 10–11, 12, 13, *15*, *16*, 17, 20, 25, 42, 142
Smith Street Bar & Bistro 122, 148
Source 186
South Yarra 47, 51, 126
Southern Cross *107*, 142
'spaghetti mafia' 39
Staley, Blyth 47
Staley, Daniel 47
Staley, Gloria *46*, 47, 109
Stefano's 186
Stephanie's *124*, 125, 128
Stokehouse 131
Sunday trading 74
Swanson Street 151, 152, 166
Swelter 151
Sydney
   bar culture 138, 141
   diners compared with Melbourne 72
   pubs and clubs 72
   restaurants compared with Melbourne 72
Symons, Michael 35
Syracuse *130*, 131, 157

Tahbilk 191
TarraWarra Estate *190*, 191
Taxi Dining Room 156, 157, *188*
Templestowe Cellars 30
temporary bars 171
Terzini, Maurice *118*, 126, 131
The European 149, 156, *156*, 164
The Galleon 113
The International 160
The Latin 39, *39*
The Press Club 156
The Society 42
The Toff In Town 166, *166*
The Walnut Tree 93
themed bars 171
Thornbury 119, 126
Thorpe, John 141–2
Tiamo 113, *114–15*
Toorak 47, 93
Top of the Town 50, 93, 147
tram car restaurant 55
Transport *188*, 189
trattorias 39, 42
Tsindos Bistro 116
Tuck's Ridge 191
Tunstall, Allan 69, *71*
Two Faces 47, 51, 57, 110, 120

University Cafe/Universita Bar Ristorante 42, 45, 95–6, *99*
Up Top 160
Usher, Rod 57, 61, 90

van Haandel, John and Frank 131, *131*
Vic Ave 122
Victoria Coffee Palace 93
Victorian Wine Industry Association 132
Vietnam Kinh Do 57
Vietnamese restaurants 57
Vigano family 50, 109
Vue de Monde 193, *197*

Wall Two 80 200
Walter's Wine Bar 157
Watson, Allan 146
Watson, Jimmy 142, 145, 146, *146*
Watson, Nigel 146
Watson, Simon 146
Weathercock 113
Wells, Patricia 72
Wilawa Cocktail Bar 142
William Street 93
Wilson, Paul 193
Windows on the Bay 93
Windsor Hotel 42, 142
wine
   cellar-door sales 186, 191
   consumption 21, 132
   by the glass 157
   internet sales 68
   tasting 30, 68
   tourism 135, 190–2
wine bars 39, 42, 113
wine lists 21, 132, 156–7
Wing Sun 54
Wolf-Tasker, Alla 186
women drinkers 145, 147

Yarra Valley 135, 186, 191, 192
Yering Station 191, 192
Young and Jackson 27, 28–9

Contributors

Claude Forell is a former senior writer, public affairs columnist and restaurant reviewer with *The Age* and founding editor of *The Age Good Food Guide*. A professional journalist for more than fifty years, he now grows blueberries near Daylesford.

Jeni Port is the longest serving wine writer with *The Age* as well as a contributor to wine magazines, including *Winestate* magazine and *Australia and New Zealand Grapegrower and Winemaker*. She is author of *Choosing Australian Wines: A Buyer's Guide*, *Crushed by Women: Women and Wine* and Australasian contributor to Dorling Kindersley's *Wines of the World*. When she's not drinking, writing or judging wine she's teaching wine communication at La Trobe University.

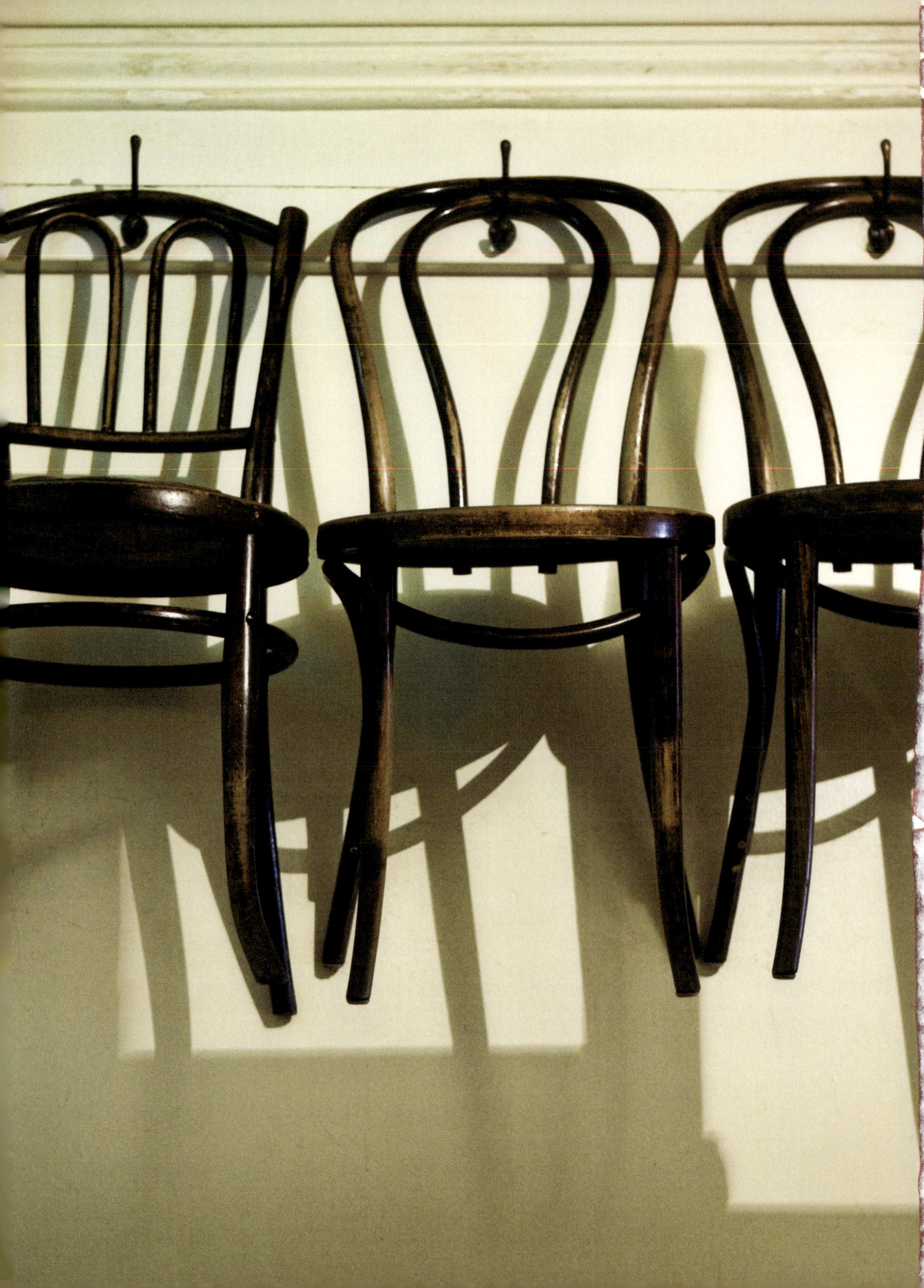